W9-BSS-020

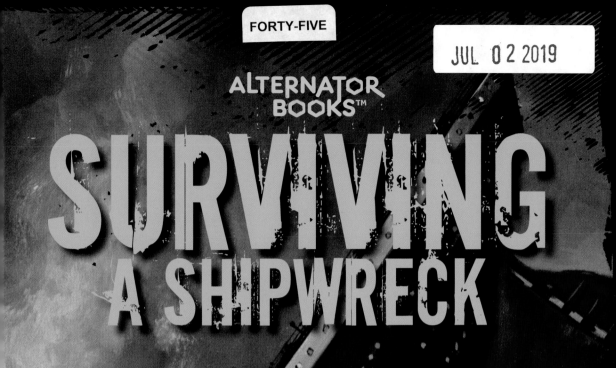

ALTERNATOR
BOOKS™

SURVIVING
A SHIPWRECK

THE *TITANIC*

BUFFY SILVERMAN

Lerner Publications ◆ Minneapolis

Lerner Publications Company
A division of Lerner Publishing Group, Inc.
241 First Avenue North
Minneapolis, MN 55401 USA

For reading levels and more information, look up this title at www.lernerbooks.com.

Library of Congress Cataloging-in-Publication Data

Names: Silverman, Buffy, author.
Title: Surviving a shipwreck : the Titanic / Buffy Silverman.
Description: Minneapolis : Lerner Publications, 2019. | Series: They survived
    (alternator books) | Includes bibliographical references and index. | Audience:
    Age 8–12. | Audience: Grade 4 to 6.
Identifiers: LCCN 2018010694 (print) | LCCN 2018013578 (ebook) |
    ISBN 9781541525641 (eb pdf) | ISBN 9781541523524 (lb : alk. paper)
Subjects: LCSH: Titanic (Steamship)—Juvenile literature. | Shipwrecks—North
    Atlantic Ocean—Juvenile literature.
Classification: LCC G530.T6 (ebook) | LCC G530.T6 S54 2019 (print) |
    DDC 910.9163/4—dc23

LC record available at https://lccn.loc.gov/2018010694

Manufactured in the United States of America
1-44425-34684-7/6/2018

CONTENTS

INTRODUCTION
DISASTER AT SEA

In the middle of the night, a jolt suddenly interrupted the smooth sailing of the *Titanic*. Many of the ship's passengers woke with a start. Then an anxious crowd gathered on the deck to find out what had happened. But even the crew didn't know what was wrong. The ships' officers tried to assure the passengers that there was no danger, and some returned to their cabins. Soon everyone on board knew they were in serious trouble. The *Titanic* had struck an iceberg!

CHAPTER 1
THE *TITANIC* SETS SAIL

On April 10, 1912, the *Titanic* left from Southampton, England, on its very first voyage. The ship stopped for passengers in Cherbourg, France, and Queenstown, Ireland, before beginning its journey to New York City. It carried 1,317 passengers and 908 crew members.

First-class passengers ate oysters, lobster, grapes, and more in the grand dining hall.

Passengers were eager to ride on the largest, most luxurious ship ever built. It carried some of the world's wealthiest people as first-class passengers. The most expensive ticket cost $2,560, or $61,000 in today's dollars. It bought a three-room suite on what people called the "floating palace." But most passengers traveled in far simpler cabins in second or third class. They were smaller rooms with bunk beds and shared bathrooms.

SURVIVAL GEAR

Most of the *Titanic*'s lifeboats were 30-foot-long (9 m) wooden rowboats. Each of these boats could hold sixty-five people. There were also four smaller **collapsible** lifeboats on board. But two of these boats were still folded on the roof of the officers' quarters as the *Titanic* began to sink. They fell into the ocean before passengers could board them.

As the ship continued on its journey, it was moving fast toward icy waters. Each day Captain Edward J. Smith ordered the crew to increase the ship's speed. When other ships sent radio messages that they had spotted icebergs in the sea, Smith changed course to avoid them. He took the *Titanic* farther south than originally planned. Smith did not expect to meet icebergs on the new route. But after four days of smooth sailing, the *Titanic* was unknowingly racing toward disaster.

Officer Hugh Walter McElroy (*left*) and Captain Edward J. Smith (*right*) aboard the *Titanic*

CHAPTER 2
ICY WATERS

It was clear and cold in the mid-Atlantic Ocean as the *Titanic* sped toward New York City. On its fourth day at sea, a nearby ship, the *Californian*, sent a telegraph message that it was surrounded by ice. But the person in charge of working the *Titanic*'s telegraph was busy sending passengers' messages to their friends and family. So the warning message was not heard.

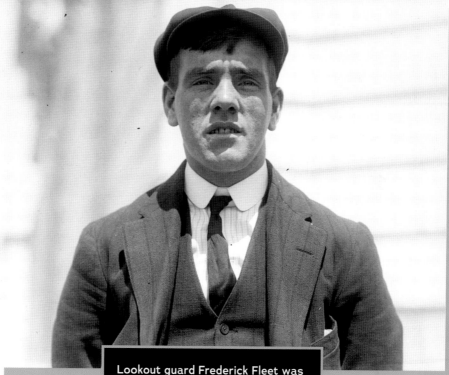

Lookout guard Frederick Fleet was the first person to spot the iceberg.

Lookout guard Frederick Fleet stood in the **crow's nest** of the *Titanic* that night. His job was to spot any dangers in the ship's way. At 11:40 p.m., he saw an iceberg straight ahead. Fleet rang his warning bell and called the **bridge**. First Officer William S. Murdoch ordered the crew to put the engines in reverse to slow the ship and turn it away from the iceberg. But it was too late. The side of the *Titanic* hit the iceberg, making gashes in the **hull** below the surface of the water.

SURVIVAL GEAR

Wireless telegraphs were common on ships when the *Titanic* sailed. They could send messages up to 500 miles (805 km) away from the ship. The operators who worked the telegraphs sent passengers' messages. They also warned other ships of dangers, such as icebergs.

Passengers and crew members put on their life preservers and waited to get into lifeboats.

Inside the hull were sixteen **compartments** made to keep water from flooding the whole ship at once. Even if four of these compartments flooded, the ship could still float. But after hitting the iceberg, water poured into the right side of the *Titanic*'s hull. The weight of the water pushed the **bow** down. The compartments' walls were supposed to keep water from moving into other compartments. But the walls were designed poorly. They didn't reach all the way to the ceiling. So water spilled from the top of one compartment to the next, until six compartments were filled. The *Titanic* was sinking.

The crew told passengers to put on life preservers and come on deck. Forty minutes after the *Titanic* hit the iceberg, Smith gave the order to start loading women and children into the lifeboats. The ship had not even held a lifeboat drill. The crew and passengers weren't prepared for this **evacuation**.

CHAPTER 3
ESCAPING DISASTER

Smith ordered the telegraph operator to call nearby ships for help. They sent this message to the *Carpathia*: "Come at once. We have struck a berg." The *Carpathia* was 58 miles (93 km) away when it received the *Titanic*'s signal. It raced past six icebergs on the way to rescue the passengers and crew of the *Titanic*.

While the *Carpathia* headed to the disaster, the situation grew more desperate for those aboard the *Titanic*. Passengers were evacuating onto lifeboats. The first lifeboats were loaded with women and children. But because of the chaos, many of the lifeboats were less than half full when they left the ship. Passengers were afraid to board the lifeboats. Many thought it would be safer to stay on the ship than to get into the small boats. The crew turned men away. Some jumped into lifeboats as they were being lowered. Others

Women and children boarded the lifeboats first.

This was the last lifeboat to make it off the sinking ship.

swam to the collapsible boats that had overturned in the water.

More than half of all first-class passengers made it onto the lifeboats. Less than half of the second-class and a quarter of third-class passengers survived. Most of the ship's passengers and crew did not escape the sinking ship.

As water flooded the *Titanic*'s lower compartments, the ship's bow sunk lower and lower. The **stern** with its three huge **propellers** lifted up higher and higher. This tremendous weight pushed against the ship's middle, eventually tearing the ship in two. The bow ripped off and sank. Then the stern rose straight up in the air. It slowly filled with water before plunging into the ocean.

Survivors watched from their lifeboats as the *Titanic*'s stern lifted up and then sank.

SURVIVOR MARGARET BROWN

Before Margaret Brown sailed on the *Titanic*, she was used to helping others. She worked in soup kitchens to feed people in need and raised funds for hospitals. Brown continued helping others during the *Titanic* disaster.

She loaded women onto lifeboats before boarding a lifeboat herself. She and other women rowed during the long, cold night. After being rescued by the *Carpathia*, Brown helped survivors contact their relatives. She brought their messages to the telegraph operator and set up a fund to pay for sending them.

Brown organized a survivor's committee while on the journey home. She was elected chair and raised money to help those who had been left with nothing. Because she spoke many languages, she could aid survivors who did not speak English. After the *Carpathia* docked in New York City, Brown stayed on the ship to make sure other survivors were met by friends or family and got medical aid.

Many considered Margaret Brown to be a hero for helping the *Titanic* survivors. She told her story to newspapers. She used her new fame to promote issues that she cared about and continued helping others.

Margaret Brown helped many other survivors while aboard the *Carpathia*.

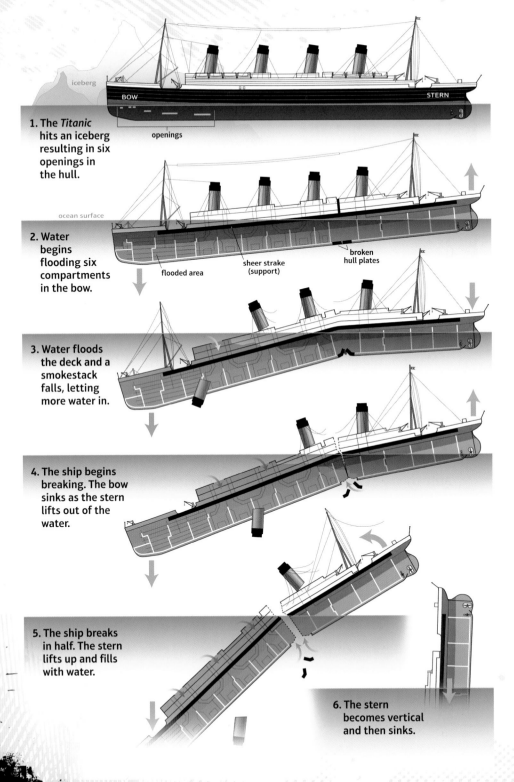

iceberg

BOW   STERN

openings

1. The *Titanic* hits an iceberg resulting in six openings in the hull.

ocean surface

2. Water begins flooding six compartments in the bow.

flooded area

sheer strake (support)

broken hull plates

3. Water floods the deck and a smokestack falls, letting more water in.

4. The ship begins breaking. The bow sinks as the stern lifts out of the water.

5. The ship breaks in half. The stern lifts up and fills with water.

6. The stern becomes vertical and then sinks.

Titanic survivors huddled on the deck of the *Carpathia* after being rescued.

Many of the lifeboats left without a ship's officer. However, Officer Harold Lowe managed to escape on one of the lifeboats and he took charge. His boat soon met some of the other lifeboats. Lowe transferred his passengers and returned to help those in the water. Lowe and two crew members were able to save twenty-five more people from the water and a sinking lifeboat.

At last the *Carpathia* arrived at four in the morning. The survivors were numb with cold, but they spent the last of their energy rowing like mad toward the lights of the ship. Eventually, the *Carpathia* picked up the survivors. One survivor remembered the moment, saying each lifeboat was "like a speck against that giant."

The *Carpathia*'s crew lowered ropes down to haul the survivors aboard. Soon the 706 survivors of the *Titanic* were warm, dry, and safe.

The World.

"Circulation Books Open to All." "Circulation Books Open to All."

VOL. LII. NO. 18,501. NEW YORK, TUESDAY, APRIL 16, 1912. PRICE ONE CENT in Greater New York and Jersey City. TWO CENTS outside of Greater New York, Jersey City and on Trains.

GREAT TITANIC SINKS; MORE THAN 1.500 LOST;
866 WOMEN AND CHILDREN KNOWN TO BE SAVED;
SCORES OF NOTABLES NOT ACCOUNTED FOR

THE LOST LINER, HER POSITION AND THAT OF OTHER SHIPS WHEN SHE HIT ICEBERG

The TITANIC
LENGTH 882 FT.
BEAM — 92 FT.
DEPTH — 94 FT.
DISPLACEMENT
45,000 TONS
VALUE (ESTIMATED)
$10,000,000

WHITE LINES ON SIDE of STEAMSHIP INDICATE LOCATION of BULKHEADS

White Star Official Admits the Greatest Disaster in Marine History — J. J. Astor Rumored Lost, but Bride Saved — Text of Olympic's Fateful Message—Partial List Is Received.

HOPE THAT MANY WILL BE FOUND ON WRECKAGE.

Virginian and Parisian Reach Scene Too Late—They Are Joined by Other Steamers, Which Find Only Debris—Capt. Smith Believed to Have Gone Down with Ship—The Saved Suffer Severely from Exposure After Floating in the Lifeboats for Eight Hours.

CHAPTER 4
A SAFER FUTURE

News of the *Titanic* disaster spread quickly, but newspapers had conflicting reports. Some claimed that all the passengers were safe. Others said that the ship had made it to Halifax, Nova Scotia, in Canada. But soon the world learned the truth. The *Titanic* was on the bottom of the ocean, and more than fifteen hundred people had died.

Carpathia's passengers and crew comforted and helped the *Titanic* survivors. The people aboard the *Carpathia* gave them food and clothing. Some gave up their cabins so the survivors would have a place to sleep and recover. The *Carpathia*, which had been sailing to Croatia, changed its destination. Three days later, it reached New York Harbor, where friends and relatives greeted the survivors.

The *Carpathia* arrived in New York City on April 18, 1912, with the *Titanic* survivors.

Soon after, both the US and British governments investigated the causes of the disaster. They called on survivors to testify. Eighty-two witnesses spoke to a special US Senate committee. Both governments decided that they needed new laws to make sure people would be safer at sea.

They called for several changes to how ships were made. Large ships needed to be built better to block out water. And ship compartments had to be designed better to help the ship stay afloat during an accident.

TITANIC TODAY

For more than seventy years, no one knew exactly where the *Titanic* lay on the ocean floor. Then, in 1985, Robert Ballard and his crew found the wreckage. Robots equipped with cameras took pictures of the sunken ship. These photographs renewed people's interest in the *Titanic*. And in 1997, a movie about the disaster became a hit. This *Titanic* movie includes many real details about life aboard the ship and its tragic sinking.

The US Senate committee spoke with *Titanic* survivors at the Waldorf-Astoria Hotel in New York City.

Radio **communications** between boats also needed to improve. New laws required that certain radio **bandwidths** had to be reserved for the navy and telegraph operators on ships. And ships' telegraph operators had to monitor those bandwidths twenty-four hours a day.

Navigating through ice fields was also a problem. So new ice patrols on the Atlantic Ocean began monitoring dangerous ice fields. Boats called cutters patrolled the shipping lanes and reported icebergs. Later, aircraft and radar tracked icebergs.

And new rules about lifeboats were put in place. Every ship had to carry enough lifeboats for all passengers and crew members. The rules also required that ships have lifeboat drills twice a month. Lawmakers hoped that a tragedy as big as the sinking of the *Titanic* would never happen again.

The survivors of the *Titanic* were changed forever by their voyage. Many had lost family members. None could forget the horrors of witnessing the tragedy. Their memories stayed with them forever, and their stories continue to grip the world.

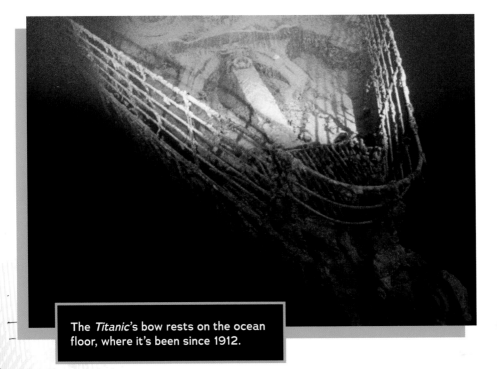

The *Titanic's* bow rests on the ocean floor, where it's been since 1912.

SURVIVING DEADLY SITUATIONS

Probably, you won't ever be on a sinking ship. But the best way to survive a dangerous situation is to prepare for it. These steps help people survive a ship disaster:

1. Know where your life preserver is when you board a boat.

2. Pay attention during a lifeboat drill, and know the steps to follow during an emergency.

3. Send a signal for help if you are on a small boat that is in trouble. Listen for an evacuation signal on a large boat. The crew will blow seven short horn blasts followed by one long one. They might make an intercom announcement.

4. Put on your life preserver before you assist anyone else.

5. Stay calm. Take deep breaths if you feel yourself panicking.

6. Follow directions. The captain or crew will tell you how to get to safety.

7. Take the quickest route to safety. If the ship is tilting, hold onto handrails or pipes to keep yourself steady.

8. When on deck, immediately go to your lifeboat. Wait in the lifeboat for a ship to rescue you.

SOURCE NOTES

16 Sean Coughlan, "*Titanic:* The Final Messages from a Stricken Ship," *BBC*, April 10, 2012, http://www.bbc.com/news /magazine-17631595.

23 Kim Gilmore, "*Titanic*'s 100th Anniversary: 6 Survivor Stories," *Biography*, April 12, 2012, https://www.biography .com/news/titanics-100th-anniversary-6-survivor-stories -20799733.

GLOSSARY

bandwidths: ranges of frequencies for sending signals on a radio

bow: the forward end of a ship

bridge: a room or platform from where a ship is steered

collapsible: able to be folded in a compact shape

communications: exchanges of information

compartments: separate sections in a ship's hull that help it stay afloat

crow's nest: a platform near the top of a tall pole on a ship that sailors use as a lookout

evacuation: moving away from a dangerous area, such as a sinking ship

hull: the main body of a ship

propellers: fanlike machine parts that spin in the water to move a ship

stern: the rear end of a ship

FURTHER INFORMATION

Berne, Emma Carlson. *Titanic*. New York: Scholastic, 2018.

Goldish, Meish. Titanic's *Last Hours: The Facts*. New York: Bearport, 2018.

Ohlin, Nancy. *Blast Back! The* Titanic. New York: Little Bee Books, 2016.

Remembering the *Titanic*
https://kids.nationalgeographic.com/explore/history/a-titanic
-anniversary/#TitanicInterior1.jpg

Sabol, Stephanie. *What Was the* Titanic? New York: Penguin Workshop, 2018.

Stewart, Melissa. *Titanic*. Washington, DC: National Geographic, 2012.

Titanic Facts for Kids
https://www.coolkidfacts.com/titanic-facts-for-kids/

What Made the *Titanic* Sink?
http://discoverymindblown.com/articles/what-made-the
-titanic-sink/

Would You Have Survived the *Titanic*?
https://www.natgeokids.com/nz/discover/history/general
-history/would-you-have-survived-the-titanic/#!/register

INDEX

PHOTO ACKNOWLEDGMENTS

Image credits: Lebrecht Music & Arts/Alamy Stock Photo, pp. 1, 14; Bettmann/
Getty Images, pp. 4–5, 17, 21; F.G.O. Stuart/Wikimedia Commons (PD), p. 6; United
Archives GmbH/Alamy Stock Photo, p. 7; Carl Simon/United Archives/UIG/Getty
Images, p. 8; Chronicle/Alamy Stock Photo, p. 9; Hulton-Deutsch Collection/CORBIS/
Getty Images, p. 10; Ralph White/CORBIS/Getty Images, pp. 11, 28; Universal
History Archive/UIG/Getty Images, p. 12; Library of Congress (LC-DIG-hec-00939),
p. 13; World History Archive/Alamy Stock Photo, p. 15; API/Gamma-Rapho/Getty
Images, p. 16; National Archives/Wikimedia Commons (PD), p. 18; Hulton Archive/
Getty Images, p. 19; Laura Westlund/Independent Picture Service, p. 22; Library
of Congress (LC-USZ62-56453), p. 23; Library of Congress (LC-USZ62-116257),
p. 24; PA Images/Getty Images, p. 25; Library of Congress (LC-USZ62-68081), p. 27;
Design elements: sl_photo/Shutterstock.com; Miloje/Shutterstock.com; Khvost/
Shutterstock; Redshinestudio/Shutterstock.com; Milan M/Shutterstock.com; foxie/
Shutterstock.com.

Cover: Everett Historical/Shutterstock.com.

UNLABEL

Selling You Without Selling Out

MARC ECKŌ

A TOUCHSTONE BOOK
PUBLISHED BY SIMON & SCHUSTER
NEW YORK   LONDON   TORONTO   SYDNEY   NEW DELHI

TOUCHSTONE
A Division of Simon & Schuster, Inc.
1230 Avenue of the Americas
New York, NY 10020

Some names and identifying characteristics have been changed and some characters are composites.

First Touchstone hardcover edition October 2013

TOUCHSTONE and colophon are registered trademarks of Simon & Schuster, Inc.

For information about special discounts for bulk purchases, please contact Simon & Schuster Special Sales at 1-866-506-1949 or business@simonandschuster.com.

The Simon & Schuster Speakers Bureau can bring authors to your live event. For more information or to book an event, contact the Simon & Schuster Speakers Bureau at 866-248-3049 or visit our website at www.simonspeakers.com.

Designed by Headcase Design
www.headcasedesign.com

Manufactured in the United States of America

1   3   5   7   9   10   8   6   4   2

Library of Congress Cataloging-in-Publication Data
Ecko, Marc.
Unlabel : selling you without selling out / Marc Ecko.
pages cm
1. Ecko, Marc. 2. T-shirt industry—United States. 3. Clothing trade—United States.
4. Businessmen—United States—Biography. 5. Branding (Marketing)
6. Entrepreneurship. I. Title.
HD9969.S6E35 2013
338.7'687115—dc23
[B]
2013023472

Illustration permissions are on page 294.

ISBN 978-1-4516-8530-5
ISBN 978-1-4516-8533-6 (ebook)

To my wife, Allison

You are the center of all that is good and beautiful in my world. I love you. You have always helped me build a canvas to create all I can imagine. Despite life sometimes being a little messy and rough around the edges, in the end we make it plenty tidy.

For Sage, Alex, and Ella!

Here's the one textbook I wish they were selling when I was in school. Though it's unlikely to be something Mommy reads to you before bedtime (forgive me for all the cussing), I'm hopeful that you eventually discover a useful key in here that may help you crack some of those stubborn problems you are sure to encounter in your life.

CONTENTS

This book breaks down the anatomy of a personal brand
as demonstrated by the Authenticity Formula:

$$AWE! = \left(\frac{Unj}{\sqrt{}} \right) \mathcal{T}^{\infty-1}$$

1   2   3

+ ‖ CAPACITY for CHANGE ⊏ ± ∃ ‖ (∃!) Ω

4   5   6

Authenticity[1] is equal to your unique voice,[2] multiplied by truthfulness,[3] plus your capacity for change,[4] multiplied by range of emotional impact,[5] raised to the power of imagination.[6]

"There is no life I know to compare with pure imagination."

—WILLY WONKA
(GENE WILDER)

"I'm absolutely positive that I'm serving the American people better if I'm maintaining my authenticity."

—BARACK OBAMA

CHAPTER 1

AWE

I am a brand, but I am not a label. My brand is Marc Eckō. You too are a brand. Whether you know it or not. Whether you like it or not. A brand is not skin-deep. Labels are skin-deep, but a brand—a true, authentic brand—is made of blood and bones, skin and organs. A brand has a heartbeat.

The anatomy of a brand, in turn, is defined by its authenticity. And just like a doctor can't describe the wonders of the human body in a pithy one-line description, a brand's authenticity can't be clearly defined in a Twitteresque 140 characters.

Hard work is required to understand, grow, and nurture the anatomy of a brand. You can't do it on the surface. You can't slap on a "Brand Band-Aid." You have to dig deep and poke around with a scalpel.

To understand the anatomy of the human body, doctors use tools. They use stethoscopes, exams, and a mountain of knowledge that dates back to Henry Grey and Hippocrates. I, too, have a tool. It's a formula. To understand the anatomy of a brand, I created a formula that explains the nervous system, the heartbeat, the spine, and the core of a brand's authenticity. It's not straightforward. It's not a tidy 1, 2, 3.

This is a book that explores the anatomy of a brand. And it uses this formula—the Authenticity Formula—to explain the cross sections of that anatomy. Each chapter peels back a layer and dissects a variable of the formula. And just as doctors use a body as an example for their students, it just so happens, coincidentally, that I have an example that we can use for our anatomy lesson: me.

My brand started in my parents' garage in Lakewood, New Jersey, where I spray-painted T-shirts and sold them for $10 a pop. I grew that brand to the tune of a billion-dollar retail business. I've built skate brands, hip-hop brands, magazine and video game brands. I've built brands that people literally tattoo on their bodies, which is "branding" in the truest sense. But the most important brand that I built was me, *the personal brand that's from my guts to the skin.*

My philosophy is simple: unlabel.

Not "un" as in the nihilist or negative sense of the prefix, but in the "refuse" sense of the meaning. Refuse to be labeled.

Fight their labels.

Ignore their labels.

Peel off their labels.

Create your label.

Unlabel.

This takes work. In the same way that you do push-ups to exercise your body, you need to challenge yourself to shake free of the herd, find your own unique voice, and create your personal authentic brand.

Find your swoosh, your Apple, your Rhino.

You're labeled in hundreds of ways by thousands of people. But how much of this have you consciously controlled? How much have you consciously created? *How much of what's known about you is* authentic *to you, and how much is merely the perception of others?*

When you unlabel, you can be an artist without being a starving artist. You can sell without selling out. To do this, you need to create an authentic personal brand that transcends the gatekeepers *(the critics, the haters) who want to put a label on you and gets right to the* goalkeepers *(the ones who vote, the folks with the shopping carts). The goalkeepers are the only judges who matter.*

How people see you, feel you, understand you, and make assumptions about you when you are not in the room are pieces of your personal brand, and this is true whether you're the president of the United States, a priest, or a plumber. Whatever your product or service, you are essentially selling you. Deal with it.

THIS BOOK IS the story of how I unlabeled myself, defying classifications so that I could grow both creatively and commercially. It's a personal story, a business story, and a prescriptive course for anyone who wants to grow a brand.

Brands are often thought of negatively as the domain of advertising, but a personal brand can be a powerful tool. In times of success, it keeps you grounded. In times of crisis, it keeps you confident. In heightened moments of critical decision making, it hones your improvisational skills. But it doesn't come easy. It takes real effort, imagination, and follow-through to create your authentic personal brand.

I'm a brand, but I'm also a creator. Are these ideas even compatible? People think of the word *creator* as something almost divine, while *brand* is almost vulgar. *Brand* is *all* Don Draper; *creator* is *all* Michelangelo. Creators do work that is noble and proud—spiritual, ethereal, and impossibly pure. There's an inherent tension between these two concepts.

I'm a brand, but I'm also a creator. I'm both an artist and an instigator.

Brand. Create. Not mutually exclusive.

CREATE *vs* BRAND

Unlabel is about resolving that tension. This requires a fundamental change in your assumptions. You must move from the mind-set of "I am a consumer and I want X" to "I am a producer and I create Y." *Create* can be anything; you don't have to be an artist or musician or inventor. Maybe you create code or create ads; or if you're a dental hygienist, you create clean teeth.

When you unlabel and create an authentic personal brand, you will broadcast yourself differently to the world. You will think of yourself more actively, not passively. You won't just *use* the social network, you'll *become* the social network. When you have a rock-solid sense of your own authentic personal brand, everything else—the graffiti you're tagging, the mix tape you're hawking, the company you're launching, the next $1 billion platform you're stewarding—will flow externally from the inside out; from your guts to the skin.

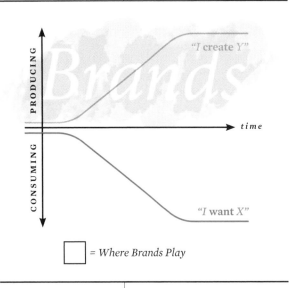

= *Where Brands Play*

People can take your job. No one can take away the brand you've created and your *ability* to create again. Let them smash what you've been saving, let them burn what you've built—when you can create, the power is yours, not theirs. What happens when your job is yanked away? What happens when your career becomes obsolete? What happens when you shit the bed—*hard*?

To me, these aren't just rhetorical questions. I've had to answer them. I nearly lost all control of my company, I struggled with crushing debt, I even thought I might lose my house. I was a media darling and then a media target.

But it was okay. I was okay. You'll be okay. Because if you do it right, your brand is still there selling for you, and when you know you can create, your brand will help you recover, get a new job, make new sheets. Your brand is your bedrock. It's there when your start-up cracks $200 million in revenue, but it's also there to help you deal with a nasty boss, swallow dire news about the economy, and it's even there if you face bankruptcy.

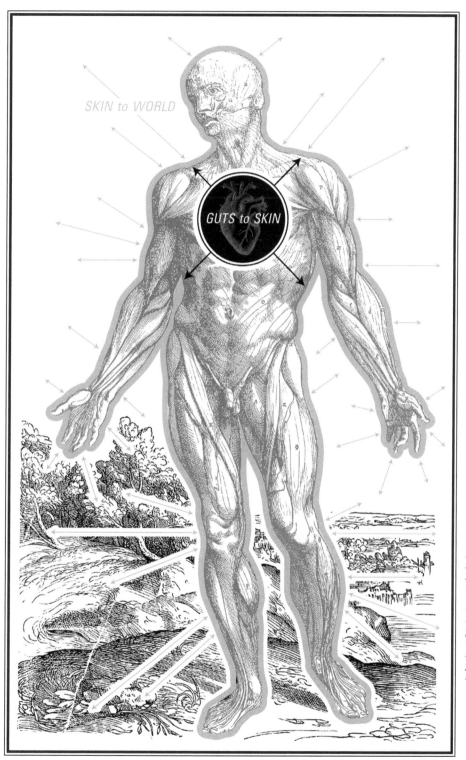

SKIN to WORLD

GUTS to SKIN

When you UNLABEL and create an authentic personal brand, you will broadcast yourself differently to the world. You will think of yourself more actively, not passively. You won't just use the social network, you'll become the social network.

Building a brand is like creating your own personal religion. You need to be willing to fight for it, defend it, die for it. It involves being something of a zealot. Honestly? I would have preferred to call this book *Creating Your Own Religion*, but the world is too sensitive to use *religion* as a metaphor for *branding*. But religions brand all the time. The Sistine Chapel? Now *that's* branding—it puts Apple's retail stores to shame. Glass cube storefront? Whatevs.

How 'bout that nave roof detail at Antoni Gaudí's masterpiece, *La Sagrada Família*, in Barcelona, Spain? That's one hell of a shopping environment.

Building a brand is like creating your own personal religion. You need to be willing to fight for it, defend it, die for it. It involves being something of a zealot.

The book breaks down each individual component of the authenticity formula, and then, throughout, you'll see each piece in action. Each chapter tackles one variable of the formula, and you'll see that my story is the formula's story, and within it are prescriptions for how you can apply it. (And while there isn't much math, there are plenty of pictures. I use visuals to process and to synthesize; that's why there are so many photos in this book.)

This isn't a fashion book. I don't care if you've never seen my clothes or have no interest in fashion, graffiti, or street wear. That happens to be the aesthetic world I came from, but the principles are equally valid regardless of whether you're promoting a new product, launching a website, or selling cars.

And this isn't a "how-to" business book about how to make millions. There are no cheesy mission statements. (But there is a manifesto I dare you to sign.) I won't spoon-feed you *7 Habits of Highly Successful Creators*, I'm not going to tell you *The Art of the Brand*, and you won't see me lose my virginity (though girls have definitely played into my motivations). I don't believe in just bragging about wins, sugarcoating, or pretending that I never fail. I've failed plenty. Unlike what I've seen of the Trumps and the CEOs and the cigar-smoking Titans of Industry, I believe in not only disclosing that failure but also robustly diagnosing it, and learning from it. This is the textbook I wish I had in college.

$$\Delta W \exists! = \left(\sqrt[\infty-1]{\frac{Unj}{}}\right) \mathcal{T} + \left\| \boxed{\begin{array}{c} \text{CAPACITY for CHANGE} \\ \text{C} \pm \end{array}} \right\| (\exists!)^{\Omega}$$

Through all my ups and downs, it was the creation of my personal brand—and discovering the seed for my AUTHENTICITY—that helped me live the American Dream 2.0.

Not just settling for the brand I was born into.

Not just checking off the boxes of what the perception of success looks like.

Not just accepting the gatekeepers' *label*.

I know that plenty of readers will laugh and say, "Wait, *Marc Eckō*, writing a book about authenticity?" It's true: my clothes have been called inauthentic, my street cred has been questioned, and my publicity stunts have been criticized. The cynics have jeered and the detractors have slung their arrows. And I wouldn't have it any other way. I wear those scars with honor. This is all part of the story.

I found success—measured in both guts-to-the-skin happiness and billion-dollar companies—only when I scrapped off the labels of the gatekeepers, ditched the boxes, and *created* my own personal, authentic brand that captured the attention of the people who count: the goalkeepers.

You don't need much to start this creation. In my case? Just some crayons, scratch paper, and a stack of comic books.

*Everything you need
to understand about
branding is on the inside.
One must not be afraid
to look or be mystified
by a pseudoscience. It's
all there.*

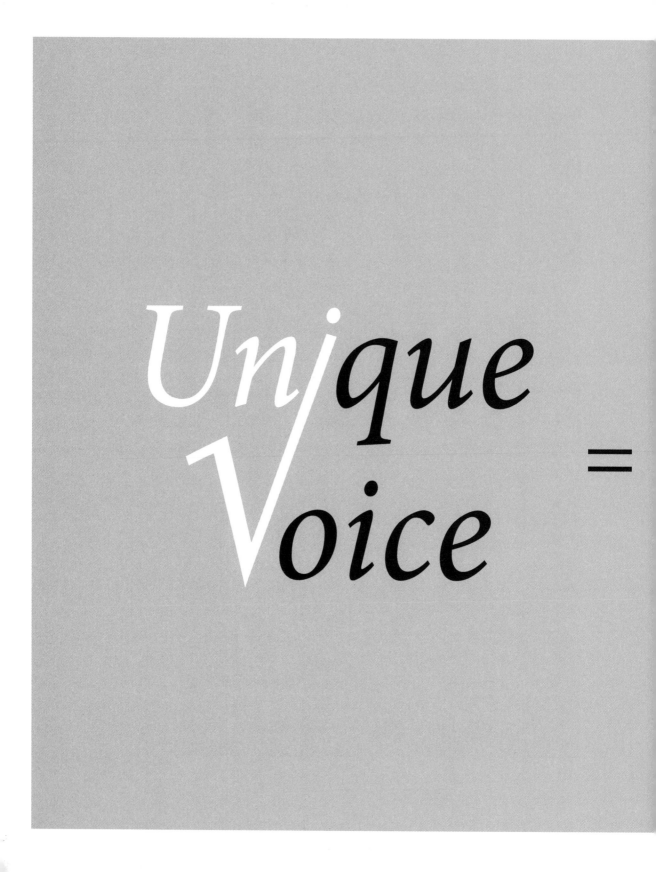

Unique = *Voice* =

$$\frac{\displaystyle\int_{0}^{100} f(\text{ACTION})\,dx - \int_{0.1}^{100} f(\text{FEAR})\,dx}{\displaystyle\int_{0.1}^{100} f(\text{SELF})\,dx}$$

"Fear is a state of nervousness fit for children and not men."

—MARCUS GARVEY

"I fear not the man who has practiced ten thousand kicks once, but I fear the man who has practiced one kick ten thousand times."

—BRUCE LEE

F E A R

Authentic brands have a UNIQUE VOICE ($\sqrt[Uni]{}$), which is a function of three variables: ACTION, FEAR, and SELF.

Before you can take ACTION, you must overcome your FEAR. This is where we begin.

***FEAR** can immobilize you, trap your creative voice, and arrest you from expressing yourself. A certain amount of FEAR is healthy. A fear of fire is stamped in our DNA. It's a survival instinct: you're afraid of fire because you respect its power. Thanks to this fear, we learned to leverage fire, to govern it, to use it for cooking meat and to keep our homes warm.*

In business, you need to have a healthy amount of FEAR when it comes to playing with the fire of debt, loans, and financial leverage. If we all had just a little more FEAR, maybe we could have dodged the credit crisis of 2008–09. But too much FEAR could prevent you from taking any risks, which you need to do to create and scale a brand. If you're going to build a UNIQUE VOICE ($\sqrt[Uni]{}$), this process is going to be painful, it's going to be dangerous, and someone, somewhere, is going to hate you for it.

When starting out, it's easy to cloak your fear in the artifice of "being above it all." We all tell ourselves lies like, we're too good for schlocky "brands," we don't want to be "mainstream," and we'd never "sell out." How much of that is your true concern, and how much of that is just your FEAR of expressing your own UNIQUE VOICE ($\sqrt[Uni]{}$)?

IN 2005 THE president of Tommy Hilfiger Corporation, Dave Dyer, asked me and my business partner to join him on his yacht.

The boat sliced through the Hudson River, and I could see the Statue of Liberty straight ahead. Dyer, a big guy from the South, turned to Seth Gerszberg and me. "Champagne?"

We nodded. He poured. We drank it all in.

"Deal's almost complete," he said. "Here's the LOI."

LOI. Letter of intent. Seth and I stole a glance at each other. We tried to keep from smiling. This had been almost twenty years in the making.

"You boys like seared tuna? Sesame encrusted?" Dyer asked.

Another nod. He went down below to check on his chef.

Seth and I mouthed the words *Holy shit.* The deal was an offer for Hilfiger to buy our company, Eckō Unlimited, for an ungodly amount of cash that I, in good taste, probably shouldn't say. Screw it: about $500 million.

Seth and I leaned against the yacht's railing. I closed my eyes and channeled DiCaprio in *Titanic.* We drank more champagne.

"We should give a five hundred thou bonus to the receptionist," he said.

"Let's make it a mil."

We clinked our glasses and talked about how we'd spend the money. Maybe buy another house? Maybe buy a jet? Sure, who doesn't need a jet. Nah, that's too self-indulgent; we'll lease one. We talked about the new company we would form.

"What should we call it?" Seth asked. "Something that reminds us to buy back these fuckers."

"B.O.T.," I said.

"B.O.T.?"

"'Buy Out Tommy.' We'll get so big that we'll buy *him* out."

Dyer served the perfectly cooked fish, the champagne turned to gin, and we finished our cruise. But then a funny thing happened. Even though Hilfiger (the person) signed off on the deal, and even though Dyer shook our hands and filed the letter of intent, Hilfiger's board of directors killed it. They said it was too "cash rich," too big. The risk was greater than the reward. The deal never happened.

At the time, our company was in great shape. It was lean. It was profitable. It was growing. When the deal fell through, we didn't cry, we just said, "Fuck it, let's get *bigger*. We don't need Hilfiger's five hundred mil. We don't need outsiders. We'll make our own conglomerate. We'll become the institution."

We decided that in order for Eckō (the company) to become that big, it would mean that Eckō (the person)—me—would need to become supersized. The world needed to *perceive* us as a giant, a Titan of Industry, a multibillion-dollar enterprise with retail stores across the globe. And perception is reality, right?

We had grown from a T-shirt business set in my parents' garage to being on the verge of Hilfigerland. If we needed to change what our company was and who I was, then so be it. But this path would prove to be a ride down a rabbit hole to *in*authenticity that almost destroyed me and the company.

But before we play that out, let's go back to where it all began: Lakewood, New Jersey.

I. *ECHO* WITH AN *H*

I WAS IN the fifth grade, playing flag football. The quarterback, my friend Ben, looked at me in the huddle. "Marc, the ball's coming your way," he said. "Post route!"

"Got it." That was a total lie. I didn't want the ball to come anywhere near me. I couldn't catch, couldn't run, and the words *post route* had as much meaning as "paper route."

"Break!" Ben yelled. We all clapped our hands, and I shuffled to the line of scrimmage, dreading what would happen next.

"Blue forty-two! Blue forty-two! Hut-hut-hut!"

I started running, and by "running," I mean that I staggered my chubby legs forward, jogging slowly, huffing and puffing, easily blanketed by the kid who defended me. *Don't throw it at me, don't throw it at me . . .*

My defender tripped and fell down, leaving me alone in the end zone. Ben spotted me—*Don't do it*—and he chucked the ball, launching a perfect spiral that cut through the blue sky in a long, glorious arc. As it sailed toward me, I was all alone, extending my arms, and I thought to myself, *You can do this*, and I felt the ball hit my hands—and ricochet off.

Laughter from the sidelines. "Good catch, Fatty!" I heard someone taunt.

The voice came from behind a chain-link fence. As I picked up the ball, I saw a short, black, bare-chested dude on the other side of the fence. He was shredded like Grandmaster Melle Mel in his prime. His name was Anthony something, but everyone called him "Supreme Mathematics."

Oh shit. Not Supreme Mathematics. I'd heard of him. Everyone had. He'd been held back a couple of grades. He was a Five Percenter (a group derived from Malcolm X's Nation of Islam, whose members believe that they are the 5 percent of the population that knows the truth about the universe), and Supreme Mathematics was his Five Percenters name. Every day he did backflips after school with his shirt off, ten in a row, and legend had it he could do one-handed chin-ups. He was the ringleader of the break-dancers.

I reached down for the ball and started to run away.

"What's up, Fat Boy?" Supreme said.

I became frozen in his grown-ass-man gaze. "C'mere, Fatty!"

Supreme pushed up against the chain-link fence, glowering at me. "What'cha doing running around playing football, Fatty? Look at you running around with your titties bouncing up and down!"

"I, um . . ." I said as a comeback.

In the distance, I could hear Ben yelling for me, asking me to throw the ball back. I couldn't. Supreme Mathematics had me in his spell. The muscles on his shoulders rippled and seemed to grow even larger. His friends started to laugh.

"I *know you*, Fatty." He narrowed his eyes. "Aren't you Jewish? Where's your little beanie? Where's your curly things?" He pointed to his hair.

"I, um . . ." When I have a good line, I stick with it.

"I've seen you on a bike, Fatty. Fly BMX bike. I'm going to fuck you up and steal your bike."

I wasn't just afraid of getting beaten up. I feared the social rejection. The sneers from the other cool kids. They laughed as I stood there, powerless, chubby, awkward. They couldn't see that I was an artist. They couldn't see that I had something to say. They just laughed at my label. And the chain-link fence was a gateway, of sorts, that kept me from the crowd of insiders. Supreme was the gatekeeper, and I didn't have the key.

Just then I heard a new voice, a female voice. *"Hey!"* My twin sister's voice.

Marci ran up and squeezed between me and the fence, shielding me. "You leave him alone!" she yelled.

"Who's this?" Supreme laughed.

"That's my twin brother, and you better back off."

"Twin?!" Supreme shook the fence, laughing. "How are you so fat and she so skinny? You must eat all her food, fat boy!"

"He doesn't eat my food!" Marci yelled, flashing him a look that somehow conveyed *I will fuck you up.* "Go. Away. *Now.*"

Supreme Mathematics seemed rattled by this refusal to back down—from a *girl*—and his fingers unwrapped from the fence. He turned and left. Marci threw her arm around my shoulder, and we walked back to the game. I wasn't yet ready to face the gatekeepers. I was too afraid. Too insecure in my SELF.

That's how I rolled: I needed my twin sister to save my ass. And I wasn't too proud to admit it. Marci often came to my rescue. It wasn't the first time that I (the baby brother) borrowed "Her Voice." I needed her ACTION to get over my FEAR. (And as I found out years later at Eckō Unlimited, she would save my ass again and again.)

M ARCI IS THE reason I have my name Echo. When my mom was pregnant, she thought she carried only a single baby. She felt the baby kicking in the lower part of her abdomen, and then, at the same time, she felt kicks in her right breast. This made no sense to her; was this some Chuck Norris baby who could do the splits? The doctor told her the second kick was just an "echo in the fluid."

So on the morning of August 29, 1972, at St. Barnabas Hospital in Livingston, New Jersey, my mother pushed! pushed! pushed! and Marci came out. But my

mom still felt something, so the doctor called for a second bassinet and told her, "Here comes the echo."

I guess I've been an instigator since birth.

We grew up in eighties Lakewood, New Jersey. An eclectic mix of Orthodox Judaism, hip-hop, black folks, brown folks, white folks, and bagels and lox. Let's say it was more stirred together than your average American suburb. I owe a lot to this hot pot. The one kid my age who lived near me was named Darren Robinson, and he quickly became my best friend. We were geeks who played countless hours of Donkey Kong and Coleco Vision Super Action Football, wearing out our Atari 2600s. Marci and I were twins, but the three of us were triplets. We did everything together, and our parents also became close. Darren's family introduced me to this whole other world of music, exposing me to artists such as Al Jarreau and James Brown. Darren's father turned an entire room of their small house into a shrine for his records, and he let me spend countless hours

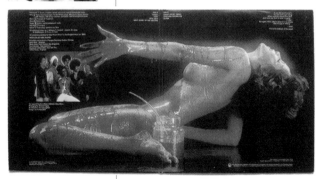

listening and staring at the artwork on the covers.

This education in music probably helped make me a little cooler, but I got hooked on the dorkiest of dork hobbies from my father's own collection: comics. Not just the typical stuff like Spider-Man, but obscure gems like *Superman vs. Muhammad Ali* and *Howard the*

Duck. I was all-in. I didn't just *read* them; I studied them, traced them, drew them, and dreamed them. I figured out how to draw a hand from the panels of Captain America. I got my first hard-on from tracing Elektra's body. I traced and I traced.

My grandma, who lived with us, made a big fuss over my drawings, cooing, "Ooooh, look what Marc drew!" and she'd stick it on the fridge.

But it wasn't *cool*. I was a goofball. Chubby, curly hair, freckles, a big gap in my teeth. I was the mamma's boy; my twin sister's baby brother. Even worse, I was *safe*. So much so that *parents encouraged* their daughters to come over to my house because I was deemed "safe to play with." I was the artsy kid. The nice kid. The one with the Ooompa Loompa face. Plus, there was a prize at the bottom of a Cracker Jack box: they had Marci to play with. So the girls got a two-for-one: their friend Marci and her safe little twin Oompa-Loompa–faced brother.

"Let me show you Marc's drawings!" Grandma said to one of the many girls who came by.

"I'd love to see it," the girl said, smiling at me.

Grandma opened a folder and took out my drawings of the Hulk, Yoda, and Conan the Barbarian.

She wasn't the best wingman. But it wasn't so bad, because for every one of those shameful moments, she made sure to slip my preteen ass a *Playboy* just

OUTSTANDING YOUNG ARTISTS · Students from across the nation submitted original works of art which were published in the first hard-bound edition of "Outstanding Young Artists in American Elementary Schools." Two fourth grade students at the Clifton Avenue Grade School were nominated last spring by ░░░░░░░░░░░ their art teacher. Pictured holding the book that contains their drawings are ░░░░░░░░░░ (left) and Marc Milekofsky, now in the fifth grade at the Princeton Avenue School. A copy of the book was purchased by the Clifton Avenue Grade School P.T.A. for the school library.

to make certain I was, in fact, "into girls."

"You like that?" Grandma would say, pointing to a set of natural, pendulous 36Cs.

"Yeaaahhhhrr."

"Good," she'd reply.

II. **THE EXTREME SPORT OF GRAFFITI**

I MIGHT HAVE spent the rest of my life as a comic-book dork if it wasn't for a trip to visit my cousin in Trenton, New Jersey.

While riding in the car with my dad through Trenton, I happened to spot freight cars covered with insane Krylon colors spray-painted on, like apocalyptic billboards. Saturated. Acidic. Spanish brown, burnt orange, hot pink, harvest gold, pastel aqua, clover green, and baby blue.

I nudged my dad. "What's painted on those trains?"

He shrugged. "That's graffiti."

A few weeks later, he took me to a bookstore, where I beelined to the art section (like always) and buried my nose in "how-to-draw-comics" manuals. Then I saw something that stopped me cold—the cover of *Subway Art* by Henry Chalfant and Martha Cooper—the most completist visual summary of early-eighties graf culture in NYC. It featured the likes of Dondi White, Futura, Lee, and Crash. When I saw this book, I saw my future. I saw the teenage Marc, not the boyhood Marc. The book practically had a label that said "Drink me."

photo © Martha Cooper.

Dondi White became a big influence. That image of him straddling the walls between two subway cars—like some sort of masked vigilante, a real-life Spider-Man—injected a whole new possibility of what *artist* could mean. He was famous for his riff on Vaughn Bode's adult-themed comic strip, called *Cheech Wizard,* that used to run in *National Lampoon* magazine. Dondi reimagined the characters as B-boys (decked out with hip-hop swagger) on the sides of subway cars. He was sampling. Just like eighties rap. Taking pieces of pop culture and mashing them together to create his unique vision. Dondi's infamous series of works, *Children of the Grave* parts 1, 2, and 3, spanned three entire cars on the New York subway from 1978 to 1980. He even sampled the name of the piece; it's from a Black Sabbath song.

It was Dondi's third piece in the series that hipped me to Vaughn Bode's work. Fascinated, I read more and I unraveled more. *Cheech Wizard* was filled with pages of these otherworldly hippie lizards having sex with voluptuous cartoon women. It was graphic, sexually and aesthetically, and most certainly not meant for ten-year-olds. I loved it.

I sensed that this was all somehow "counterculture." Even though I didn't have the vocabulary to articulate it, I felt it in my gut. And graffiti—like hip-hop at that moment, or more specifically, Dondi and also MC Shan, who sampled the Ohio Players on his single "So Def"—would be a sort of gateway that allowed me to discover art and culture, from Pablo Picasso to Spike Lee. After all, Picasso said, "Bad artists copy. Good artists steal," although with sampling it's not theft,

An early √ision for the Future

photo © Martha Cooper.

because the sampler acknowledges the source material. This would launch me into universes far, far away from Lakewood.

My next small step was at Darren's cousin's birthday party, where I heard Run-D.M.C.'s self-titled album for the first time. I had listened to earlier rap, but this was the album that established the four elements of hip-hop:

1. The DJ
2. Break-dancing
3. The MC
4. Graffiti

This was the codification. Well I couldn't rap, I couldn't MC, I was too fat to break-dance, but I could draw my ass off.

This cultural sampling—from both music and art—along with the *extreme sport* *of graffiti*, became a way for me to communicate with my peers. My art was no longer a G-rated girl repellent. Both in terms of the music I listened to and the art that I studied, this sampling became a clear "best practice" of creating, and I became more conscious of its use and existence. This was the first bit of kindling for creating my own personal brand.

MY FIFTH-GRADE art teacher held a drawing competition, and instead of handing in the usual family portrait or landscape, I did the King of Pop.

Michael Jackson's impact on the browning of American pop culture is undeniable. I had a *sense* that I was tapping into something. I illustrated a pencil portrait of MJ sitting on a throne like a king, based on a magazine cover I'd seen at the time. Everyone loved it! White kids loved it, black kids loved it. Even Supreme Mathematics bigged me up. And I was thinking . . . "This feels good."

And then I followed it up by spray-painting the Lakewood Airport with a two-hundred-foot image of a screaming rhinoceros. C'mon, I was *ten*, I

---

* When I say "extreme sport," I'm not talking about the X Games, Tony Hawk, or whatever connotations you have for snowboarding or "bros." Graffiti, thanks to the need to climb and reach dangerous places, was forbidden and testosterone fueled, much like how extreme sports took surfing from the Beach Boys and made it counterculture.

didn't do anything close to that. I started small, but I put in my hours, shifting into deep practice-makes-perfect mode. First comics, then Dondi (or what I imagined of Dondi)—drawing obsessively until my eyes blurred past the marker's chiseled nose, scribbling my name on school desks and bathroom stalls. My parents were incredibly supportive of my new borderline-delinquent interests. They weren't hippies, but they did believe in me, Marci, and our older sister, Shari; they almost wanted us to fail a bit in order to learn.

Note, my name belt was Marc backward or "CRAM." I was still vetting "ECHO" as a moniker.

I inched closer when I found some old Krylon spray cans in the garage, and soon I splattered every piece of plywood with the letters of my name. I was what graf artists would call a bona fide "toy": someone who had an incompetent style. I was wack. But I was oblivious to this; being a toy was all relative because in Lakewood, I was king.

I needed a "tag" name. A proper alias. An aka.

My first idea was a simple, one-word, four-letter name: "Cram." That's M-a-r-c spelled backward.

Craaaaammmmm?! I thought to myself. *Wack.* Cram wasn't going to cut it.

I thought back to who I was *the very second I was born*—by definition, the time I was most fearless—and I realized that my parents, on that night in the hospital in 1972, had handed me my street moniker on a silver platter.

Echo. With an *H.* Marci's twin. I was the Echo.*

Did I have a vision of how graffiti would emerge as a cultural force? Did I have a tingling sense of a billion-dollar industry that I would help to create? No. I just wanted to paint a T-shirt. My "vision" didn't start with billions, my vision started with a can of spray paint and what I could do with it in the next thirty minutes. Entrepreneurs lose sight of that. When Steve Jobs and Steve Wozniak built their first motherboard, they didn't envision the iPhone. Visions

---

* I later added a line over the *O*—Echō—in an homage to Stussy, who tagged his name Stüssy.

24

can start small. Visions *should* start small. They're incremental, like building Legos:

Snap one block to the next.

Snap another block.

Repeat.

(ACTION) > (FEAR)

Having an overly majestic *"vision"* can cripple you with pressure. When I started with graffiti, I thought about my next eighteen hours, not my next eighteen years. Free yourself to do the same.

III. **MR. PRESIDENT**

IN SEVENTH GRADE, they introduce student government in Lakewood Public Schools. My friend Darren, the most popular kid I knew, encouraged me to run for class president. At first I didn't want to do it. I was no longer getting bullied, due partly to my newly forged graffiti handle, and I was even getting head nods from some of the cool kids in the hallway, so why would I want to start going *backward* on the cool meter? I had no interest in school politics or giving a speech about "free chocolate milk for everyone!"

But as Darren was quick to point out, this could be my way in to getting girls to actually talk to me—or at least look at me. And I definitely had the urge to merge. Despite the chicken pox scars, the pimples, the 38-inch waist, maybe I could use my art as a tool to change the way I was perceived.

My campaign for class president promoted *zero* policy. It was just me and my art. I tapped into my first "Unfair Advantage."

THE iPOD VS. THE iBELIEVE

Was I any more qualified to be class president than my opponent? Did I have any more right to win? Better ideas? Grander plans?

No. That didn't matter. I had something more important. I had tapped into the greatest technology that exists. A technology greater than any shiny LED, greater than any social media algorithm, greater than anything ever produced in any factory.

I had tapped into the *iBelieve*. Thanks to my newfound faith in my illustration and a growing awareness of what was happening right then in music and culture, combined with an instinct to blend it/sample, I knew that I could *make*

them believe. This philosophy trumped any device or gadget. I knew that my images were different, and I knew that if I put them all over school, then people would see/take in, and they too would believe.

My ads for the election had a simple formula that I still believe in to this day: TITLE, HEADLINE, PROMISING IMAGERY, ACTION.

For my election:
TITLE: Marc 4 Prez!
HEADLINE: Vote for Marc for Class President

PROMISING IMAGERY: Cheech Wizard–style B-boy picture of me. Cosigned and designed in the hand of my new alias, Echo. This looked *nothing* like what everyone else was doing. The image set me apart.
ACTION: Vote next week!

This framework can be used whether you're a seventh grader, a corporation, or trying to inspire ten million people to vote on the fate of Barry Bonds's record-breaking home run ball (more on that later).

We were allowed to hang as many campaign posters as we wanted on the hallway walls, and the school—according to its own rules—could not take them down. I happily exploited this loophole. I made posters and created a simple, evocative ad campaign. Me, as in my Dondi'ed-the-fuck-out cartoon version of me—arms crossed in a B-boy stance—standing in front of wildstyle letters that read "Vote for Marc for Class President." Conveniently signed and promoting "Artwork by Echo."

I did one. Then five. Then ten. Then I went to the local Quickie Press, and $5 later, I had stacks upon stacks of campaign posters. So I bombed the school hallways with my artwork. In graffiti terminology, I got "up."

I won in a landslide—and won again the next year. In fact, I won it every year until I graduated in 1990—six years in a row. I discovered the art of advertising without even knowing the name George Lois, the legendary adman who created "I Want My MTV."

This is what you need in life. In building your personal brand. In any advertisement. No amount of slick packaging, production value, or shiny gimmicks can mask the absence of belief. In your product. In your idea.

If you can't express your idea convincingly in black and white and slap it together on a Xerox machine—I mean low-budget—then your idea is not believable. Worse still, it means you yourself don't *reaaalllllyyyy* believe.

It's ideas, not dollars. Artfulness, not computer graphics. Not models. Not celebrities. Believable, defendable ideas.

IV. **THE (WANNABE) SHIRT KING**

WHEN I WAS twelve, during a Dig Dug binge at the 7-Eleven, I stumbled on the latest issue of *Black Beat* magazine. It had L.L. Cool J on the cover. But that was not what stopped me dead in my tracks. It was what he was wearing: a sweatshirt painted with an airbrushed photo of, well, L.L. Cool J as a B-boy version of himself. And the wildest part was that the article wasn't about LL but about the artists who made the shirt: some guys called the Shirt Kings from Queens, New York. My mind was blown.

It would serve as exhibit A.

L.L. Cool J and the Shirt Kings

I practiced my spiel, looked in the mirror, honing my powers of persuasion. "This will be a good experience for me. This will pay for itself." And that night at the family dinner table, before I took a bite of my dry-ass turkey, I just blurted it out: "Can I get an airbrush and air compressor?"

My mom half squinted at me. "A what?"

"It'll pay for itself, because I'll use it to paint T-shirts, and I'll sell 'em for a profit—"

"How much does it cost?"

"I can make money—"

"How much?" my dad asked firmly.

I couldn't meet his eyes. "All in? Two hundred fifty max."

"You know that would blow all your bar mitzvah money," he said.

I knew that money was tight. My dad had quit his steady gig as a pharmacist to get a real estate license. My mom was also in real estate. Sales were up and down, and by that I mean down.

A couple of days later, my dad said to me, "That airbrush? How can your mother and I know you're serious about this? Remember that saxophone?"

That stung. Yeah, I remembered it, and how much I dreaded playing, and how I ended up blowing it off.

"If you really want that airbrush, and if you're serious about earning some money," my dad said, "then prove it to me."

The next day, armed with Exhibit A in the case to prove it, I placed the copy of *Black Beat* on the kitchen table. "Check out that sweatshirt," I said, index finger squarely on L.L. Cool J. I proceeded to explain to him that those very airbrushed sweatshirts, like the one in the photo, were "desirable."

"This is hip-hop. I love hip-hop. This is what we wear in hip-hop. You can't get this in Lakewood. After all, Shirt Kings are out at Kings Plaza in Jamaica, Queens. *No one* makes this in Lakewood. I could fill that gap. I can."

This was a sort of verbal business case. It was crude, but it had one thing going for it: a believable thesis.

In the class election, I had leveraged my artwork to win. My art had sexy legs in an otherwise mundane world. So I could then reason that if the kids liked my art enough to vote for me, they'd like my art enough to buy it on T-shirts. Or at least some of them would, right?

PROVE IT TO ME

It doesn't matter if you're twelve and want an airbrush or if you want millions of dollars or a hundred dollar line of credit to fund your mature business. You need the Prove It to Me. A lot of people forget this, especially creative types.

Where's the history? Where's the data? What's your thesis? How does what you've done in the past prove what you are about to do? A good idea isn't enough. Everybody's got good ideas. You need to show that *in the past, I took X, and did Y. Now, with X+3, I'll do Y+3+3.* That burden is on you.

Just because you're an artist, or a thinker, or an athlete doesn't mean that you can get around the math. When I evaluate business proposals today, I always look for the how and the why. I do the math, did you?

Prove it to me.

My parents were finally persuaded by my logic and an unlikely ally, my uncle Carl Asch. He was a blue-collar guy, a hands-on guy, crusty. He was a diesel engine mechanic professionally and the go-to fix-it guy for the family and extended family. Uncle Carl believed in *learning by doing*, and he thought that I'd learn more with this airbrush, sink or swim, than I would in any classroom that claimed it as a curriculum.

T HE NEXT WEEK, my parents cashed out my bar mitzvah money savings account and bought a Paasche VL-3W airbrush kit and the Sears Craftsman air compressor.

And in the next year, guess how many shirts I sold?

Zero.

I had no intention of going to market half-cocked. I recognized that I was still a toy.

First I needed to get *good*.

I set up shop in my parents' garage. It wasn't even a *garage*, really. And I had the use of only half of it. We lived in a brown bi-level on a cement slab. With Uncle Carl's help, my dad had converted half the garage into a den. It was called the "Blue Room," and had a blue, black, and white-speckled shag carpet and embossed, faux-wood, white-paneled walls. I'm 99 percent sure that I was conceived in the Blue Room. It had so much swag.

Invented in 1876, the airbrush lets you maintain precise control while spraying different textures. Impressionist artists such as Wilson Irvine used them in the 1890s. Airbrushes have been used for cars, photo retouching, murals, and by street artists.

Shag carpet was a big deal. Here's a seventies-era ad—we bought the blue one.

Shag carpet was a big deal. Here's a seventies-era ad—we bought the blue one.

Deleted scene from The Empire Strikes Back

The Blue Room had a bar that Uncle Carl made, and the bar had this marble-patterned mirror behind it. Oddly, the bar itself featured a random nautical sailing theme. It was also home to my dad's comic-book collection, the Kodak *Library of Creative Photography*, the collection of *Playboy* mixed-drink recipe books, and a collection of rhinos carved out of driftwood.

In 1980, the holiday season after *The Empire Strikes Back* came out, Darren got a vinyl Tauntaun action figure as a present. I didn't. So I'd plopped my Han Solo on the back of one of the rhinos and bowled over Darren's Tauntaun and Luke Hoth. Corny but true.

Uncle Carl helped me transform the non–blue room half of the garage into my studio-office-factory-temple. From scratch he built an industrial, over-sized easel on which I would tack up any old fabric, T-shirts, and old sheets and pillowcases I could get my hands on and practice.

At first it was very basic stuff. Mostly I painted my graf name, Echo, again and again with different hand styles and bubble letters. Soon the space started to look like the scene from all psychopath movies, the walls plastered with images.

I was laser focused though, and this was a new feeling. (I don't know that anyone is laser focused in life until he or she has a stake in the fate of the outcome.) This wasn't like the quickly dropped interest in the saxophone. I wanted to get good, and I needed to pay my parents back; pride was on the line. I wasn't mindful of creating an authentic brand at this point. I was more focused on whether or not this could be a vehicle to help me get to second base with the opposite sex. But painting quickly became a full-time job outside of school. I came home and hunkered in the garage for seven- to nine-hour stretches, no matter how hot or cold it was.

I probably spent a thousand hours in that garage before I sold a single T-shirt. (Maybe there's something to Malcolm Gladwell's 10,000-Hour Rule. For the rest of my career, the time invested in this garage gave me a massive advantage.) I had a hunch that beach scenes would be popular on T-shirts, and

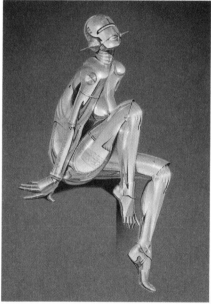

there's a certain technique that you use to airbrush a palm tree. To create a palm leaf, you start far from the surface, and then you bring the airbrush closer and closer so that the line diffuses from a fat, soft line to a tight, sharp pencil point. I would sit there like a Rain Man doing the same thing over and over, painting palm leaf after palm leaf.

My creative inspirations all oozed together in one primordial stew: Dondi, early hip-hop like U.T.F.O. and Slick Rick, and *Airbrush Action Magazine* which had some amazing stuff from Mark Fredrickson and erotic illustrations by the likes of Hajime Sorayama and Olivia De Berardinis. And by "amazing stuff," I mean what damn near qualified as porn.

By the time eighth grade rolled around, I was like a battle-hardened Danielson, waxing on, waxing off. I was getting good. Not yet a master, but I knew I had chops. And I knew I had tapped into a style that people wanted.

But would it sell?

Airbrush Action Magazine happened to be published in Lakewood, NJ (small world).

V. **NOT IN KANSAS**

MY FIRST SHIRTS were all loss leaders; I literally gave them away. I wanted something more important than a quick buck: I wanted walking billboards, I wanted a showcase for my brand.

At first I was afraid to wear them myself. I was afraid to wear a shirt without a known label. What if they looked goofy? What if the art wasn't good enough? I feared that every conversation would go something like this:

Random kid: "Where'd you get that shirt?"

Me: "I painted it."

Random kid: "That's *your* art?"

And then would the kid be impressed, or would he snicker?

Screw it, there was only one way to find out: I wore the shirt to school—feeling eyes on me—and I didn't get any snickers. Then I wore another. Then I did it again. And to clarify, these weren't subtle designs: people noticed. I was painting big, bold, loud B-boys on the shirts, just like the L.L. Cool J photo that first inspired me. My classmates saw me wearing a sweatshirt with *a painting of me* on the front, and that's just not something you see on the average eighth grader.

My first sale was to a girl in my class who asked if I could paint . . . a palm tree. Seriously. Market research had paid off.

It was a slow build, but it started to add up: $10 here, $15 there. Beach scenes were big. Lots of TLFE ("True Love Forever") couples shirts. Bubble letters, wild style, lots of B-boys, Cheech Wizards. I was flush with Queen Nefertiti portraits—I even created stencils for the really popular motifs just to keep up and increase my production pipeline. I could rock a dead ringer of Michael Jordan in forty-five minutes. Black Bart Simpsons? Gizmo and the gremlins? Easy.

I did have one rule: when I custom-painted, the client needed to bring me the actual clothes. I didn't want to be responsible for a bad fit or bad fabric.

Why take that risk? I couldn't. After all, I didn't have a car or the cash to go buy the stuff. Funny how necessity breeds invention. (I wish I had muscle memory, as that lesson would have served me well later. Reduce risk, lower your required capital, and focus on what you're really good at—and hire others for what you are not.) This is something you should think about in any business: don't try to do everything. You aren't the best at everything. Find out where you have an advantage and stick to that.

G OING INTO FRESHMAN year of high school, I sold more shirts, which meant that more kids *saw* more of my shirts, which meant that they *bought* more of my shirts. Another positive feedback loop. I paid back my bar mitzvah money and coined a name for the company: Echo Airbrushing. I made business cards, designed some custom-made snapback hats that said "Echo Airbrushing" across the front panels. I even cobbled together some early biz-dev deals: I sold the T-shirts at school fund-raisers, splitting the profits with the school.

Graffiti had put me on the social map. But I still couldn't really talk to girls—like Meredith the hippie girl, the *hot* hippie girl, the girl with just one dreadlock in her hair. And get this: she was Jewish. That rocked my world. She was like a Jewish Lisa Bonet from *The Cosby Show*. I was in heavy lust.

What was holding me back? I looked at myself in the mirror and realized that maybe it had something to do with the baby fat. I was probably pushing two hundred pounds.

The summer before sophomore year, I dropped fifty pounds. All I did was airbrush and lose weight. I ate tuna damn near every day; no more binges on chocolate chip mint ice cream and *Conan the Destroyer*. When I wasn't painting,

Before *After*

Closer to fighting shape

Darren and I would play nonstop basketball, lowering the rim for slam dunk contests. When those really hot August days rolled around, I would cut holes in a plastic garbage bag and wear it over my body while I painted. I tried to justify this as a "smock," but, really, I wanted to soak myself in sweat and burn the calories. I went from a 40-inch waist to a 34.

Right before school started, I went to the mall and got a brand-new, fresh left ear piercing and a pair of acid-washed Guess jeans. What?!

Girls looked at me. And then I did something miles from my comfort zone: I tried out for our school play. Not just any school play but one put on by Mothers Against Drunk Driving (MADD). A goody-two-shoes play. It was a version of the musical *The Wiz*, which was, of course, the soulful rendition of *The Wizard of Oz*. This was Lakewood, after all. Not Kansas.

The first time I took acid . . .

I was chosen to play *Toto*. No shit.

Yes, Dorothy's dog, Toto. He didn't have any lines. He was written to just scamper around and look cute. I said, "Screw that, I'm making Toto *my Toto*." So I pulled out my bag of sampling tricks to make the *hip-hop* Toto. A mix of "(You Gotta) Fight for Your Right (to Party)"–era Beastie Boys with a flash of Budweiser mascot Spuds MacKenzie. Toto was proper B-boy, complete with a borrowed gold dookie rope chain, snapback hat, and Lee Riders jeans with the patch on the cuff.

F.R.E.S.H.

In the middle of a scene, I jumped out with lines like, "*Daaaaamn*, that's fur-*resh*!" Okay, so maybe that wasn't winning any Tonys, but the high school crowd ate it up.

I also made and wore an airbrushed sweatshirt with a painting of me, Marc, as Toto. I stole the show. Toto became the star. When we took the show to the middle school afterward the teacher in charge raced up to me and said, "Marc, you can't go outside!"

THE POLISH

What finally swung the cool meter, though, was nail polish. The summer of my junior year, a college-age friend of Marci's stopped by the garage to ask if I could paint her nails.

I agreed, but the only problem was that my setup was a little different from a salon. My kit wasn't set up for enamel-based paint, which is what you need for nails, so I hacked it and sprayed her hands completely with paint until her fingers and palms had streaks of gold, blue, and cherry all over. Then I carefully applied a clear protective coating just over the fingernails.

The final step was washing the paint off her hands. Thanks to the protective coating, the paint on her nails remained. The girl looked at me like it was magic. It was this very physical and artistic interaction.

She told her friends, and they told their friends, so pretty soon, around prom season, my garage was packed with hot girls who wanted me to paint their nails.

It wasn't some salon-like atmosphere. I had early Beastie Boys blasting while I painted. Darren and my other buddies were shooting hoops in the driveway. It should have been a music video.

I met girls and made $35 a pop. It was a New Jersey fairy tale. I'd finally cracked the code and could speak to girls without cracking my voice. My junior year, I went to two proms—junior *and* senior. Eventually I even dated Meredith.

"Why not?"

"Fifty kids want your autograph!"

I bolted past her, and, sure enough, there was a crowd of girls screaming, "Toto! Toto! We love you, Toto!!!!"

It was my first taste of fame. Even if "fame" meant adulation by a mob of seventh-grade girls.

Are we really in Kansas?
Lakewood High School students Marc Milecofsky and ▓▓▓▓▓▓▓ perform in special Wizard of Oz" last night as part of the school's Becoming Aware of the Dangers of Drugs

That was my Justin Timberlake moment; my crossover moment. I started to walk through the halls with this force field of my art and my newfound

RANGE OF EMOTIONAL IMPACT

Playing a mute dog in an "antidrugs" school play is not, typically, the core of any business plan, but it did more to grow the awareness of my business than if I'd printed another two hundred fliers. Emotional "touch and feel" moments can come in surprising places.

popularity. I could hang with the skaters, hang with the hip-hop heads, hang with the BMX biking kids. People knew who I was. I had started to peel off my label and create my own brand.

KIDS BOUGHT MORE of my gear, I could raise my prices, and my clientele grew and changed. There was this kid who was our school's Mr. Best Dressed: he was clean-cut dapper, had a high-top fade, and rocked polka dots like the rapper Kwamé. The ladies loved him. He got turned on to my clothes and started coming to me again and again. Once I got his endorsement, the other kids wanted in.

I sold to some shady characters, too. Stoners. Dealers. Sometimes I traded my gear for a bag of weed, and while working at Kmart pushing carts, I met a guy named Chance, a former basketball star, who, let's say, was "entrepreneurial" like me. Only the product he sold wasn't legal. He was older, and he had connections and started introducing me to people outside of Lakewood, in Newark and in East Orange. My world was getting bigger. New clientele.

VI: **FEAR**

GRAFFITI HAD HELPED me overcome my social anxiety, my fear of getting left behind, and my fear of girls. I even conquered my fear of bullies, as just before graduating from high school, I got in my first and only fistfight. A kid named Jake, who dated one of my exes (Meredith, in fact), ambushed me, beat me up, dislocated my shoulder, and kicked my ass so hard that I literally shit my pants. So as I geared up for college, you would think I was ready to take a bigger leap with the artwork and salesmanship. Well, I leaped all right.

Right into the Rutgers University Pharmacy School.

It seems ridiculous now, and it felt ridiculous then, but I got caught up in the messaging around me. My parents were in real estate, and the real estate market had imploded.

While my dad never talked about money, I could just *feel* the anxiety. Late at night, when the house was quiet, I could hear him waking up, I could hear the snoring go in and out, I could hear the way he tossed and turned.

My cousin had gone to pharmacy school, and my dad had gone to pharmacy school. My family never pushed it, but I knew that pharmacy school meant a *guaranteed salary of $60,000.* I did the math. I'd have had to paint a lot of fingernails to make $60,000.

There's good fear and there's bad FEAR. In creating your own personal brand, you need a healthy amount of the former, and you need to overcome the latter. At the point I graduated high school, I was finally starting to hit the right balance, but I gave in to the greater FEAR of living without a security net.

It's one thing to take risks, it's another to be suicidal. I had big dreams for my art, my T-shirts, and my brand, but I also had a dose of reality, and I knew I wasn't ready to be a starving artist. The FEAR still had a hold on me. For now.

$$\frac{Unique}{Voice} = \frac{\int_0^{100} f(\text{ACTION})dx - \int_1^{100} f(\text{FEAR})dx}{\int_1^{100} f(\text{SELF})dx}$$

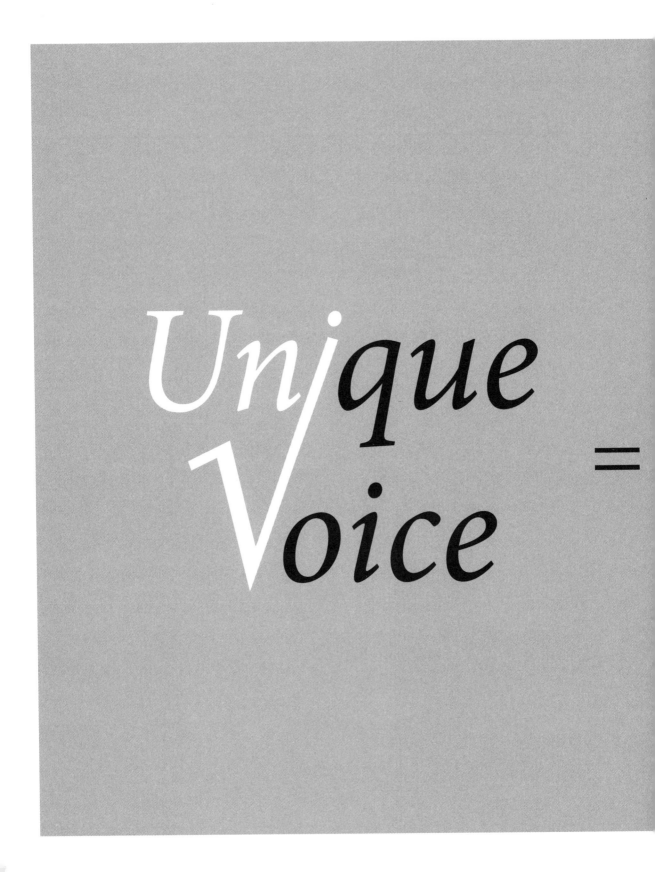

$$\frac{\displaystyle\int_0^{100} f(\text{ACTION})\,dx - \int_{0.1}^{100} f(\text{FEAR})\,dx}{\displaystyle\int_{0.1}^{100} f(\text{SELF})\,dx}$$

"Action is the foundational
key to all success."

—PABLO PICASSO

CHAPTER 3

ACTION

ACTION: *An authentic personal brand is more than just an idea. It's not static. It's not enough to say I have a brilliant idea and then lock it in your laptop. And it's not enough to just talk about it, tweet about it, blog about it. Talk is cheap. An authentic, unique voice is a doer.*

Unlike the other components of UNIQUE VOICE ($\sqrt[Unj]{}$) (FEAR and SELF), it's possible to have an ACTION value of 0. (No one is completely FEARLESS or FEARFUL, and SELF can't be 0, since you can't be completely SELF-less unless you're dead.) But ACTION? If you're not careful, you can let weeks, months, and years slip by without ACTING on your passion. And when you finally take this ACTION, there's no guarantee that your critics, peers, or even your friends will like it.

This chapter is about taking real action. Global action. Not small stuff. Lots of people "do stuff," but it's not material. Take the action that's difficult. Take the action that pushes you.

It's tough to find famous examples of companies, artists, or individuals who have a low ACTION score (close to 0, say), because by definition, if you've heard of them, they probably took plenty of ACTION. The better example is the thousands of companies and millions of people you haven't heard of: the artists, entrepreneurs, creators, and would-be instigators who talked a good game but never backed it up.

I. PHARMACY SCHOOL DROPOUT

Jodeci was always on my Walkman

MC Serch, my lost twin?

"**M**ARC, I CAN still see a shit stain!" a frat boy yelled.

In my first year at Rutgers, I was cleaning a toilet bowl and listening to the song "Lollipop," by the Chordettes, a syrupy 1950s tune that goes: "Lollipop, lollipop / Oh, lolli lolli lolli / Lollipop!" This wasn't by choice. It was my tenth toilet of the day, and the twenty-fifth time I heard "Lollipop."

Welcome to pledge week 1991 for Alpha Zeta Omega, the coed fraternity for Rutgers's Pharmacy School.

I looked up from the toilet to see Satan. Or so it seemed. There was this six-foot-six senior, and when he got stoned, he liked to saunter through the halls and growl in this evil, demonic voice and pretend he was the devil.

He towered over me in the bathroom, flipped off the lights, shined a flashlight to his face, and snarled, *"You. Will. Worship. Satan."*

"I'm just cleaning the toilets, Satan," I said.

"I. Am. The. Devil." His eyes glowed a fiery red, and then he stalked off to terrorize another pledge.

It's safe to say that I never really fit in the frat scene, or the college scene in general, for that matter, and part of it had to do with race. They called me a "wigga." White on the outside, black on the inside. They also called me "Serch," as in MC Serch from the white hip-hop group 3rd Bass. I had grown up in the quasi–melting pot of Lakewood, but my new classmates had grown up in walled-off cultural gardens: either all white or all black.

Maybe it was the way I dressed. I didn't do Rutgers preppy. I wore my pants slightly baggier and my hat cocked a little to the side. Or maybe it was all the bass spilling off my Sony Walkman: a mix of Jodeci and the Jungle Brothers. Back then, before hip-hop went fully mainstream, that wasn't the music they expected from a kid who looked like me.

And it wasn't just the white kids who had issues with me; the black kids were suspicious too, rolling their eyes and asking, "Why all the extra slang? Where are you from? Who raised you?" I wasn't parroting them, I certainly wasn't mocking them, and I wasn't trying to get anyone to accept me as their own or give me a pass, either. I wasn't dropping "Yo"s for the sake of "Yo"s—it was just who I was; it was where I grew up. My taste in pop culture was informed by black culture and the environment I grew up in.

Believe it or not, I actually went to class, but I still sucked at pharmacy school. I just could never focus in that lecture hall format. The only time my intent—my "chi"—was truly sober was in front of the airbrush. When I got an *A* in organic chemistry, it blew (and still blows) my mind.

I thought that if I joined the "academic pharma" frat, I could meet tutors, which would create an academic umbrella, that could help me get through the program. AZO was supposed to be a secret handshake to 24-7 tutors. It wasn't. It turned out to be, at least for the time I was there, just another fraternity.

Squandering my time with the frat did more than humiliate me; it kept me from the course of ACTION that I so desperately wanted to take. It sapped away the time I needed for studying, creating, and hustling. I didn't have the time to study *and* airbrush *and* binge-party (or clean toilets) with AZO. You have only so many minutes in every day—so many ticks on the clock—and every action you perform means, by definition, you're *not* performing some other action. You have to make choices, and it was time I made mine.

I needed to leave AZO to get back on track with school, with painting, and with my passion for building a fledgling Echo Airbrushing.

But I did it in the most *in*authentic way possible.

My mother has naturally thinning hair; it's a condition called alopecia areata. So I sought out the biggest gossipmonger in AZO, and I told her that I needed to tell her something confidential.

"Hey. Can you keep a secret?" I asked her.

"Of course, Marc. What is it?" She looked concerned.

"It's kind of personal. I don't want it to get out."

"I won't tell anyone," she said, nodding. "Promise."

I took a deep, deep breath and tried to look her in the eyes. "It's my mom. She has cancer."

It's easily the worst lie I've ever told. Just as I expected, she let the cat out of the bag, and in less than twenty-four hours, everyone in AZO bombed me with condolences. Even Satan dropped character and said, "I'm really sorry about your mom."

So with that as an excuse, I left the frat. The following year, when my mom visited Rutgers, my old AZO friends would call out to her, "Mrs. Milecofsky! I'm so glad to see you doing so well!" and my mom, who didn't know about the lie (until now; sorry, Mom), thought they were the friendliest people in the world.

Was the lie crass and childish? Sure. If I had to do it again, I hope I would man up and tell them the truth. It was the wrong means to an end, but it unshackled me from the frat, it let me laser in on what I cared about, and it let me take ACTION.

II. **KOOL DJ RED ALERT**

BRAND MANAGERS OFTEN try to carve up the world into a nice, neat matrix, which might look something like:

	MALE	FEMALE
WHITE		
BLACK		
OTHER		

Opposite:
Close-up of Urban Identity Crisis

The advertisement for my artwork licensed for reproduction as posters

I've never liked this oversimplification, and it's partly because of my time at Rutgers. If a black kid sees Tony Hawk land a 900, doesn't he have the right to think it's cool? And can't a white kid listen to Talib Kweli? Why does cool need a color?

In my sophomore year, I received one of the greatest gifts a college student could ever ask for: a dorm room to myself. (My assigned roommate got into some trouble with the law. The details are fuzzy, but it supposedly involved a gun, and when they never replaced the dude, I sure as hell wasn't going to tell anyone.) Not having a roommate meant that I could keep the light on all night, literally drawing until dawn.

One early piece was called *Urban Identity Crisis*. It's a self-portrait of me crying into a pool of my own tears, and the reflection in the pool is me, but black.

Another is called *Either Way It Hurts*, where my body is split in two, sitting on a bus alongside two other riders. On my right side, I'm white, next to an older

black man, who's looking at me in my Bo Jackson kicks and disapproving. On my left side, I'm black, next to an older white lady who's clutching her bag, worried I'd steal it.

Friends coming by my room had mixed feelings about the sketches. But I was just putting it all out there, and I didn't expect anything *but* mixed feelings— I was trying to provoke a conversation. I was even on some KRS-ONE shit (Knowledge Reigns Supreme Over Nearly Everyone), as I built an ECHO acronym:

Either Way It Hurts,
acrylic airbrushed on
bristol board

Educating
Change to
Heal and
Overcome

I used the dorm as a showroom. I hung designs and prints all over the walls, and then I'd show the options to my classmates, who would tell me which ones they wanted airbrushed onto T-shirts or jackets. Then, on the weekends, I drove back to my parents' garage at Lakewood and pounded out the clothes.

It was a good gig. I could pick and choose my clients, and I cleared around $500 per weekend. Not bad for a college kid who just needed to buy music, art supplies, and weed, but I sensed that I was still riding a bike with training wheels. Many of my Rutgers friends freestyled, and some of them wrote lyrics, and we'd all crack up and have a good time, but for most of these guys, it was just for kicks.

T HEN I FINALLY met someone who shared my creative appetite: Cale Brock, an aspiring R&B singer. He was a year younger than me, and, man, he could just *croon*; a real throwback to Sam Cooke, but modern. Cale could give Wanya Morris, the lead from Boyz II Men, a run for his money. He had chops.

Unlike a lot of kids who *talked* about becoming a star, Cale actually did something about it, he took ACTION, and he was always in the studio recording tracks. We both saw the world as something bigger than Lakewood, and he was the first person I felt comfortable sharing my dream of being sold in Macy's.

Why did I dream of Macy's? Because that's where Polo was. Why Polo? Because that's what Slick Rick rapped about: "I got the Johnson's baby powder and the Polo cologne. Fresh dress, like a million bucks." For a kid who grew up in the Jersey suburbs, Macy's meant success. It's what I knew. I didn't grow up in the hipster ecosystem of ultra-niche boutiques, and I knew that if I wanted to be a real brand—a mainstream megabrand—then someday I would need to crack Macy's.

We were both *relentlessly obsessive*. We played in the intersection of culture, emotion, and intuition. And we weren't afraid to let the world see it. We weren't afraid to dance goofy, sing off-key, or be the guy who rocks sunglasses indoors. We gave ourselves the freedom to play with that creative putty, not worried about "checking boxes." We were in the minor leagues of pop culture, the minor leagues of What's Next, and we both hungered for the bigs.

I pushed Cale to send a tape to Michael Bivins. Biv, a member of New Edition and Bell Biv Devoe, was the Simon Cowell of early-1990s R&B; he had a knack for discovering young talent, taking chances, and making stars out of nobodies like three Philly kids who became Boyz II Men. He would go up to strangers and say, "Sing for me right now, and if I like it, I'll sign you on the spot."

One weekend Cale took me to visit a friend out in Vineland, New Jersey. It turned out his apartment served as the hub of this emerging scene in R&B music, filled with talented artists rising up through the black church: people like a chubby sixteen-year-old kid hunched over an old drum machine, laying down beats. The dude was good, and I introduced myself.

"Whaddup? Rodney. Rodney Jerkins," he said.

I had no way of knowing that Rodney Jerkins, aka Darkchild, would go on to produce for Lady Gaga and Michael Jackson and Katy Perry, but, in a way, I'm not surprised. That scene had such a brash energy; it oozed from every pore and made you want to match the tempo. I became hooked on the magic of music production, and I felt a kinship with this class of hustlers who were hell-bent on getting up and taking action.

So I went even deeper. Then came *The Low End Theory*, the sophomore album of A Tribe Called Quest. I remember listening to Q-Tip on "Verses from the Abstract": he rhymed over this hypnotic bass sound that was so obviously acoustic. "Thanks a lot Ron Carter on the bass, Yes my man Ron Carter is on the bass—"

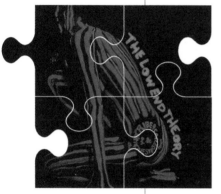

Wait, was that a sample? Ron Carter? Who's that? I scrambled to the liner notes of my CD and learned that it was the legendary jazz bassist Ron Carter, playing live. I proceeded to deconstruct the samples on that record. It blew my mind. They sampled from the endless gold mine of black music. The track "Scenario" alone drew from a who's who of black music. Miles Davis, Kool and the Gang, Ohio Players, jazz organist Jack McDuff, and the Jimi Hendrix Experience all on one record? Crazy.

So I followed the rabbit hole into jazz music. Proper jazz music. (My Dondi sampling all over again.)

My next question was "Who manages Tribe?" and deep into the five-point type in the jewel case notes, I saw a management company and name.

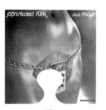

The endless gold mine: A Tribe Called Quest, Ron Carter, Jack McDuff

"Violator Records? Baby Chris Lighty?" I felt like I'd heard that name before.

Oh, right: Red Alert name-dropped Violator and Baby Chris all the time. He turned out to be the business manager and one of the shepherds of the Native Tongues, a cohort of Afrocentric, positive lyricists who waxed deeply on jazz-oriented sampling and beat creation and led to what became, according to many, the Renaissance of hip-hop. For me, this was the relevant counterforce to mainstream rap, which, at the time, was a cheesy soup of MC Hammer and "Ice Ice Baby."

I started mailing out drawings, hats, and T-shirts to all the musicians and producers I looked up to and wanted to emulate. Kool DJ Red Alert was first. Back then he was one of, if not *the*, most dominant DJs in hip-hop, and *Rolling Stone* magazine would name him as one of the fifty most influential people in music. He also was a part of Violator Management. Every weekend night, in an era before iTunes and Spotify, *everyone* listened to Red Alert on the New York radio station 98.7 Kiss-FM, the audio bible of hip-hop.

Ba-zerk—
Ba-zerk—
Ba-zerk—
Y-Y-Y-Yeah—
Yeah—when you in Manhattan—
the Bronx—Yeah—
Queens—Yeah—
Staten Island—or—Yeah—
Upstate—Yeah—
Long Island—Yeah—
Connecticut—Yeah—
New Jersey—Yeah—
Where ever you going—Yeah—
You going to be cranking it up like—Yeah—
Thisssssssssssssss is WRKS-98.7 Kisssssssssss FM.

DJ Red Alert, New York City's voice of early nineties hip-hop

I couldn't wait until his Friday-night show. Red was famous for doing shout-outs. I had no patience for waiting on hold and doing the dial-up thing, so I went to my strong suit of communication: my art. During his radio show, I camped out at the Kinko's and straight-up spammed his fax machine with "Echo Airbrushing" promos. Black-and-white pen-and-ink illustrations of MCs standing encircled in a rap cypher. Or images shot from the floor to the sky, showing MCs jumping across the stage. All the images were unapologetically self-promotional—SELF-referential—and clearly branded and signed "Echo."

And then one Friday night I'm listening to 98.7 like always, drawing in my black book, and I hear something on the radio.

"I gotta shout out my man *Echo* for blessing me with this fly gear! Yo, he got the fresh airbrushed jacket, the craze snapback hats! My man Echo Airbrushing, yeah, yeah, Big Up Lakewood, New Jersey, and my man Echo, artwork is crazy."

Whoa, what!?

I called Cale right away. "Did you just hear that?"

I called my sister next. "What should I do next? Send more? Should I go to his studio?"

I seeded my brand with the bona fide artists and instigators of pop culture. The motivation wasn't as simple as "I hope they wear this"; it came from a desire to educate them, to land on their aesthetic radar, and to build a literacy of who I was and what I was trying to accomplish. Don't think of this as sending "fan mail." This is a professionally produced, hypercustomized presentation. When you send me (or anyone) a solicitation of your idea, or your product, or the marketing materials of who you are and what you're trying to sell, *work backward* from the experience of cracking open the box from its taped seal. Ten things to *never* do when building your swag bomb:

1. Never Send Directly to Someone's Home

I've had that happen. It's fucking creepy. Everyone has a business address, and in this day and age, they're sufficiently accessible.

2. Never Expect Your Intended Audience to Even See It

So make it good enough that even if it gets to only his or her lieutenant—which will often be the case—you still make a material impact.

3. Never Send Just the Stock Shit

Think deeply about what you will send them, and work hard at customizing the content so that the end user will recognize this as an amazing, highly personalized gift. And it's just that—a gift—so . . .

4. Never Have Expectations, as It's Just a Gift

The joy and purpose has to come from the confidence that you did it; you took ACTION. Not everyone will acknowledge receipt. That's okay.

5. Never Handwrite Your Marketing Materials

It's one thing to send a handwritten cover note (preferably a 6" x 4.5" stock postcard) that's less than twenty words. Fine. But it's something else to send an all-handwritten business proposal that looks like it came from Son of Sam. I don't care how legible your writing is. *Type.*

6. Never Use Secondhand Packaging Materials

A used Trapper Keeper folder—with maybe a sticker over the dents so that you pass it off as new—ain't cutting it. Why should I take your idea seriously if you're not even willing to make a quick trip to Staples?

7. Never Stalk

If you have a phone number or email of an executive assistant, fine, it's okay to call *once* in advance and then again *once* in confirmation of receipt. (You can also send it with a certified receipt, so you know who signed for it, and when.) But don't call repeatedly like some psycho. Not cool.

8. Never Forget to Include Your Name, Email, and Phone Number

Don't presume that anyone is going to read a long letter. If the visual impact and the overall wraparound isn't there, you're dead. So make sure it looks good, feels good, and that it emotes your goals. And make it as clear as the sun who sent it.

9. Never Send a Picture of Yourself Fan-Boying Out

Again, creepy. Let the content and the *high* concept speak for you. Don't send some weird head shot.

10. Never Gush

Notable figures don't like being fawned over. Be careful to whom you say—and how often you say—"I love you." (Good rule for life in general.) Don't tell them, "You are my idol." Speak matter-of-factly, and acknowledge the traits or practices that you respect and admire.

The shout-out tasted good. It tasted like the first time you have chocolate. I wanted more. At Marci's urging, I didn't get complacent and didn't let it fizzle as a one-shot thing; I had an instinctive grasp of the *power of inertia*, so I doubled down and sent him more. And not just Red Alert, but also Public Enemy's Chuck D. Q-Tip. KRS-ONE. Essentially, I sent packages to all the cultural pioneers who inspired me.

I could quote *Do the Right Thing* and *Mo' Better Blues* backward and forward, so I sent Spike Lee some gear too. I heard he had a new movie out—a biopic of Macolm X—so I sent him a sweatshirt with a meticulously painted portrait of Malcolm X on it. I must have spent two days on that one. I never really expected to hear anything back from any of these guys. But a kid can dream, right?

Spike Lee graciously sent me a thank-you note—an actual signed letter from *Spike! Fucking! Lee!*—and that felt good. "Ya-dig? Sho-nuff."

I knew that I was on the verge of something. I knew because it *felt authentic*. I could sense that the timing was right and that I needed to take it to the next level. But how?

Part of a swag bomb for Spike Lee

THE RED ALERT shout-out was big, and it made me even more convinced that Cale needed to do the same thing with Bivins. He needed to send him one of his mix tapes.

"I'll do it," Cale said. "But only if we bundle it with one of your jackets."

Deal. We literally packaged our dreams together. Maybe Cale was a little afraid to pitch Bivins—that goes back to the FEAR variable—but that's okay; a certain dash of FEAR is normal. You get over it, Cale got over it. Everyone gets some stage fright—don't let it stop you. Cale didn't.

We spent two weeks making this custom package for Biv; Cale went deep into his studio, and I went deep into mine, painting this elaborate denim jacket. We planned to give it to him at a Bel Biv Devoe concert in Holmdel, New Jersey, at the Garden State Arts Center.

A jacket I made for Cale when he became officially a part of "The East Coast Family" and signed to Biv 10 Records

We pinned so many hopes on that moment. A short handwritten note (with my contact info) taped to a Maxell cassette tucked into the left chest pocket. I made the jacket in the Blue Room of the garage, using a canvas of Swarovski crystals I had copped from a rummage store. Black, pewter, red, and clear. I

Hats made for DJ Red Alert

bedazzled the hell out of that thing, one crystal at a time. And then finally, on the night of the concert, I couldn't go. Instead, I went to the hospital for a long-scheduled and inevitable surgery to correct my perpetually dislocating left shoulder.

So maybe it was a slow news day for the Asbury Park Press, *but it ran a photo of my jacket for Biv.*

But the show would go on, and Cale gave me the full details. The concert was packed, and at the end of "When Will I See You Smile Again?"—the one slow jam on BBD's *Poison* album—my older sister, Shari, ran up to the stage in a cattle call of women. Unlike the rest of the gaggle, she wasn't waving panties and flowers at Biv. She was armed with the package; one jacket, freshly painted and barely dry, with the Easter egg of Cale's cassette in tow. He stopped at the lip of the stage, acknowledged Shari, and held up the jacket to the audience, like a trophy. The yellow lights converged on my sister—and the jacket—in a dazzling spotlight. Even Bivins couldn't have choreographed it any better; here was this beautiful, adoring woman giving him a fly present. He gave her a kiss.

SECTION **E**

INSIDE

Underdog *Last-place CBS vows to get back to the top.* ◆ *page* **E3**

Stepping Out *JCC raises $30,000 at auction.* ◆ *page* **E4**

Asbury Park Press

PANORA

Press pho

Jacket designed by Marc Milecofsky, Lakewood, was given to Michael Bivins of Bell Biv DeVoe during concert.

$$\int_0^{100} f(\text{ACTION})dx$$

Cale and I were so excited that Bivins had actually *received* the jacket. But would he even notice the tape? Would he read the letter? Would he just chuck it in the trash can? It was such a long shot.

That night I sat at home and nursed my shoulder, talking on the phone with Cale, and we wondered how long to wait before following up with Bivins. Weeks? Months? Maybe never?

At three o'clock in the morning, the phone rang.

"Yo, is this Marc? This is Biv." Biv's signature gravelly voice.

"Hi, um, yeah, this is . . ." I tried to remember my name.

"I want to hook up with your man Cale. Tell him to be at the Sheraton in Red Bank in thirty minutes."

Three thirty. Cale didn't chicken out. Cale jumped on a once-in-a-lifetime opportunity. Cale took ACTION.

III. **NUT-HUGGERS**

T HE BIV CONNECTION changed everything, or so I thought. He ended up signing Cale to his newly formed imprint on Motown Records, called Biv 10 Records. And they soon released an "East Coast Family" single, "1-4-All-4-1," which prominently featured Cale.

When Biv was in town for a concert or whatever, he, of course, invited Cale, and Cale, of course, invited me. Suddenly I had *access*. Soon we were going on tour with Boyz II Men, where Biv would hook us up with hotel rooms, feed us, and invite us backstage. My first taste of *the life*.

It was so seductive. Biv threw himself a birthday party in New York City and invited Cale and me. So, like any good self-promoter, I rolled up in my Echo Airbrushing hat and an airbrushed tie. Red Alert was DJ'ing. I wandered around aimlessly, introducing myself to the emerging stars.

And then there she was. Shorter than she looked in the movies, but looking as hot as when I saw her on-screen on her back, having Mookie (played by Spike Lee) apply ice cubes to her nipples in *Do the Right Thing*.

"Whassup? My name's Echo." I gave her my hand.

"Rosie Perez."

"I want to marry you. For real."

She laughed and pivoted straight off my handshake into the crowd, probably a little creeped out.

The beautiful Rosie Perez

Across the room was a smooth, crisp, impeccably groomed black man. He wore an oversized white linen shirt, white linen pants, and it looked like he'd just stepped off a Gulfstream jet just returning from the Caribbean.

The white linen man seemed to be socially engineering the room, dipping in and out of conversations as he whispered in people's ears like some kind of Svengali. Even though it was Bivins's party, you just *felt this guy's presence*; it was like he owned the room. He seemed to make people feel a certain way.

I nudged Cale. "Who's that guy? White linen?"

Gatekeepers stand between you and your chosen path. Or at least they *think* they do. They imagine themselves as the Big Boss at the end of a video game, like Bowser from Mario Bros. They're the anointed ones. The thought leaders, the sage shamans, the final arbiters of taste and merit. Understand what you are playing for. The value of the endgame needs to be what matters to you and your intended audience.

Playing for a questionable value, in a currency you can not bank on, is the wrong path! In fashion, the ultimate gatekeeper would be *Vogue* magazine's Anna Wintour; in hip-hop, maybe Kanye West. But before you get to the Big Boss of Anna Wintour, you need to go through the gatekeepers of fashion critics, publications like *Women's Wear Daily*, or organizations such as the Council of Fashion Designers of America (CFDA).

Most of this is not real, it's *imagined*. The gatekeepers are not the goalkeepers. The goalkeepers are the ones who actually keep the score. This is the endgame. In fashion, it's the people wearing your clothes. In music, it's the people listening to your creations. In business, it's who's buying your products. Goalkeepers matter. Gatekeepers *think* they matter. Perception versus reality.

Opposite:
Life is not a linear game like Super Mario Bros. The gatekeeper thinks that he's Bowser and that he's keeping you from Princess Peach, but that's not the only path. Life is more like a sandbox game. An open world. You don't just go from left to right—you can go up, down, over and around to rescue the princess.

"That's Puffy."

Apparently this "Puffy" character had just produced Mary J. Blige's multiplatinum debut, *What's the 411?*, and would soon sign a young Biggie Smalls to his own record label, Bad Boy. He ushered the group Jodeci, the spicier Boyz II Men, around the room. Where Boyz II Men were all about tartan plaids and a preppy look, Jodeci was dipped in all-black military fatigues and Timberland boots. I didn't talk to Puffy that night, but I knew from that instance he was worthy of studying. And clearly had the Jedi powers I sought. Years later I would engage him, but for now he was just the mysterious guy decked all in white linen.

I drove back to Rutgers a little starstruck and a lot ambitious. How can you go from a party with Rosie Perez to organic chemistry? How can you go from first class to coach? It was time to capitalize on these connections; it was time to create a business plan; it was time to take it to the next step. And clearly, there was only one catalyst for this action: Michael Bivins.

He could make a star out of Boyz II Men and Cale, so he could make a star out of me, right? That's how it works: the road to success goes through the gatekeepers.

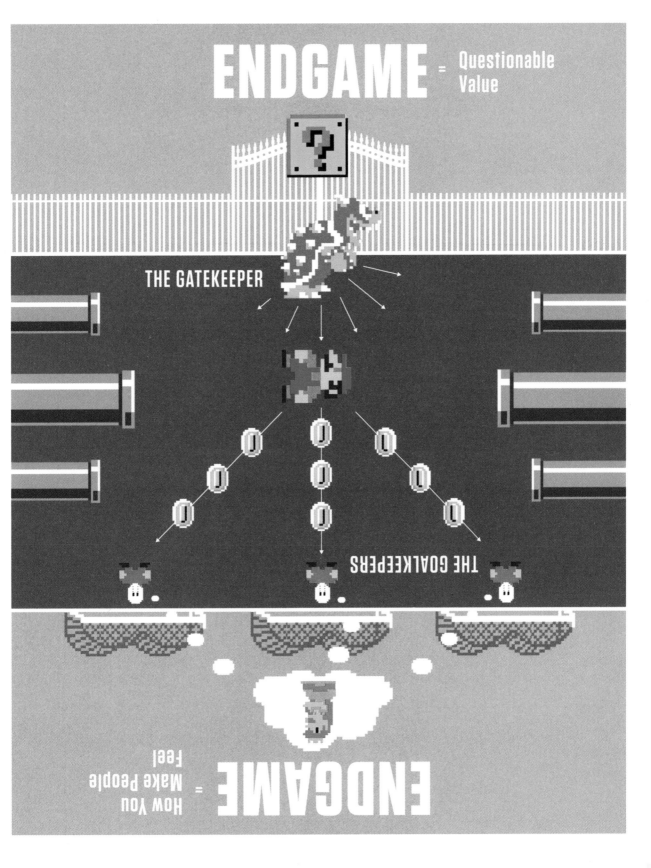

DEVELOP YOUR LEFT HAND

To some extent, when you're pitching a new idea, your "technical rigor" isn't what ultimately matters. When I'm asked to invest in a project, what I look for is the *believability* that there's a problem that needs to be solved in the marketplace, and that this is a problem that can be solved only by the person pitching. There needs to be something that makes me feel that this kid's tone and UNIQUE VOICE ($\frac{Uni}{V}$) feel relevant, necessary, and almost clairvoyant.

My business plan for Echo Airbrushing might have been technically naive, but it did have this much going for it: my personal brand was massively authentic and believable. I made a case that "I am authentically connected to street art." My story fit my business. The personal brand that I had created—from my guts to the skin—was in perfect alignment with the external company brand. I cut my teeth by spray-painting T-shirts in my garage, and this was something authentic that couldn't be replicated (or taken away) by a corporate fashion team, perched on the fifty-seventh floor of a Manhattan skyscraper, saying, "Okay, fellas, now how do we do this 'street' thing?"

That said, it's important to show respect for the technical rigor. I didn't have that rigor—yet—and knew it was my weak left hand. You should also at least understand and address what you don't know. I could drive hard to the hoop with my right, but when I went left, I turned the ball over. Over the years, I worked on my left, sharpened my game, and cut down my turnovers. That's what I look for in young entrepreneurs who pitch me: they need to have that transcendent quality of an authentic, UNIQUE VOICE ($\frac{Uni}{V}$), but they also have to know their weaknesses and show a willingness to fix them.

My next play was to create a business plan that I would eventually pitch to Bivins. It was so naive. I believed that my unique view of the world, and the art that I projected from it, would clearly have a niche. I couldn't be alone in my experiences. I just needed to *say it* and *show it*, and others would want to *hear it* and *see it*. My plan noted that Russell Simmons, the cofounder of the label Def Jam Recordings, was launching a clothing company called Phat Farm; that Cross Colours (led by Carl Jones which featured bright, saturated colors—one of the first brands to market heavily to the African-American community) was doing $100 million in business; and that Tommy Hilfiger was on a path to $1 billion.

The plan was so vague. There was nothing technical or rigorous about it. I didn't contemplate supply side or how to actually mass-produce my ideas.

No conversations around merchandising, product variation, or assortment. I don't even know if it had the word *fashion* in it. And worst of all, there was no material proposal for how this new company would be configured. Who would own what? At what percentages of the company? Who and how would it be capitalized? And when would it begin to generate revenue? At Scale? *Scale?* The only scale I knew was the one I rarely stepped on to weigh myself.

I WORKED ON the plan for most of the summer of 1992, back in Lakewood, once again setting up shop in my parents' garage. An old high school friend named Perry Landesberg—the son of my high school art teacher—fueled my ambitions of mass production. Perry was a great connector. He suggested I meet his buddy Seth Gerszberg, who might be a viable investor.

"You need to meet Seth," Perry told me. "He's got money. He's always starting new businesses."

Seth sounded like an urban legend. Supposedly, he spent most of his time in Vienna, Austria, running an architectural artifact excavation and resale business. High-end pawning. He was a drama major in college, but apparently he never went to class and managed to hustle other acting and drama majors into going as him—convincing them that it was a great way to study and learn by doing. He was an Orthodox Jew. He was the son of a hardnosed businessman and lawyer (the late Shep Gerszberg, who even had buildings in Lakewood named in his honor). He owned a landscaping business and, legend had it, he had an  army of twenty kids running around on tractors and lawn mowers, making him money hand over fist. Who was this guy, a Jersey Keyser Söze?

All this, and he wasn't old enough to buy a beer. The idea that someone my age could organize twenty people to do *anything* seemed so bizarre; I didn't own a passport, and my most far-flung destination had been a family vacation to Quebec. I hadn't been on a plane since I was ten.

A red Ford Mustang convertible roared into the driveway, kicking up dust and blasting Bruce Springsteen's "Dancing in the Dark." I could hear him change the gears and pop the brake, and then he climbed out the Mustang's window like he was on *The Dukes of Hazzard*, and jumped from the car, his boots landing with a thud.

This short and muscular buzz-cut guy comes up to me and shakes my hand. "Seth Gerszberg."

Firm shake, all business. His hands were callused and dirty, the kind of hands you get from a life of work. He looked a lot like an Orthodox Jewish Tom Cruise, with a yarmulke and tiny, nut-hugging jeans shorts. Jus' saying.

He seemed to notice his dirty hands. "Sorry, just came from Georgian Court University. Big client. Fucking arborvitae."

"Yeah, I heard you're into landscaping?"

"Some." He shrugged. "I'm usually in Vienna. I resell marble and artifacts from old buildings."

I nodded as if I did that too.

"Perry tells me you want to start a business," Seth said.

"Yeah, like Stussy," I said, referring to the godfather of the street-ware industry. "I think it could be a thirty-million-, maybe fifty-million-dollar company." I pointed to some of my designs squared away neatly in a wannabee business plan binder I had made for Biv.

He grabbed the binder, and I almost asked him to wash his hands. He flipped through the pages and licked his finger and kept flipping. "This is good," he said, and then licked and flipped more pages. "This is good."

He turned to me. "So what do you want to do?"

"What do you mean—"

"Do you need money? How much?"

I stammered a bit. "Uh, I'm still working on the plan, I'm not sure."

"You got cash-flow projections?"

"Well . . ."

"Where are you going to manufacture? What's the valuation?"

His questions made me uncomfortable and started to piss me off. "Evaluation?" I said.

"*Valuation*," he corrected me.

He asked me all these things that I had no fluency in. And honestly, it scared me; it scared me that someone roughly my own age could have such a leg up in knowledge, and I couldn't help but read him as a charlatan, or maybe a shark, who could take advantage of me. Also, he just wasn't *that cool*: those nut-hugger shorts, plus he hadn't heard of Stussy or Michael Bivins. His whole character didn't make any sense to me; it seemed too much of an anomaly. A red-Mustang-driving, jeans-shorts-wearing, dirty-hands Orthodox Jewish kid who exported artifacts from Austria? It didn't compute. He wasn't famous, so how could he be rich? Those two go had to go hand in hand, right?

I did what a lot of creative types do when they don't understand the business: I hid behind the art.

> I did what a lot of creative types do when they don't understand the business: I hid behind the art.

"No, no, no, you don't get it," I told him. "I don't need any 'basis for evaluation.'" I pointed to a design. "It's about the *art*."

"Right, I get that," Seth said. "But to determine the necessary quantity of capital, we'll need to—"

"*You* don't get it," I said, and I could feel my blood rising. He was calm as fuck. Confident. I was shook.

"Hey, I'm interested," Seth said. "Just tell me what you need."

"I'll get back to you."

I never wanted to see the kid again.

IV. **LYRICIST LOUNGE**

I FOCUSED ON the sexier stuff, prepping my plan for Bivins. I tried to get a sit-down, but apparently his office ran through his aunt, a supernice lady who told me to "put down what you want in paper, dear," and that she'd set up something. So I waited.

In addition to hooking me up with Seth, Perry Landesberg also turned me on to the geographic ground zero of emerging hip-hop: an event called the Lyricist Lounge, founded by Anthony Marshall and Danny Castro, which took place at the Supper Club, Tramps, and other downtown New York venues. They had an open mic night, and the place vibrated with the industry's emerging talent.

I rolled in with Perry, and as soon as we opened the door, we started coughing. The place smelled like a stoner's Christmas, with all the weed that was burning. I happily lit up and joined in.

This was nineties backpack hip-hop. All you could hear were these deep, deep drums. Everyone wore five-panel caps or had young dreds, walking around with JanSport backpacks and hoodies and vests. The host, Anthony Marshall, bounded onstage, and the crowd hushed. "Give it up for . . . Mos Def!" The room exploded.

Mos Def took the mic, and we settled in. Perry pointed out Talib Kweli and Biggie Smalls. There were also some record company reps that all the rappers were trying to impress in the hopes of landing a record deal. In the far corner was Matty C, aka Matt Life, who, when he wasn't writing for the *Source*, was an A&R man for Loud Records and produced for Mobb Deep. I felt like this was both the culmination—and the beginning—of something. It *clicked* at a very deep level in my gut, deep beneath the skin and into the bones, and I needed to be a part of it.

After the show, Perry introduced me to Marshall and Castro.

Trying to keep my cool, I handed them my black book of my work. I might have walked into the Lyricist Lounge as a fan, but I wanted to walk out as something more.

"This is some good shit," Anthony said, flipping through illustrations and photos of shirts I had done. "What'd you have in mind?"

This was the beginning of our relationship. With Marshall's direction and connections we would eventually release mix tape compilations called *Underground Airplay*, which would feature rappers from Biggie to Doug E. Fresh.

I RACED HOME to my college apartment to share the news with my buddy Ben and my other roommates. "Dude! I'm going to be painting this giant canvas alongside the rappers, and—"

"Uh-huh," Ben said, not looking at me, his eyes only on watching *The Simpsons*.

"This is huge. You should come."

"Eat your words
but don't go hungry
Words have always
nearly hung me."

—TOM TOM CLUB,
"Wordy Rappinghood"

The digital grid of Twitter, Facebook, blogs, and Tumblr give the illusion that you can "create a brand" just by typing 140 characters. A brand does more than tweet, a brand does more than talk, a brand does more than just cultivate perception. Think about what your brand is *without* the crutch of social media and words, and make sure that it can stand on its own actions. Talk is cheap without action.

Words. Action. Two different things. Know the distinction, and quit talkin' loud and sayin' nothing. The great equalizer for WHAT YOU SAY is how you will EXECUTE.

"You're like a dull old knife
that just ain't cuttin'
You're just talkin' a lot
and sayin' nothing."

—JAMES BROWN,
"Talkin' Loud & Sayin' Nothing"

My friend Sunil ignored me and said to Ben, "You wanna order pizza?" How could they not *get* this? I tried one last time.

"You guys'll love it. Mos Def will be there—"

"Nah," Ben said, "I'm not coming."

"Me neither," Sunil said.

"I don't get it," I said, and I really didn't. Ben was a guy I'd known since I was a kid. He had DJ'd my seventh-grade Valentine's Day party. He had always bigged me up in the Lakewood days. Now that all the stuff we'd sandboxed in was becoming *real*, not just talk, it seemed like he was disowning me.

"Don't you guys want to make a go of it?" I asked. "What's not to like about this?"

"Dude . . ." Finally, Ben looked at me. ""DJ'ing is just for fun. And now you're trying to go all 'professional.' You think you're better than us?"

Sunil didn't say another word. He just turned off the TV, stalked into his room, and slammed the door behind him. Ben did the same thing. Seconds later, I heard the locks click. And that's how my apartment would stay for the next several months, with my roommates—my friends—in their rooms with the doors shut.

This made me question everything. How could I move forward when I had lost the confidence of my peers? Clearly, I was no longer credible to people like Ben, and therefore I had to be a fraud to everyone else, right? I was fake to them, corny, nothing but a toy. What right did I have to paint in a club like S.O.B.'s, where real New York rappers performed? *You're not New York, you're Lakewood.* Years ago, I had discovered the iBelieve. Now I became tormented by the iDoubt.

I couldn't shake these fears, and they came close to shutting down my ACTIONS. They chased me and choked me until the very day I was supposed to paint at the Lyricist Lounge.

Fuck them.

If my friends couldn't back me, then I didn't have time for them.

Now that I had an opportunity, I couldn't squander it by being too afraid to act. This wasn't a game or hobby anymore. I knew it wasn't a game for Cale. I knew it wasn't a game for Lyricist Lounge cats or anyone who performed on their stage, or rocked on our *Underground Airplay* mix tapes. Unlike my roommates, they weren't into hip-hop and street art because they wanted to shoot the shit or get laid. They were serious; they were real. So was I.

V. "COULDA, WOULDA, SHOULDA"

I COULD FEEL it. The energy was right and my actions were right, but I still had three problems:

1. I had no capital.
2. I had no capital.
3. I had no capital.

Oh, and there was a fourth problem. By now, I spent the bulk of my time promoting Echo Airbrushing, painting at the Lyricist Lounge, launching a hip-hop bazaar at the Rutgers student center, and working on *noncommercial* artwork, which was starting to get traction: a distributor of high-end posters wanted to license my art, saying it reminded her of Romare Bearden. *Really?* I knew my name didn't belong in the same sentence as Bearden, one of the most legendary African-American painters of the twentieth century. The comparison was ridiculous, but it felt good.

But here's what I *wasn't* spending my time doing: going to class. I was on the brink of dropping out of Rutgers, and even if I didn't want to count pills for a living, I still desperately needed those student loans as a financial lifeline.

One day I got a phone call from Michael Bivins's aunt. "Marc, he can see you tomorrow."

Finally! Game on.

I got to Biv's office early, having brought a stack of T-shirts, samples of art, my business plan that I'd made at Kinko's, and a fresh embroidered hat that said "Biv 10."

This man, Michael Bivins, was the man who *made stars*. All of my work connecting myself to the gatekeepers was now destined to pay off.

Biv invited me into his office. Back then his whole persona was like a more street-edged version of *The Fresh Prince of Bel-Air*: the glasses, the clean-scrubbed appeal, the college-bound vibe that even let the nerds feel cool. He had a real fresh, preppy swagger. He decorated his office like a classroom, and even his desk was the kind of kiddy desk you have in third grade.

"So, ah, Russell Simmons is launching Phat Farm," I began, and I could feel my armpits getting swamped.

He looked at me like I was lost, and I was.

Finally, when I finished stumbling along after only a few minutes, he gave me a noncommittal nod and said, "Just speak to my aunt."

I thanked him and left. *Speak to his aunt*? Was that a yes or a no?

The aunt was equally cryptic, so I went back to waiting by the phone. Days ticked by, and no one called. Days turned to weeks; weeks turned to months.

Finally, the phone rang. This must be Bivins, right, telling me to be at the Sheraton Hotel in thirty minutes?

"This is Echo," I said.

"No. *I'm* Echo," the voice said.

Pause. "Who is this?"

"This is the *real* Echo," the voice said again.

Michael Bivins from his early days with Bel Biv Devoe

Here's a little reference from my comic-book roots. Every once in a while, they do a crazy, balls-out story line where, say, Superman has to battle five other fake Supermen: a robot Superman, a Lex Luthor Superman, a black Superman, whatever. That sort of happened to me.

"The only difference between me and you," the voice on the phone said, "is that you've got a 'dash.' But I got the *crown*! I'm going to get it—and take it from you. *"Yo, let's battle!!"*

"Dash"? Does he mean the long mark over the o? (For the record, it's called a *macron.) Crown? Battles?* What was this dude talking about? I sold jackets and

T-shirts, that's it. It turned out that he fancied himself the "real Echo" because he was a hard-core graffiti writer from the Bronx who thought I was selling out by selling *anything*. To him, and many in the "hard-core set," selling graffiti in any form—whether it be a T-shirt or canvas—was effectively selling out and inauthentic. He wanted to claim the street moniker Echo for himself. I had never heard of him.

He wasn't alone. Maybe no one else wanted to "battle" me or beefed with my very existence, but there were others who claimed the Echo "name." There was an Amsterdam graf artist Echo, another clothing line named Echo (more on it later), and even a girl graf artist Echo. That's the thing about graffiti: sometimes naming conventions just aren't *that* original.

The other Echo disappeared eventually. When you're commercializing a craft—be it art, cooking, or masonry—there's always going to be people who consider themselves *more hard core* than you or *more real* than you. But real by whose standards? Authentic by what laws of compliance? A school? Training? Creation can't be bound by some esoteric code of ethics that ends up limiting your vision or putting constraints on how far you can stretch or grow. Besides, this other Echo, as a creator, was interested only in two-dimensional creation, and there's nothing wrong with that. I had my scopes in 3-D on things much farther than the surfaces I painted on.

But before I could go 3-D, I needed capital. Bivins was looking like a lost cause, so I thought about another possible investor: Spike Lee.

Clearly, Spike had to be interested. Right? After all, I'd sent him that sweatshirt with Malcolm X on it, he'd written me back a nice letter. And Spike was a business-savvy guy, so I just *knew* that he had to be ready to plunk down some cash.

My friend Terrence joined me as we navigated the subway, and we took the dollar van to Brooklyn to visit Spike Lee's lieutenant, Jeff Tweedy, who ran his 40 Acres & a Mule clothing store. They had featured my Malcolm X sweatshirt that I sent in my swag bomb in the window, so a partnership with me seemed all but inevitable. My friends—okay, maybe not Ben or Sunil—said things like, "Yo, your shit's hanging in Spike's window!" and that gave me the sense that this was *destined to happen*.

(ACTION):

"Yo, let's battle!!"

Creation can't be bound by some esoteric code of ethics that ends up limiting your vision or putting constraints on how far you can stretch or grow.

The whole ride, Terrence and I talked about what it would be like to work with Spike. Back in the day, when Spike worked on his films, he promoted them with production hats and jackets. Maybe I could design those?

I found his office, waited outside, and finally went in for the sit-down.

The meeting lasted all of seven minutes.

When Spike Lee sent me that letter to thank me for the sweatshirt, this is what I wanted to read:

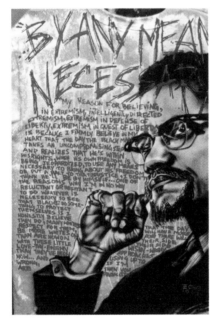

Yo, Marc,
Thanks for the fresh sweatshirt.
Love it. I'm gonna hang it in my
store's window! Let's get together
and figure out how you can make
more like this for me.
Thanks again.
Spike

But as far as I can remember, the letter actually read something like this:

Marc,
Thank you for the gift. I appreciate
it. It's always great to hear from the
fans, and it means a lot to me.
Spike

Above:
Spike Lee's
Forty Acres and a
Mule logo

Right:
The sweatshirt I
made for Spike

Terrence and I took the subway home together.

We rode in silence.

I now know that this is normal for every entrepreneur. You're always pitching. You never stop auditioning. Even for Spike, even Mark Zuckerberg, even for the president. You will always keep pitching, and you will always have to deal with rejections. This doesn't mean you should give up; it means you're human and you have a pulse.

NO BIVINS. NO Spike. I was losing hope of paying rent or even buying more paint for my airbrush, as I was only a few dying gasps of air away from failing out of school and losing my student loans. If I left Rutgers—at that point, at least—the Echo Unltd. baby would die in the womb.

In a last-ditch effort to save my ass, I had a meeting with the head of the pharmacy school, Dean John Colaizzi.

The dean sat down across from me and leaned back, crossed his legs, and slouched very unprofessorially. Is a dean allowed to slouch? This threw me off: where was the starch?

"Dean," I began, "I know that my grades have been—"

"Let me show you something." He cut me off, and I braced for the Academic Bullshit. "You see that?" He pointed to a painting hanging in the lobby. I had airbrushed a painting of pills for the school's anniversary, and apparently Dean Colaizzi proudly hung it on display. Huh.

"My grades—" I started again.

"Marc, you have a skill set," the dean said. "Tell me. What do you really *want* to do?"

Pills, *an airbrushed painting I did that hung in the Rutgers College of Pharmacy*

Was this really happening? I opened up and told Dean Colaizzi all of my plans for Echo Unltd., my financial problems, and how I was afraid to take the ACTION that could leave me broke or slingshot me to a very different reality.

The dean stared at me in silence. Then he said something that I'll never forget. "Marc, you don't want be forty years old, saying 'coulda, woulda, shoulda.' If this is what you want to do, you need to go for it."

"But there's no way I can grow my business while also taking classes."

"Here's what we'll do," the dean said. "We'll create a customized, one-man curriculum for you. We'll call it 'Medical Illustrations.' You'll still learn here in the Pharmacy School, but it won't be as classroom intensive.

"COULDA, WOULDA, SHOULDA."

—Dean John Colaizzi

This way you can stay enrolled but continue with it, along with your passion for art."

It was one of the most generous things that anyone has ever done for me. But it was more than just generous, it was a smart, effective way to inject me with academic motivation. Dean Colaizzi created a hands-on, learn-by-doing, practically applied curriculum based on my gateway drug to all learning: art.

He created an environment that let me take ACTION.

Beyond relieved, I thanked him and drove back to my apartment. I thought about what I should do next and realized I had only one last play.

I'd been blowing him off for months. I'd been chasing the high-profile gatekeepers, mistaking them for the goalkeepers. It wasn't their fault. Shame on me and my unrealistic expectations. I'd been blowing off the one guy who had believed in my vision from Day One. He was the one person who had sniffed out the Prove It to Me in my business plan and thought that I had proved it.

I made the call.

"Yo, Seth. You still interested?"

$$\frac{Unique}{Voice} = \frac{\int_0^{100} f(ACTION)dx - \int_{01}^{100} f(FEAR)dx}{\int_{01}^{100} f(SELF)dx}$$

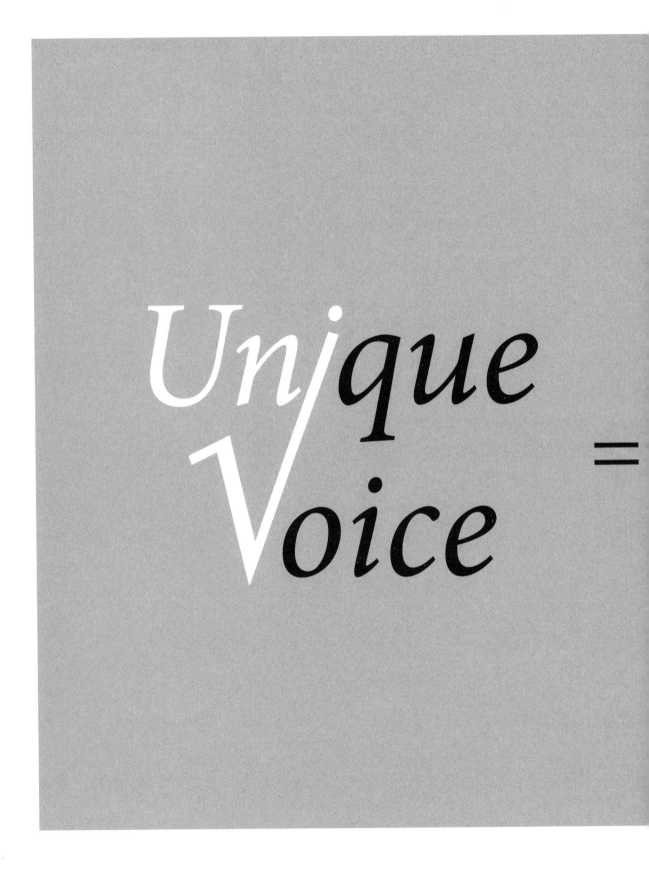

$$\frac{\displaystyle\int_0^{100} f(\text{ACTION})\,dx - \int_{0.1}^{100} f(\text{FEAR})\,dx}{\displaystyle\int_{0.1}^{100} f(\text{SELF})\,dx}$$

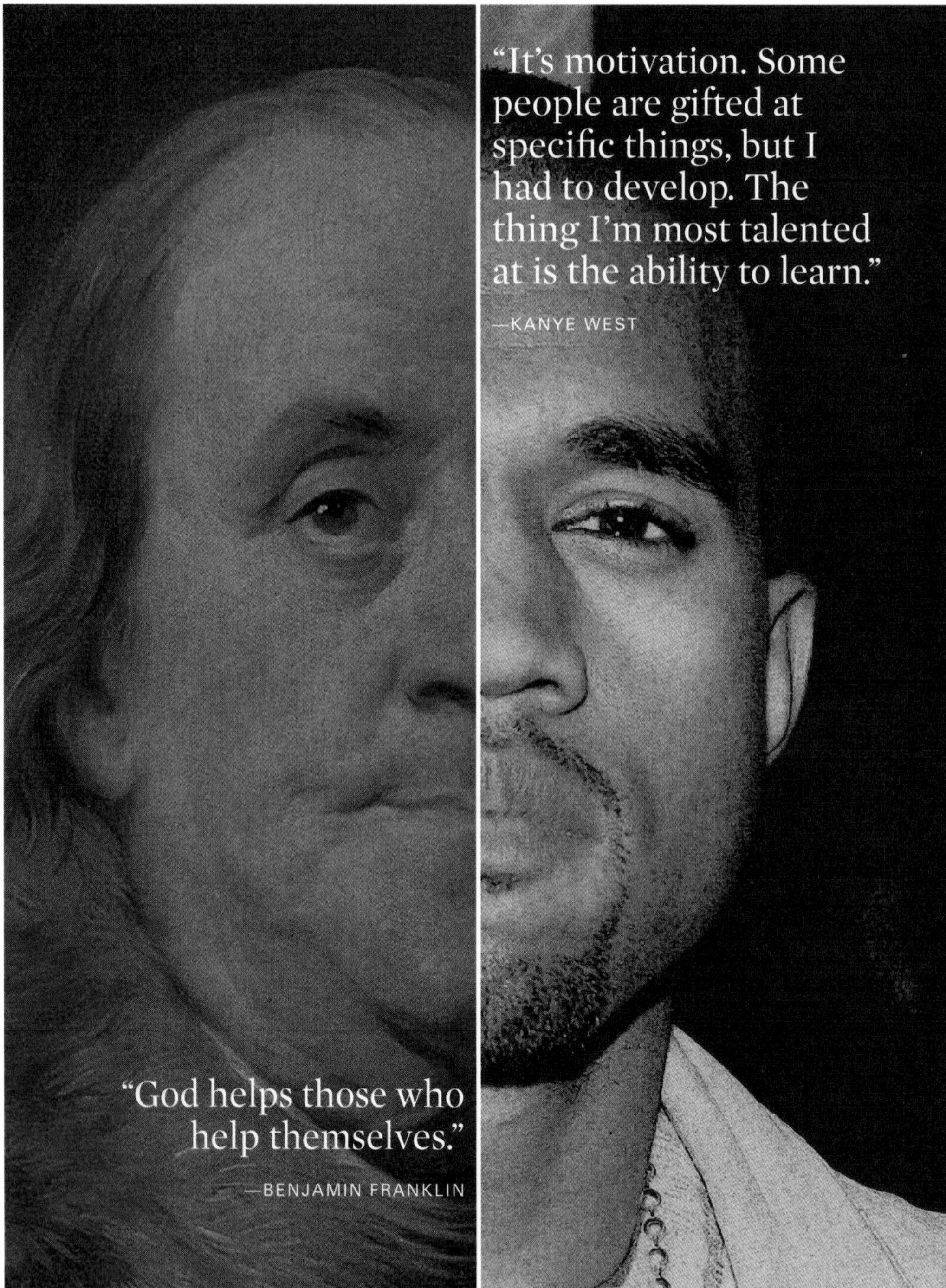

"It's motivation. Some people are gifted at specific things, but I had to develop. The thing I'm most talented at is the ability to learn."

—KANYE WEST

"God helps those who help themselves."

—BENJAMIN FRANKLIN

CHAPTER 4

SELF

SELF: *The word* SELFISH *has an ugly implication, but a strong sense of* SELF—*both internally and externally—is the engine that powers your brand. You need to dig deep, into your flesh and bones, to discover this core sense of* SELF, *and then you must own this* SELF *from your guts to your skin.*

In the formula, you can't have a SELF *score of 0, because no one's completely selfless unless dead. But you can be really, really close to selfless, like a Gandhi; let's say he's a 0.1. Or you could be at the other extreme. You could be so selfish—at a 100—that no matter how many advisors you have, you don't hear anyone but the voice inside your head. Sort of like a Hitler. Or if that's too heavy for you, maybe Jabba the Hutt.*

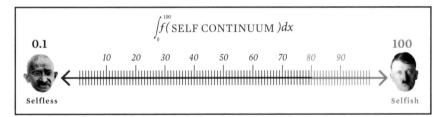

$$\int_0^{100} f(\text{SELF CONTINUUM})dx$$

0.1   10   20   30   40   50   60   70   80   90   100

Selfless   **Selfish**

Be as close to your singular purpose as you can. Gandhi knew who he was; he was at perfect peace with himself. Nike, for instance, knows what it is; regardless of the product or sport, everything has its clear and common purpose. You get in trouble when you get split against yourself. Like when Microsoft cranked out the Zune, just because it thought it should. Or that kid who comes back from spring break with fake dreadlocks. Or athletes who rap. (Sorry, Shaq.) You're better served when you're authentic to your nature and not the pomp or perception.

I. APSCO

S ETH PULLED UP in a bright red landscaping truck, which he had already decked out with a big Echo sticker plastered on the side, the way a plumber would promote his business. He hopped out of the truck and handed me a bag stacked with $5,000 cash. All in twenties. Just like his hands, the bag was dirty, but the cash was clean.

I looked at the bag and realized two things:

1. I'm responsible for this.
2. *This is real.*

Echo Airbrushings's mobile headquarters

"Do you want a receipt?" was the only thing I could come up with as a reply.

Seth laughed and gave me the marching orders: "Take this to APSCO, in Brooklyn. Ask for Big Phil. Use my name."

Five thousand dollars, that's all we had. That was the sum total of our capital. I had told Seth we would flip his $5,000 investment into $50 million, and somehow he believed me. The "plan," if you could call it that, was to use this cash to print my first run of T-shirts, based on six designs. Up to that point, I had only painted custom T-shirts one by one, by hand. To expand the business, we needed to use a big-boy production shop, like APSCO, to scale the operation. We'd then sell the shirts into local retailers, invest the profits into a second line, crack the larger retailers, and then things would snowball, right?

I navigated the subways to First Avenue and Fiftieth Street in Brooklyn. It was an industrial stretch of monoliths, a block ripe for a midnight brawl straight out of *The Warriors*. Immediately I liked it. Feeling a thousand miles from Lakewood, I entered the factory and took a freight elevator to the fourth floor, listening to it hiss and creak.

It was the middle of summer, hot, and I could smell the heavy odor of epoxies, plastic, and rubber-based pigments. I announced myself to a teenage receptionist who was half-asleep, and off in a corner was this big guy, six-

foot-something, and straight out of central casting for *Goodfellas*. He talked on a big, clunky cell phone that, even then, was old school.

The PA system blared, "Big Phil, pick up line three."

"I don't got fucking time! Put Little Phil on it!" he barked.

Big Phil hung up and shot me a glance. I could see a small pistol tucked into his waist. *How does Seth know these characters?*

I managed to say hello, but he ignored me and went back to flipping through his paperwork. I tried again.

"Um, Seth Gerszberg sent me," I squeaked.

"Seth?" Without looking up from his clipboard: "You got cash?"

I opened the bag of $5,000, letting him peek inside. He nodded.

"Kid, have you cut your screens?"

"Screens—?"

"The film. You got color separations, right?" He put his arm around my shoulder and ushered me toward the plant.

I had no idea what he was saying. He rattled off questions while I stared at his pistol.

"How many SKUs?"

"SKUs?"

"Styles! You know SKUs. Styles! How many ink colors?"

"Six colors. Maybe nine," I said.

"Nine colors? Try six, kid." Big Phil casually touched his pistol.

"Six T-shirts. I have six designs that I want to print as T-shirts."

He gave me a look as if I'd said something completely ludicrous, like, "Hey, can you sell me a strawberry ice-cream cone?" I was such a newbie. I didn't know anything about screen printing, or water-based inks, or color separations, or halftone dots; I knew nothing about the mass production of T-shirts. I thought the process amounted to handing over my artwork, and they printed it on shirts.

Little Phil walked in. He was much smaller and kind of looked like Bob Odenkirk, the actor-comedian from *Mr. Show*. "You're with Seth?"

I nodded.

"Okay then." Little Phil barked into a walkie-talkie, "Bodie!"

A creature seemed to crawl out from under the machinery. A skinny, young Billy Corgan–esque kid who looked like he was born in the factory and had never seen the sun.

"Bodie, will you unfuck this kid?" Big Phil asked, pointing at me.

Bodie nodded and then took me on a tour of the factory. He was clearly the technical guru behind the operation: the guy who knew precisely how every gear should be calibrated. He was to become my Yoda in my new quest for *the perfect color separation*.

I came to learn that the key to crispy-looking shirts was a properly deciphered color separation. No matter how good my original art looked, if it printed with low resolution, it would look cheap and lose its appeal. And as I learned from Bodie and the Phils, the quality of the image hinged on the quality of the color separation.

I quickly gleaned that Bodie was the only one who could help me, so I made him my new best friend. The Phils let me shadow him for weeks, learning the trade, watching their operation obsessively, and I readied my six designs for production. It blew my mind watching him cut the halftone-dot pages into photo-resistant Rubylith masking film, which was used to produce the individual printing screens. It was so time consuming. I kept asking, "Isn't there a better way than this???"

"No. Now you do it." Then he'd hand me the X-Acto blade to cut the film myself.

An old-school manual screen-printing press. In each station, someone pulls his own squeegie.

The factory backed right up to the Gowanus Bay. It was so raw. Especially the shit that went down on the abandoned piers. I loved it. Every day at lunch, like clockwork, you could look out the west windows on the second floor and catch a glimpse of police officers getting blow jobs from prostitutes. They did it in their squad cars. One o'clock—you could set your watch to it. We ate our subs and drank our Snapple and watched the show. No wonder Big Phil carried a pistol.

After weeks of priming my screens, getting my blank shirts on deck, they were finally ready for the factory's production cycle. I stood by the side of a metal, octopus-like screen printing machine, nervous, waiting for them to pull the first shirt off the line.

Once they spray adhesived it down, they pulled the shirt away from the wooden pallet.

It looked like shit.

The shirts were muddy and drab, and they gave me an empty feeling in the pit of my stomach. No way I was going to settle for that quality. On the other side of the factory, where they processed the bigger orders from the likes of the NHL, I'd seen T-shirts with crystal-clear, photo-quality images. Why couldn't mine look like that?

I knew I wasn't the NHL. But I also knew that I wasn't going to compromise on the presentation of my art. It needed to look right. It needed to look authentic.

I grabbed a New York Rangers T-shirt and brought it to the Phils. "*This!* Why can't my shirts look like this?"

Frisk: *one of our first six T-shirts*

"The NHL can afford Serichrome—" Little Phil said with a shrug.

"But you can't." Big Phil completed his sentence.

While I separated six colors, it was *possible* to use higher color separation that printed up to twelve, but that meant I needed more than Bodie's wisdom and skills. I needed to outsource to Serichrome.

$$\text{Un}i\text{que } \text{V}oice = \frac{\int_0^{100} f(FEAR)\,dx - \int_0^{100} f(ACTION)\,dx}{\int_0^{100} f(SELF)\,dx}$$

"Figure it out your- SELF."

Fine. If that's what it took, I was willing to do it. I called up the Serichrome office, in Dallas, and the rep gave me a quote: $5,000.

"Five thou?" I tried not to panic. That wouldn't leave us anything left to actually *print* the shirts. "I'm not the NFL. I'm not Reebok. This is important. This is about the art. You have to see my art, and you will understand why you need to help! Don't you have student rates?!"

"Yes, as a matter of fact we do," the sales guy said.

"How much is that?"

"Five thousand dollars."

I hung up and reached out to Seth.

"We don't have more money," he said.

"These are terrible," I begged. "Fucking Bodie. We need Serichrome."

"We're printing at APSCO. Quit crying about it."

"They're destroying my art, man!"

"Figure it out yourSELF."

I TOOK ON the challenge, and I leeched every drop of knowledge from Bodie, vampiring him. Eventually I learned every spell in the sorcery of color separation. I discovered that I could improve the resolution through a ridiculously tedious manual process.

The solution I came to was to sit at my desk for hours at a stretch, alone, trying obsessively to improve the patterns. To cut the screen, you use a rubber knife that's called a squeegee, and I bought a new squeegee—bigger than Bodie's. I called it "Bodie's Bitch" and treated it with the same reverence that a chef has for his trusty Japanese knife. I worked that squeegee like my life depended on it.

I created one of the six shirts that way. If I took photos of the artwork and then separated every color, elliptical halftone by painstaking halftone, I could get eight colors instead of the customary six. It was not the twelve colors I wanted, but it gave me a second skin tone and a flash of a highlight white. This allowed me to create deep, richer reds and add a glisten in someone's eye.

The shirt was called *Powerful Potion*. The day that I finally had it ready, I sent it through the production line, and the entire factory came to a halt, curious to see what it would look like. Even Big Phil came over and hung up his clunky cell phone.

The shirts came off the line and finally looked crisp. I held up one like it was the Stanley Cup. Oooohs and aahhhs.

"That's gonna sell the fuck out," said Big Phil.

And it did. The first summer the shirt was available, it sold fifty thousand units. To this day, it *continues* to be one of our best sellers, as we've probably sold one and a half million units over the years. Those early shirts were intentionally self-referential, incorporating the spirit of "Echo" prominently into the designs themselves.

Powerful Potion, *our first juggernaut*

But no matter how good those early shirts looked, no matter how self-referential, that operational process simply wasn't scalable. Unless Seth could invent a cloning machine, there was no way for me to spend the endless hours on each and every T-shirt unless my new goal in life was to compete with Serichrome, and that wasn't exactly the endgame.

The original line was selling *okay* with the average color seps that the APSCO team could process, but my core sense of SELF didn't want okay, and we couldn't afford the only alternative. Even if we had more capital, Serichrome would add an extra $12 to the retail price of every T-shirt, a price the market couldn't tolerate.

Something would have to be done.

DECIPHERING THE PERFECT COLOR SEPARATION:
A Quick Primer

It's something that 99 percent of the world never thinks about. But I had to. When I came to the marketplace, almost all of my competition (from the skate and street arenas) printed their art in flat-spot colors. Very rarely did they use halftone dots, or shading.

My form was using an airbrush, which is dependent on shading, and not line in reproduction, and therefore the halftone dot.

But most of the screen printers at the time (like APSCO) lacked the technical knowledge or computer software to generate these complex color separations. Only the very large sporting goods brands (which had cushy licenses with the NFL, NHL, and so on) deployed the technology.

These complex color separations were expensive to produce,

and the knowledge to create them was limited to niche prepress companies, like Serichrome, dedicated to providing transparency films for screen printers. So the NHL could pay Serichrome to do the color seps; then Serichrome would make a customized film and then send it to a screen print shop for production.

If you couldn't afford Serichrome—most couldn't—then your end around was to print in CMYK (cyan, magenta, yellow, and black). But this limited you to printing only on white T-shirts, as the ink is water based and translucent. I wanted to print color on dark-colored T-shirts so that I could play with the different colors popping off the dark surfaces. The only way for me to do it at that time was to separate the color. It

was what unlocked the code from average to great.

If you do it the old-school CMYK way (like how Bodie ended up temporarily solving the problem, at least with the white shirts), you have to decompose, or color separate, the original image into several individual "plates" represented by halftone dots. The magic happens when these individually composed plates layer on top of one another and then intentionally *over*print onto the dark-colored surface of the T-shirt, which creates yet another dimension of shading. The more granular the color separation—which carefully masks and intentionally overprints certain colors—the better the photo-realism of the final product. The more clumsy the color separation, the more the final print will look muddy and poor.

Before Photoshop had "layers," only the few companies that had broken the code of alpha channels held the keys to great color separations. And a newbie like me certainly didn't know the code. Yet.

Opposite:

Powerful Potion
(pen and ink, 1992)
From the very first book I ever finished writing.

Flat two-color printing on black fabric

Full color printing on black fabric

II. **THE AUSTRIANS**

I SPLIT MY time between APSCO and our "corporate headquarters"—the living room of my new apartment. I had moved out of the joint I shared with Ben and Sunil—enough with the silent treatment, enough with the closed doors—and found digs in New Brunswick, on 72 Louis Street, renting a railroad apartment that was downstairs from the Rutgers rowing team. I split the place with a new roommate who would always have my back: Marci. She was at Rutgers studying to be an elementary schoolteacher, and it was this training—dealing with kindergartners—that gave her the patience to deal with Seth and me.

We lived hand to mouth. It was technically my fourth year at Rutgers (thanks to my patron saint Dean Colaizzi), so I still limped by on student loans. I designed shirts in a small bedroom, stashed our inventory in the garage, and the UPS guy showed up at the driveway for pickups.

Things moved so fast. That's how it feels when you're in the early phase of rapid growth. As soon as we had cash in the register, we immediately spent it on marketing, buying cheap classified ads in the back of the *Source* magazine and then *Thrasher*, the skateboarding magazine. (Already I was starting to merge these two worlds, hip-hop and skate.) We were so bare bones that we advertised a 1-800 number that came to *my apartment*. The magazines had an international readership, so we got calls from all around the world at all hours of the

night. I left an outgoing message on an old-school answering machine that went something like: "Yo, you've reached Echo Unlimited. Leave a message after the beep, and if you want to submit a song for *Underground Airplay*, send me a tape."

THE CALLS TRICKLED in, and soon we started to move product. My old friend Terrence helped out by stuffing shirts in a knapsack and going door-to-door to retailers, trying to crack the mom-and-pop record shops. But I had bigger plans.

I wanted my product where *I* shopped. Real stores. I bought my Jordans and Timbs from places like Dr. Jay's—a large,

DON'T SLEEP ON THE "CLASSIFIEDS"

Look for the early adopters. Back in the early nineties, for my set, they read and were led by *Source* and *Thrasher* magazines. Instead of blowing money on full-page ads, we bought ads in the classifieds, trying to reach the true gearheads and hard-core locals. When we could afford larger ads, we still resisted the temptation for splashy full-size pages, as we knew that we'd be outgunned in production value by the Nikes of the world. Instead we bought one-third pages, but did three pages in a row, and then correlated the ads so they all spoke to one another. Since you don't have the budget to compete with the leaders of your space, talk to the supply side of your culture. This gets you in the conversation. If you're a fledgling computer science engineer, and you've got the vision for the next Facebook, it's okay to be another code ninja on GitHub. If you think you're the next XX or the Killers, it's okay to post your availability for a local gig on ReverbNation. "Soapbox it" where the trade talks.

two-floor, New York–based chain store with real size, real brands, real customers—and wanted to play on that field. Why couldn't I sell Echo there instead of just to the trustafarian hipster shops that cherry-picked me into obscurity? Yes, it was cool to be in the Patricia Field boutique in Greenwich Village or in X-Large, which had ties to the Beastie Boys, but I wanted to be next to the latest Jordan releases. This wasn't a betrayal of SELF, this wasn't "selling out"; it was exactly what my self wanted and needed to do. How did it make sense to keep my worldview so small? When I wanted clothes, I went for Ralph Lauren. Where was Ralph? In Macy's. So why couldn't I be in Macy's?

But to crack Macy's, you need volume and to get that, Seth argued, we needed more capital. "Look, I know some guys, some investors," he said. "From Austria."

"Investors?" I was confused. I already had Seth. *He* was my investor.

"We need real funding. You need to meet Rade and Josef."

Rade? Josef?

"They said that if I'm in the deal, they're in the deal. They just want to meet you," Seth said, excited. "If the meet goes well, they can give us sixty thou."

We went to our first trade show at New York's Jacob K. Javits Convention Center to meet with Rade Dzdiravich and Josef Pondl, these two Austrian guys

Selfishness needn't be defined as doing something at the expense of others. It's not a measure of greed. As it relates to UNIQUE VOICE, the great brands learn how to be self-referential without being predictable, overly indulgent, or creatively lazy. With stunning persistence, the great brands create moments that elegantly refer back to their core values, delighting their consumers time and time again. They constantly loop back to their brand's point of view, instead of just "making stuff." The best-in-class authentic brands—whether they're people, products, or services—do this effortlessly and relentlessly. But don't think this was a coincidence or magically improvised. It wasn't.

The ten most unapologetically self-referential people, places, and things:

1. Rappers

All of them. Ever heard a selfless rapper? Of course not. Rappers have to establish their UNIQUE VOICE among fierce, almost WWE-style competition, all while referencing the "culture" and somehow casting themselves above the fray. From Lil' Wayne to Rakim, from the Beastie Boys to Run-D.M.C., studying rappers—the self-boasting, the almost psychotic pursuit of notoriety—is a master class in building authentic personal brands. Just ask Ben Horowitz. A mega venture capitalist (Jawbone, Rap Genius, and Skype), he frequently references hip-hop to explain business and even quotes rap lyrics to other executives to help them make decisions.

2. Andy Warhol

For the young reader, you know enough to know that he was a cool motherfucker, even if you don't know exactly what he did. That's the power of his brand; even in death he's an unlabel. Andy was the master of *controlling his environment*, best represented by the Factory, his studio that flung together artists, celebrities, and an assortment of offbeat notables. (A concept that would inspire me years later.) Whether it was the tireless white wig he rocked or his nonstop postering of pop-culture icons, Warhol, like the contents in his famous Campbell's soup can, understood which ingredients to serve again, and again, and again.

3. Jesus

This one's controversial, I know. And this has nothing to do with the pros or cons of any organized religion; I know less about theology than I do about advanced calculus. All that said, building a personal brand looks more like creating a religion than creating a marketing deck. If you want to observe the ultimate execution of deploying a self-referential marketing tactic, look no further than Christianity. As an iconic symbol, it's tough to top the Boss on the Cross.

4. Alfred Hitchcock

From the specific cinematic devices he used time and time again, to his recurring themes, to his "hidden" cameos in all his films, Hitchcock was a badass self-promoter. He's also a story of "It's never too late," as he didn't direct his first American film, *Rebecca*, until he was forty.

5. Oprah

What's so interesting about her is that her ability to be self-referential—whether in books, shows, her magazine, *O,* or even on the Oprah Winfrey Network—makes us all more aware of our *own selves*. She makes us forget that she's a billionaire who rolls with celebrities. By baring all her

$$\text{Unique Voice} = \frac{\int_0^{100} f(\text{FEAR})\,dx \; - \; \int_0^{100} f(\text{ACTION})\,dx}{\int_0^{100} f(\text{SELF})\,dx}$$

scars and her battles with weight, she's fearlessly self-referential in a way that makes her human.

6. The USA

What a brand. It has it all. Dramatic story with all sorts of violent twists and turns. Sick logo. Red. White. Blue. Stars. Stripes. It even has a catchy soundtrack and strong merch! It has everything from the rockets' red glare to the apple pie to the pursuit of happiness. The brand's still standing, unwavering, after generations of cultural and tectonic shifts over 230 years later. Your brand has done something right when it can pull that off. Ask Ralph Lauren; he even tried trademarking the flag. Badassery.

7. Star Wars

George Lucas, more than anyone else I can think of, managed to create an entirely new mythology that has a self-perpetuating, self-referential engine at its heart. (And that's why Disney bought them. Yoda is the greatest invention since Mickey Mouse.) This is the reason "the force will be strong" forever. Some critics have panned Lucas for extending his brand too broadly. That pisses me off and makes me want to go on some saber-and-blood-soaked revenge fantasy to destroy the rebels. What George created in creating all these strains of his brand—from the Lego Star Wars partnerships to the animated series *The Clone Wars* to Industrial Light & Magic to The Old Republic MMORPG multiplayer online game to even wack-ass Jar Jar Binks— was a pop-culture virus built on being self-referential. He never falls into the trap of getting lazy. It's still fresh. It still works.

8. Will Ferrell

The most self-referential comedian. There's a reason we all love Will Ferrell characters, as the only thing that distinguishes one from the other is the wigs, the makeup, and the mustache. Practically every one of his characters, whether George W. Bush or Ron Burgundy, is a reckless narcissist who, through brilliant timing and the escalation of his voice, will suddenly start *talking very loud*. Most important, these characters all share something else in common: Will Ferrell's face. There's absolutely a "Will Ferrell brand" in the DNA of each of these characters, from Chazz Michael Michaels in *Blades of Glory* to Frank the Tank in *Old School*.

9. AARP

If you were to write the business plan for AARP, you would laugh it out of the room: "We're going to be this brand for old people. We're going to be the Nike for the elderly." But whatever you think about AARP—good or bad—you have to respect the shrewd and persistent way that William Novelli, its badass CEO, has created mechanisms to promote the brand, whether it's insurance products or the AARP logo or positioning the organization in both culture and politics.

10. M.E.

Not just any "me," but Marc Eckō. This is my book, and this is my formula, so I'll be damned if I don't include myself in a "Selfish" list that includes Yoda, Frank the Tank, and Jesus.

who looked exactly the way I imagined Austrian guys should look. "Good to meet you, *ja*?" Rade said.

Rade was six foot four and looked like a young Clint Eastwood from *Every Which Way but Loose*. He wore a double-breasted blazer over his shoulders, like a cape, along with beautiful hard-leather shoes. He didn't speak very good English and delegated every tactical question to Josef.

"You make trousers, *ja*?" Rade asked.

"Yeah, one day I'll make trousers," I said.

"You can paint artwork on trousers?" Rade looked confused.

He pointed to merchandise at the trade show, asking if I could print my art on different types of materials.

"You make denim, *ja*?" Rade asked.

I flipped through my black book and showed him some designs, geeking out a little, and I told him that, yeah, once we get bigger, I could embroider my designs on trousers, denim, linen, whatever he wanted.

"Can you do leather?" He pointed to some leather 8 Ball Jackets hanging in a booth.

"Why not!" I said, laughing. "I can make leather jackets!"

"Suits, Marc? Suits?!"

"Yes! We'll do suits." It all seemed so ridiculous; I had only a crude line of six T-shirts with low-res separations, and he was talking about stamping my art on every fabric on the planet. It was an absurd vibe; a good vibe. He believed in us.

Rade became one of my unlikely mentors: key people throughout my life that helped me along, people like Uncle Carl and Dean Colaizzi. Rade and Josef later came to my family barbecue in the summer—that time he wore a linen blazer over his shoulders—and he watched me airbrush in my studio. Seth was about to get married (he was always ahead of the curve), so he and Rade bonded over what it's like to be a groom. It all clicked. Seth negotiated a forty-sixty split. They would be silent partners who invested the cash; we would split our 60 percent fifty-fifty.

Still . . . that little problem about volume. How would we get it? We needed to create brand awareness. We needed to be in the right scene at the right time.

Our eyes turned south. To Atlanta.

III. **JACK THE RAPPER**

ATLANTA HOSTED A hip-hop convention called Jack the Rapper. The industry's flagship event, it drew everyone from Snoop to Tupac to 2 Live Crew, so just like with the Lyricist Lounge, I had a gut sense that *we needed to be there.* We could set up a booth, move our product, showcase the brand, and earn some industry bona fides. Or at least that's how I pitched it to Seth. My actual thoughts were more like, *Snoop! 'Pac! My bottomless bag of chronic!*

This was a big test for how Seth and I would work as partners. The jury was still out. Prior to the Rade deal, we had little more than a handshake agreement and a paper bag of cash. (My cousin Mickey, a lawyer, reviewed our sloppy paperwork, telling us, "This is big-boy stuff; you sure you want to do this?") Seth knew his numbers, and I respected his work ethic, but c'mon, not to be a dick, but this is the music and fashion industry, and perception is reality, right? And with his jeans shorts and yarmulke, how would he socialize with my friends like Terrence or Anthony? I felt guilty for thinking this way, but I was almost embarrassed for people to see him around my work.

We invited Terrence, Anthony, and a few other friends to help, and loaded Seth's pickup truck with the shirts. Unbeknownst to Seth, I brought the biggest bag of weed ever. You need sustenance for a road trip, right? And after all, it was *Jack the Rapper.*

As soon as we arrived in Atlanta, Seth unpacked the boxes and started to set up the booth, but a few us of slipped upstairs to smoke out. When I returned downstairs and picked up my airbrush, Seth looked at me, looked at Terrence, and then grabbed me by the shoulder.

"In the hotel room," Seth said, hard.

We walked to the elevator in silence, and I felt like I was being dragged to the principal's office. "Seth . . ." I started to say, but he ignored me. We stood in icy silence, all the way up the slow, slow elevator.

"Seth."

Nothing.

Once inside the hotel room, he slammed the door.

AGREEMENT made and effective this 6th day of July, 1993, by and between BEX USA, INC. (hereinafter referred to as BEX), a domestic corporation authorized and doing business under the laws of the State of New Jersey, with its principal address as ██████████████████, Teaneck, New Jersey 07666, and MARC MILECOFSKY (hereinafter referred to as MARC), residing at ██ ██████████████ Lakewood, New Jersey 08701.

W I T N E S S E T H

WHEREAS, BEX and MARC agree to form a corporation hereinafter known as Echo Unlimited, Inc. (hereinafter referred to ECHO).

WHEREAS, BEX and MARC have an authorized capital stock of 200 shares, without par value, in the corporation known as Echo Unlimited and the Shareholders are the owners of all the issued and outstanding shares,

WHEREAS, the Shareholders of BEX and MARC have agreed that their execution of the within agreement would be in the best interests of the Corporation and would promote harmonious relationship among directors and shareholders of BEX and MARC with respect to the conduct of the affairs of the Corporation;

WHEREAS, BEX was primarily established to do business development for RADIVOJE DIZDAREVIC and JOSEF POANDL the principals ██

WHEREAS, BEX brings to ECHO Unlimited monetary support and its experience in finance.

2

Dear Cousin Mickey,

I appreciate you reviewing this contract. I put some notes on this copy. I don't understand a lot of the → "standard mumbo-jumbo." You can reach me at ███████████.

FONDLY—

Marc

1

Note my keen use of legal language: "Standard mumbo-jumbo." (fig. 1) Also, the contract was so vaguely worded, that if you look closely at the last page, it almost looks like they're pledging us unlimited financial support. (fig. 2)

"Terrence is stoned," he said, matter-of-factly.

"Yeah, but—"

"*You're* stoned." He crossed his arms.

"Dude, I'm not 'stoned.'"

Seth grabbed my collar with both hands. He shoved me against the wall and got up in my face. "We are *partners*!" he said, almost yelling.

"I know, I know—"

"This isn't fucking spring break! We are *partners*!"

"Dude, it's no big deal—"

$$(\text{SELF}) = \uparrow 100$$
(too high)

He shoved me again. "You just drove across state lines with a bag of marijuana. Drugs. On a business trip! They'll prosecute you for that shit. Not just you, Marc. Me!"

"I get it, I get it."

Seth's eyes were red, and his voice was filled with emotion. "We could both go to jail!" He was almost screaming. "I'm getting *married*! What you just did could fuck up my life! This is not how you do a partnership! This is not how you do a business!"

Finally, he released me from the wall, like Darth Vader releasing one of his lackeys from his clutches.

I slumped down and sat on the floor. "I'm sorry, man," I said, meaning it.

"Where is it?" he asked.

I fetched the bag of weed from the bottom of my suitcase and handed it to him. He took the bag and dragged me into the bathroom.

"Flush it," Seth said.

I emptied out the bag and shook the weed into the toilet. I gave it a flush and then watched as every bud disappeared down the drain.

"If you ever do something like this again, I'm out!" he said, and left me in the hotel room, alone, still crumpled on the floor.

The convention was a shit-show, for me personally and also for the trade show as a whole: that weekend became infamous for alleged gunshots and knife fights. Years later, I realized how much respect I gained for Seth that day. *This* was our contract. *This* was our paperwork. He showed me so much steel and resolve; he had bet his career on me, and I'd treated the trip

WHO'S MORE CREATIVELY SELFISH— APPLE OR MICROSOFT?

Let's look at two different UNIQUE VOICES: Apple and Microsoft. SELF doesn't just mean selfish, as in "wanting more money," so you wouldn't say that Bill Gates and the late Steve Jobs both wanted to rake in billions and therefore they're both equally selfish. Look deeper. As a brand, Apple is constantly self-referential, with the iPod, iPad, iPhone, iEverything. Microsoft had an equal opportunity to leverage itSELF across the same types of products—the Xbox, the Zune, and the Windows operating system—but chose not to. Go even deeper. Since the 1980s, Apple restricted its operating system to it*self*, branding it, nurturing it, and controlling every aspect of its own ecosystem. Microsoft took a different approach: the company opened up Windows to the larger world, and, yes, it's still a massive platform, but in the long run, that proved to be a less successful strategy. Apple's more selfish way served its brand and consumers better in the end.

like it was spring break. Seth knew who he was. He had a sense of self and was a pro.

Break's over.

You need to have a strong sense of SELF; without it, there's no distinction between you and anyone else, and it's impossible to have a UNIQUE VOICE. But this needs to be tempered. And sometimes only outside voices can help. Too high on SELF? You can get flushed down the toilet.

IV. **FIFTY-FIFTY-FIFTY**

WE WERE SO disorganized. I was knee-deep in product development and spending most of my time at APSCO, still depressed about our dicey color separation. Seth handled the sales and marketing. But we had no one to manage the office, answer the phones, and do the day-to-day brass tacks.

Everything was done by us, so making a little mistake had major consequences: like leaving out a zero in the check register and overdrawing our bank account. "Inventory management" was always a challenge, since we lived in our office/warehouse and had to move boxes out of the way to eat dinner. Sometimes Marci asked the Rutgers rowing team guys who lived upstairs to help move boxes, and when we had larger orders, we had no choice but to stage the boxes on our driveway. Seemed like a good idea until it started to rain.

"Customer service" was a novelty: Marci once had to soothe an upset mother who called our apartment/business line to complain about the fact that we used Vanessa del Rio, a porn star, in an Echo advertisement that we ran in *Big Brother* skate magazine. Over the phone, Marci explained calmly to the mother that del Rio was an appropriate choice, since the mag was also running a contest to see which reader could poop the most in his hat. It's too bad we don't have that conversation on tape.

Sales ticked up, so we allowed ourselves to hire employee number one, Mitch. He was a friend of Seth's who was a bit of a misfit, but, hey, we weren't some stodgy corporation. Mitch would work out just fine.

Seth, me, and Marci:
the three musketeers

Mitch didn't work out just fine. Our books were a mess, the numbers never squared, and we mysteriously missed a bunch of calls. Sometimes we would ask Marci—who's always had more common sense than me, and who I think of as my Ghost of Reason—to look at the books and help us restore order.

"Guys?" Marci said one afternoon, flipping through our invoices. "This doesn't add up."

It added up when we realized that Mitch—Seth's charity case—had "borrowed" $3,000. When confronted, he squirmed and said that he'd taken it just "for the weekend as a loan." Once he was busted, his panicked father wired $3,000 to our accounts to make us whole, but what's done was done.

Mitch was out. We needed someone reliable that we could trust.

It wasn't a long job search. I knew who had to be employee number two.

I gave her my pitch back in Lakewood, in the car, while we were on the way to get groceries. "Marci," I said. "We need you."

She laughed. "All you need is someone who hasn't flunked high school—or doesn't have a criminal record."

"No we need *you*." I pulled the car to the side of the road, and the traffic roared past us. I turned to face her. Like me, she hadn't taken any design or business courses, but she believed in the brand, believed in *us*, and she would do anything to help us out. (Bonus? Whenever I pouted or said that something couldn't be done, it never fazed her, since we had been playing and fighting since birth.)

"Marc—"

"Look at this." I pulled out a knot of cash. "We've had a good summer, Marci. We made a shit ton of money."

"And I'm happy for you."

"And we want to share the company with you . . . equally. As a partner. You, Seth, and me, fifty-fifty-fifty."

"Marc, that doesn't add—"

"I'm joking, Marci. Thirds. You, Seth, and me. You're practically a partner already, with how you help us."

"I still have a year of school."

"Drop out of school. We're going to be so successful."

She looked at me, laughed a little, and said something that would take me nearly twenty years to fully absorb: "Marc, define *success*."

Define success? That was easy. Getting rich, getting famous, getting clothes and art plastered around the planet. Creating not just a brand but a megabrand. Wouldn't that prove I'm a success? I laughed off what she said that day, but many years later, when I found myself unable to sleep feeling *plastic* and inauthentic, while running a billion-dollar company, I would think about her words: *"Define success."*

Seth and Marci in the early warehouse

V. THE HAMMER

I WAS STILL taking a few token classes at Rutgers, thanks to the dean's "Medical Illustrations" program. But most of my time was spent at APSCO, trolling mom-and-pop shops for sales, and prepping for wholesale-to-retail trade shows.

When Seth cold-called retailers, they laughed him off the phone, but before they hung up, he would ask them where they bought their product. The answer was always the same: trade shows. In terms of our actual product, we still had that lingering problem of weak color separation—which meant that unless

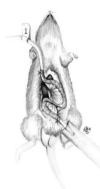

My illustration of a laboratory rat that I drew in my medical illustration class at Rutgers College of Pharmacy

I could replicate myself or reinvest in Serichrome, I'd have to change the aesthetic of my art—but nevertheless we went to the Action Sports Retailer (ASR) show in San Diego to hawk what we had.

Seth and I roamed the halls of the convention center wide-eyed, scoping out the competition. There was Stussy, which had a massive booth blanketed in black-and-white photography of the exotic places where Shawn Stussy had traveled. There was Oakley, which was literally full of smoke and mirrors—and neon lights that must have cost $250K to build out.

"Where's our booth?" I asked Seth.

He looked at our printout. "Booth 8,243E."

We made our way to a box smaller than most jail cells, but even jail cells have a toilet and a cot. It was an empty slab of concrete that didn't even have a folding chair. I looked at it and wanted to go home.

"You fucking kidding me?"

"This'll do," Seth said, nodding. "This'll do."

I paced back and forth on the concrete, wondering if it was too late to get a refund on the convention.

"Wood," Seth said. "We need wood."

Seth dragged me to go find the forklift operators, who were hauling in all these thousands of booths, and we swiped a bunch of wooden pallets. Then he dashed to Home Depot, where he bought some paint, some hangers, and a folding table. He even managed to wrangle some Police Line—Do Not Cross tape.

At the time, our best-selling shirt was called *Frisk*, which featured a guy getting patted down by the cops with the yellow Do Not Cross tape printed along the bottom of them.

"We're going to build a wall with the forklift pallets," Seth said. "We'll do an homage to *Frisk*, and you can paint on the wood while we showcase the shirts."

Seth, you magnificent bastard. Wearing sockless barbeque sneakers and his patented denim shorts, Seth plunked down the pallets and started hammering away, covering the walls with wood. About five minutes into the hammering, we heard:

"Hey! Hey! Hey! You can't do that!" A convention security guard rolled up on a bicycle, waving his clipboard at us.

Note the jeans shorts.

Terrence and me at our booth at the Magic Convention.

Opposite:

Our classic raggedy-ass trade show aesthetic. I painted that mural in the booth and sold it for cash. (Back then, I made more from the murals than the T-shirts.)

"It's just a hammer," Seth said.

"That's union work. If you want to do any construction, you need to use a 'licensed construction operator.'"

Seth and I looked at each other. Was this guy for real?

Just then, a second security guard rolled up on his bicycle and then a third. Soon there was a small platoon of security guards who pedaled around on bikes, enforcing every anal-retentive rule, shaking us down for fees.

"Okay," Seth said, trying to keep from raising his voice, "how much does a 'licensed construction operator' cost?"

The guard broke it down for us: $100 an hour, minimum of ten hours. Or $1,000 that we couldn't afford.

"We'll think about it," Seth said, putting down the hammer as if he were a robber holstering his gun—*Nice and easy, so no one gets hurt*—and the guards cycled away.

I looked at Seth, hoping that he had some brilliant scheme.

"Wait here," he said.

I watched him saunter off into the distance, looking kind of suspicious. He didn't come back for almost an hour. Enough time for me to start wondering if he'd just said, "*Screw it*," and gone home.

An hour later, my partner returned riding a security guard's bike, complete with a banana seat and a handlebar bell.

"Where'd you get that?" I laughed.

"Don't worry about it," he said, taking off his yarmulke and impersonating a guard. "You start hammering while I provide cover."

We finished the booth, hung our shirts, and I busted out my airbrush and air compressor and started painting.

So how'd the booth turn out?

In the Hollywood version of this story, the entire convention catches wind of our swashbuckling exploits, admires our scrappy can-do attitude, and we're lauded as the darlings of the trade show. Shawn Stussy himself shows up at the booth, sees my shirts, and gives me The Nod. Rosie Perez strolls by and says that, yes, in fact, she will marry me.

In the real version of the story, the buyers were sorta fifty-fifty on it. That's the thing about ACTION and SELF. The mere fact that you *take* ACTION doesn't mean that everyone's going to love it. The mere fact that you showcase your SELF is no guarantee for triumph.

Then again, we did move product. We had just enough orders to keep us staggering forward. Like always, the shirts printed on black—where the shoddy color separation was more obvious—didn't set the world on fire. That was killing me. But it was a start.

VI. **LIFE SAVERS**

F OR THE NEXT year, we pounded the pavement and hit more mom-and-pops—selling on consignment, which is the most emasculating way to do business—and eked out more sales. But it wasn't enough. We were still not with the big boys, we were still not in Macy's, and the clock on my one-year college experiment to extend my student loans was about to stop.

We hit the San Diego trade show once again. Make that trade shows, plural. San Diego had two overlapping events in the same week: Action Sports Retailer, the larger commercial one, and 432F Streetwear Show, the freckled-step-child convention, which was supposedly "more authentic" and grafficentric. Seth and I divided and conquered. He manned ASR, while I painted murals at the 432F, selling them for as much as $3,000 a pop, often to Japanese clients.

The hard-core trade show for the emerging street wear scene: 432F

A FTER BUMPING ELBOWS and egos with the skate set at 432F, I'd sprint across town to meet up with Seth, since the Action Sports Retailers convention stayed open later. I'd ask him what's selling.

"Usual," he'd say.

The *usual* was the white T-shirts. That was only two of the six. How could I become known, crack the big retailers, if I couldn't show off my art as I designed it? The art looked great on canvas, but it didn't translate into sales. It made me so depressed.

SELLING VERSUS SELLING OUT

At 432F, I connected with other graf artists—guys like Katch One, a graf genius from Hawaii—and it pushed me to step up my game. I was in awe of Katch. He was doing what I was doing, but on a giant scale and with *aerosol*, which was far more challenging than airbrushing, since it's harder to control the can. He would paint these gigantic murals and take photos of them, and then they'd print the photos on T-shirts for a brand called Con-Art. The guy was brilliant, and his work was epic.

432F raised the old question that cuts to the bones of AUTHEN-TICITY: whether I was a sellout. A lot of the other artists thought I wasn't *real* because I used an airbrush, or because I sold my gear in larger stores like Dr. Jay's, or because I had a vision of something bigger than street and skate. This was a real challenge to my sense of SELF.

These *gatekeepers* of street-wear fashion, in a foreshadowing of what I'd see later with the CFDAs of the world, viewed themselves as the *goalkeepers*.

The gatekeepers think that they're the anchors, or the brackets, that hold the shelf at the altar of relevance.

But they're not. At the end of the day, there's only one goal-keeper who matters: the folks who pay at the cash register. Sounds cynical. Vulgarian. But they keep the score. Know that.

Eighteen months later, most of the companies at 432F were out of business. (And it's a shame because many of them were worthy of success.)

Even Izzy Ezrailson, the legendary retailer who cofounded the Up Against the Wall fashion chain, could tell that I had a problem. He swung by our booth at ASR. When he saw that the four dark shirts—67 percent of my line!—weren't selling, he said, "How are you going to do this? These prints aren't working. The numbers don't lie." He chuckled at our naïveté. I didn't have an answer. I was so fucking frustrated.

He was right. It wasn't going to work, which meant that our *entire company* wasn't going to work—at least not the way I envisioned it, and not how we were doing it. We couldn't afford to pay Serichrome, but we also couldn't afford to *not* pay Serichrome. We needed some kind of technological break-through, or we were dead.

And then, at that very trade show, literally right next to me, I stumbled onto the one thing that could save us: marijuana.

The booth next to us at Action Sports Retailer belonged to a brand called Eighth Day, as in, "On the eighth day, God created weed." Yes, they were a bunch of potheads, but somehow they sold these beautiful, high-end shirts with dark, tie-died, photo-quality illustrations. Their quality was impeccable.

How were these guys doing it? They looked as broke as Seth and Marci and me; no way were they paying Serichrome.

I introduced myself to the owner, a dude named Drew, who was a skinny, hippieish, No-Cal kind of guy with dirty jeans and Chuck Taylors.

"Hey, man," Drew said lazily.

"How'd you do this?!" I pointed to his shirts, geeking out. "Who did this for you?"

"I did it myself." Drew shrugged.

"How?!? How is that possible?"

"I used Photoshop," Drew replied, leaning against the wall.

This was 1994, and I had never heard of Photoshop. I didn't even have a computer; we did the books with calculators and legal pads and (lots) of Wite-Out.

"They're perfect," I said in awe, feeling the fabric of his shirts. "Yo, can you get up in my black book?" I asked him, referring to the sketchbooks that graf artists carry. This was unprecedented—asking a *nongraffiti artist* to sign my black book.

"Sure, man." Drew seemed amused by my idolatry. He was the most relaxed dude I've ever met.

"Teach me," I practically begged. "I'll do anything. I'll do whatever you want. I'll clean your toilets; I'll cut your wife's toenails."

All Drew asked from me was a big bag of weed. Without thinking, I'd promised him that it was the best in New York.

"Come to my house in Tahoe," Drew said. "Stay with me for a week, and I'll teach you everything you need to know."

So I got home and immediately packed my bags for Lake Tahoe, Nevada, my Dagobah, to train with Drew, my new Yoda of color separation. But where would I find this best weed in New York? And how would I get it to Tahoe without landing in jail?

Screw it. These were the risks I had to take; this stoner could be the key to unlocking the potential in the product. So I went to my usual "guy" and got "the premium" stuff, but then I packed it meticulously—surrounded by rolls of minty fresh Life Savers candy. My theory: the candy, and more specifically

the spearmint flavor, would help me smuggle it through airline security. I knew it might taste different, but I hoped Drew wouldn't notice that.

I checked my luggage at Newark—so far so good—and then, at the Reno airport, I went to pick it up at baggage claim. I watched the rest of the flight's luggage scroll by on the carousel. No sign of mine. More bags plunked onto the conveyor belt, but still I was waiting, waiting, waiting.

Where were they? The crowd thinned, and soon I was one of only ten people waiting. Then Seven. Then just a few of us. Then I was alone. No bags.

Then, finally, my luggage dropped onto the belt.

And just as I was about to step toward it, I heard the low, menacing growl of a dog.

A cop with a dog walked through baggage claim, sniffing around the luggage. Oh shit. I took a few steps backward and thought about leaving the airport. Could they trace the bag back to me? Did I have fingerprints? *Fingerprints?* What the fuck was I thinking? They didn't need fingerprints; the bag was tagged with my name on it. I visualized Seth visiting the prison and glaring at me through the bars.

And then the dog turned and walked away.

I grabbed my bag and got the fuck out of that airport.

At Drew's place, I caught my breath, but there was still the issue of my weed that he expected to be the best in New York.

Drew greeted me at his door with a bro-hug.

"Hey, man," he said, sounding like he'd just woke up. "Any problems at the airport?"

"Nah," I said. I unpacked my bags and showed him the packs of Life Savers. He picked up the box of candy and shook it, frowning, looking as confused as if I'd just given him a My Little Pony.

"What the fuck is this?" He sniffed the Life Savers.

"That's how we do in the East."

I took out a pack, and we lit some of the weed. He inhaled and started coughing. "This shit's terrible!"

"It's Jersey style; it's an acquired taste," I said, trying to keep a straight face.

Drew coughed some more. "You can't tell me that RZA smokes his weed like this, or that Ghostface Killah smokes his weed like this."

Drew gave me a hard look, considered, and then burst out laughing. I laughed too.

"Fuck it," he said, chuckling. "Menthol."

For the next week, I crashed on his couch, we smoked East Coast menthol, and Drew unlocked the secrets of digital color separation. He sold me a computer—building computers was a side gig of his—and he taught me how to hack alpha channels in Photoshop. While we worked, another of his buddies ran a tattoo shop in his living room. He'd be drinking Jack Daniel's straight from the bottle while working on guys' full sleeve tattoos.

I took notes like I'd never taken notes in my life, studying harder than I ever did for any class on organic chemistry or pathophysiology. I knew that I was in front of greatness. Drew was my next unlikely mentor: a guy you can't judge by appearance or labels. He saved my ass, and he helped me unlock massive value in my brand by getting my final products to look like how I conceived them.

When I flew back to New York—without any drugs—I was ready to redesign my entire line. I finally had a way to let my product match my art.

That was a watershed moment. Using Serichrome would have added $12 to the cost of each T-shirt. Now? I could do it for $0. I no longer had to use clunky handmade color separations: I could do it digitally on my computer. Here was my new process: I made a digital file that I then dropped off at the printing facilities of the *Daily Targum*, the Rutgers student newspaper, and for fifty bucks they made me transparent films, which I then sent to APSCO. (Serichrome would have charged me over $2,000.) I built an assortment of new shirts around the new tech, and it took off. Then I went back and redid the four dark T-shirts that wouldn't sell, and even those worked a lot better.

> I took notes like I'd never taken notes in my life, studying harder than I ever did for any class on organic chemistry or pathophysiology. I knew that I was in front of greatness.

Behind every great fortune is a crime. (Or in my case, maybe a misdemeanor.) Behind every Eckō there's a Drew in Tahoe. It would have been easier not to worry about the color separations. Instead of going to Drew's place in Tahoe, I could have spent a week rolling with graf artists, and we

FIND YOUR UNFAIR ADVANTAGE

Technology doesn't have to be in the form of zeros and ones, but it needs to affect your consumers' emotions as they consume your product. It isn't about bits and bytes or algorithms. Technology should be pursued to create more value, more efficiencies, or other currencies to you and your brand's shareholders. In my case, this was the pixel resolution of graphic T-shirts; it was a technological advantage from my competitive set.

It wasn't like I was the only one tapping into street culture, but, unlike many of my early competitors, I discovered a piece of technology that would change the way people viewed, and felt, my product. Literally.

It was a subtle thing. The consumer wouldn't be able to look at the shirt and say, "Hmmmm, he must be using fourteen colors, not six!" But the shirt just looked better, it felt better, it washed better. The colors were more intense; they could see my art better!

That's important in any business. When I launch new ventures, I don't presume that my brand alone is enough. I'm constantly asking myself, "What's my unfair advantage? What's my technological advantage?" Is it a supply-side technology? Is it a sales technology? Is it a technology in the way that my people communicate to the consumers?

Don't underestimate a retailer's affinity for brands that can do what consumers may dismiss as mundane or "not about the brand." For instance, in fashion, retailers look for suppliers who have systems to fulfill stock in an array of uneven sizes. This is called "replenishment systems." Brands like Polo Jeans, Guess, and Levi's invented the best practices of the industry. These computer systems are able to ship you denim in the right size. There are so many possible combinations: 30-inch waist, 30-inch inseam, 30/32, 30/31, 32, 33—all those SKUs (stock-keeping units). It gets very complicated very fast, and your inventory can

break. Having these world-class systems means a lot to a brand's promise, both to the consumer and retailer.

Best-in-class guys had inventory management systems—basic by today's standards—but at the time, they gave Ralph Lauren's Polo Jeans and Tommy Hilfiger's Tommy Jeans the competitive advantage, coupled with good design and pricing, of course. In the 1990s, when I showed a denim line to retailers, no one took me seriously. No matter how good it was, they knew that because I lacked the supply-side technology, I could never service the volume they needed. I didn't understand that.

This is stuff you have to think about; not just the romance of a new idea. You can't just say, "Oh, we just have a great idea." The unsexy stuff—the nuts and bolts—matter: operations, supply, inventory, technology.

What's your unfair advantage? You have to ask that. Otherwise you're just in the business of selling cogs.

could have bigged each other up. But I needed to reframe SELF, both for me and the brand, as something with a larger worldview.

And I had earned my unfair advantage.

VII. **THE RHINO**

FOR THE FIRST time, we felt the wind at our backs. Thanks to Drew and my new dark sorcery of hacking Photoshop, I had rebuilt my assortments and could see the results. Sales picked up, we cracked more retail stores, and we finally moved out of my garage and into a real (if small) office.

As we started to grow, I realized we needed a new logo. That became clear at the larger trade shows such as the Magic convention in Vegas, which packs in the big-boy brands like Levi's and Timberland. I looked up at the walls, and I'd see a giant alligator: Lacoste. I walked farther, and I'd see a giant pony with a guy on its back: Polo. A few booths down, I'd see a big swoosh: Nike.

Where was our swoosh? Where was our crocodile? What would visually define our SELF?

The original logo was just my graf moniker that spelled out "Echo Unltd.," in hand-drawn type. It worked well enough—four letters in one word balanced against the five in the other; you could stack the two words on a hat; it had good symmetry; and Seth and Marci wanted to keep it—but I sensed that we needed something more.

We needed an actual *image* to which people would add their own meaning. This would let us become more visually self-referential, just like with Nike and the swoosh. It so happened that every once in a while, I still painted where it all began: in my parents' old garage in Lakewood. It was still a comfortable place to lose myself in deep production. One day my eyes locked on those old rhino wooden figures, the ones Darren and I played with as kids. That was it: the rhino.

I immediately mocked up a rhino logo and painted a rhino T-shirt. We unveiled it at our next trade show, and people hated it.

"Is that a dinosaur?" asked one buyer.

"I don't get it," said another. "Where's the graffiti?"

"Keep the hippos," said another. "Gimme the graffiti shirts."

People thought it made no sense. "Isn't the rhino for outdoor brands?" "Are you guys now selling hunting jackets?" I had a different take. If a street brand is defined by something that's obviously street, you don't have as much room to grow. By picking something more oblique, something that makes you think, it lets you fill the symbol with new, surprising meaning.

The meaning of the rhino logo, like all good logos, goes deeper than the skin. Yes, from a graphic design point of view it works: it's symmetrical, it has good line weight, it reproduces easily. The anatomy of the rhino reflected the values that we embraced: crunchy on the outside and soft in the middle. It has a tough skin, muscular heart.

I didn't let the critics faze me; I knew that we had found our mascot. From then on, when we hired street teams, we would plaster stickers of rhinos all over, and they would *pop*; they were not what you expected to see from the guy who airbrushed intricate illustrations at trade shows. It was simple in comparison.

This felt so true, so authentic. It gave me the confidence to ignore the critics. This object from my youth had such a pure connection to my values—the ruggedness, the stubbornness—that I knew my path was right. It felt like warm energy, like the power of the sun, and I knew it came from an authentic place.

Maybe two years earlier, while still finding my voice at Rutgers, these critics would have wounded me, maybe they would have made me doubt, and maybe I would have abandoned the new logo. But I was past that point.

It was manna from heaven—when you do something that you *know* is authentic—embrace it, run with it, and trust your SELF before the critics.

VIII. **IT WAS HAPPENING**

"MARC," MY SISTER said, "look at this."

She showed me the calculator.

Two million dollars.

We were sitting in a booth at a diner after wrapping up the first day of Vegas trade. *It was happening.* I was on the phone with my mom, and I lost it. I could feel myself starting to cry.

"Marc, are you all right?" my mom asked.

I wiped the tears. "We just booked two million dollars in sales."

Seth and I made eye contact, gave each other The Nod, and I could hear my mom crying. I was still tearing up.

I wasn't tearing up because of the money. Not really. I couldn't have expressed it in these words at the time, but I had sensed a validation that now, finally, I had established a UNIQUE VOICE for myself and for my brand. SELF. I had it. I had conquered the paralyzing FEAR, I had taken ACTION, and I had dug deep beneath the body's skin—by honing my skills, by studying with Bodie and then with Drew—to create my foundation of SELF. We had our UNIQUE VOICE.

"Marc," my sister said, looking up from the receipts again, "those rhino shirts are really starting to pick up."

It was happening.

Or was it? We sold $2 million that day. And the next day, we sold $3 million. But as Seth and I would painfully learn in the next year, "taking orders" didn't mean "fulfilling orders," and revenue didn't mean profit. I had no idea how empty and hollow and inauthentic that $2 million figure was. I hadn't yet contemplated the infinite-truth $(\vec{\mathcal{T}})$ portion of the authenticity formula.

$$\text{Unique Voice} = \frac{\int_{0}^{100} f(\text{ACTION})\,dx - \int_{0.1}^{100} f(\text{FEAR})\,dx}{\int_{0.1}^{100} f(\text{SELF})\,dx}$$

$$\tau^{\infty-1}$$

INFINITE TRUTH

IV

$$\frac{\text{"What you Do"}}{\text{"What you Say"}}$$

"It depends upon what the meaning of the word *is* is."
—BILL CLINTON

"Never let them know your next move. Don't you know bad boys move in silence."
—BIGGIE SMALLS,
"Ten Crack Commandments"

CHAPTER 5

WHAT YOU

SAY

INFINITE TRUTH: WHAT YOU SAY. *What else is branding other than a promise that needs to be delivered? The notion of truth is the crucial part of expressing an authentic brand. Social media and Wikipedia and truth-by-Google make it very difficult to discern between perception and reality, actions and words. One of the worst lies ever told is that perception is reality. I hate that* phrase. Reality *is reality.*

The INFINITE TRUTH $(\bar{T})$ is the great governor: it ensures that your deeds are greater than your sentiment. Even when UNIQUE VOICE $(\sqrt[Uni]{\ })$ is tempered by INFINITE TRUTH $(\bar{T})$, it's still a constantly iterative number. You (as a person or a company) are always changing, and your brand is always changing. This can be both good and bad.

Great brands are nothing more than streams of connected promises that always deliver. It's critical that these "promises" be truthful. Talk can be romantic, but talk alone is cheap. It's easy to get wound up in the art of creating the slick veneer of "brandspeak," but great brands aren't built on snappy copy or slick graphic design. They're established through the relentless repetition of promising something and then delivering on what they promised, often beyond expectations.

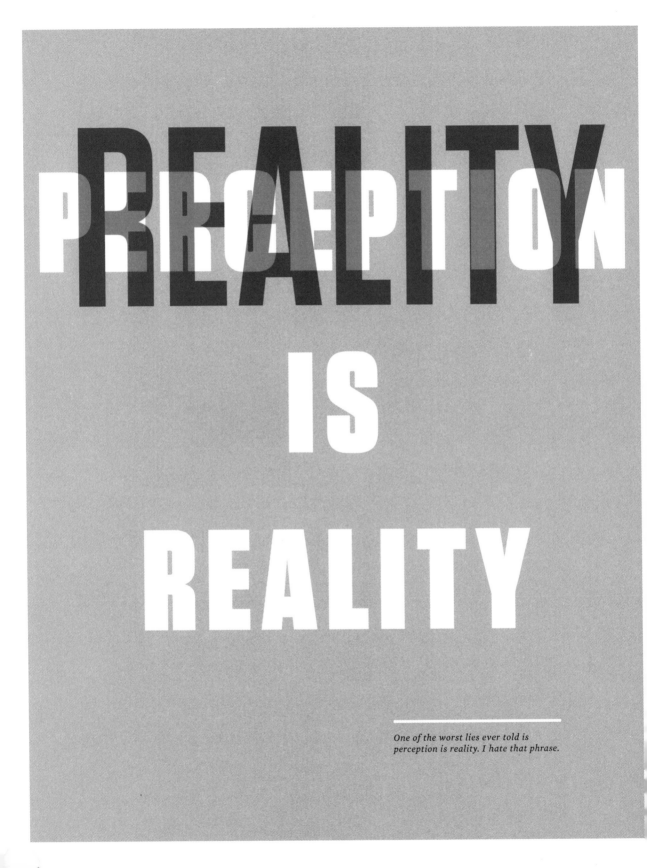

PERCEPTION

REALITY

IS

REALITY

One of the worst lies ever told is
perception is reality. I hate that phrase.

I. COMMON CREDIT

A Vegas party. Like all our parties, funded with credit cards

IN 1995 WE produced, hosted, and managed a party for the tastemakers and buyers of fashion at the San Diego trade show. I cohosted it with my old friends from the Lyricist Lounge, flying in artists from all over the world, like Common, the Beatnuts, DJ Honda (Japan), and Serch (from 3rd Bass) as the MC.

Common took the stage, shouting into the mic, "Yo, what's up, San Diego? Yo, what's up, Echo?"

He launched into "I used to Love H.E.R.," and the crowd went bonkers. A red banner emblazoned with the stencil rhino logo hung on the stage behind Common. Echo stickers, Echo T-shirts, and Echo product adorned every wall. Models flitted through the crowd, and the line to get in stretched around the block.

We had an even bigger event two weeks later in Vegas. We were on fire. This one featured the Roots and Black Moon. It was expensive, and we were using credit cards like bank loans, but it was Vegas, baby!

We had so much momentum. We had gone from trade show newbies (with the wooden pallets) to trade show darlings, with the right parties, the right booths (like a re-creation of an NYC subway station, turnstile and all), and a *presence* that said we're on the up-and-up.

Today he's known as Common. Back then, "Common Sense." Rocking the Echo.

We had established the rhino. The T-shirts were still mostly sold in mom-and-pop stores—those were the little engines that could—but we finally started getting placement in better boutiques and even landmark department stores like Macy's Herald Square. Our staff had grown to about four dozen. We

MC Serch, aka Michael Berrin, played a crucial role in the "golden era" of Echo marketing. We even made a limited-edition alarm clock.

CHEAT TO WIN? YES AND NO:
First Impressions Matter

We finally did it. A big retailer of ours was Dr. Jay's, and buyers from Macy's—scouts, essentially—trolled Dr. Jay's and could see that our gear was selling. They gave us an early test order at Macy's Herald Square. Just a tiny order of a "four-way," which is a four-way metal cross on a pole, with shirts hanging on each of the four arms. This was a sink-or-swim moment. If the four-way sold, we might get more orders. If not, better luck at the mom-and-pops.

So we did what any responsible company would do: we secretly paid street teams to *buy back our own product*. That four-way sold, and soon Macy's ordered more four-ways, and those sold too, even without our street teams. We were off and running.

What's the takeaway here: Should you cheat to win? Yes and no. Long term, no, it'd be unscalable, unethical, and inauthentic to cook your books or buy your own inventory. That's bullshitting the world and bullshitting yourself.

But when you're launching a business, and you believe in the fundamentals, think of it like a date; you want to make a good first impression on her (in this case "her" was Macy's.) You pull out the chair, hold the door, maybe even whiten your teeth beforehand. At the restaurant, maybe you "cheat" by secretly tipping the maitre d' for a prime table. You don't lie about your core personality or make any false promises, but you do what you need to do to make a good first impression.

even put MC Serch on the consulting payroll as a marketing director. He helped orchestrate our advertising campaigns, funneling our product into the hands of hip-hop royalty, and soon our ads featured Q-Tip, Busta Rhymes, and KRS-ONE. This was just an evolution of the product placement I had started at Rutgers, now multiplied with assortment and scale.

The trade magazine *Sportswear International* named us one of the "Top 10 Brands to Watch." There was a sense in the community that *"These guys could be players."*

Potential. Perception. We had it.

Could we back it up?

eCho UnLIMiTeD

Designer Marc Milecofsky conceives a collection as if it was a storyboard from a comic book or movie. In his head, the graphics he creates plays out a story and each part of the line is a subplot.

"When I design a line, I try to have unity," said Milecofsky. "You rarely see a collection in this industry where all the pieces make sense—and that are wearable and can be merchandised."

Perhaps, that's why the merchandise director for the "Jurassic Park" sequel has com-

"we don't want to see the line stuffed in the young men's section"

missioned a collection from Echo. It's among the many coups in a pivotal year for the three-year-old company. The launch last fall of a complete line, including outerwear, has multiplied sales five-fold in the seasons since. It has also sparked the rapt attention of major retailers.

Fortunately, Milecofsky and his partners—sister Marci Milecofsky and Seth Gerszberg—had already set up production in Southeast Asia in mid-'94. Although the three share hats, for the record, Marc is CEO, Marci is vice president and Seth serves as president.

Gerszberg hooked up with the Milecofskys when Marc decided in his third year of pharmaceutical studies at Rutgers that he "didn't want to count pills forever" but instead wanted to concentrate on his art. As a street artist during the turn of the decade, Milecofsky airbrushed denim for Spike Lee, Chuck D. and KRS. Through a mutual friend, they met Gerszberg now 25, who had been working as a construction broker for U.S. companies in Austria.

Since their first ASR Expo in late '93, the trio has concentrated on positioning Echo as a major player in the sportswear market. That is, sportswear with an alternative flavor, notes Milecofsky. "We don't want to see the line stuffed in the young men's section, but featured in in-store shops." A website is also

part of the trio's broader plan.

So, what's with the name? Marc's street artist tag and family nickname tracks back to his birth. What the doctor deemed a sonogram echo when his mother was pregnant with Marci was really a twin brother. The two celebrate their 25th birthdays at the ASR Expo this year.

ECHO UNLIMITED
120 Jersey Ave., New Brunswick, NJ 08901
908/247-3322, Fax: 908/247-9746
Contact: Marci Milecofsky, Marc Milecofsky, Seth Gerszberg **Year established:** 1993
Employees: 15 • **Designers:** 1 • **Sales reps:** 15

II. SEX, MONEY, POWER

WE HAD CLEARED $7 million between the Vegas and San Diego trade shows, the demand for the name was gaining traction, and we had established the right tone and pitch for our brand's UNIQUE VOICE. Our tiny business was about to go global.

The key was the rhino. Or, more specifically, the power of the rhino logo, which helped us begin to express a lucid brand voice. The rhino helped us solve our "T-shirt-only problem."

Since the very beginning, ever since I peddled T-shirts at Lakewood High School, the only thing distinguishing my apparel from Brand X, Y, or Z was my art. That's it. Cracking the code of color seps meant that my art would look better and feel better, but at the end of the day, it was still about taking what was inside my black book of illustrations and transferring that onto gear.

This worked well for T-shirts, sweatshirts, and hoodies, but how do you translate that to jeans? Polo shirts? What about backpacks, fragrance, or shoes? If I wanted to scale my aesthetic, I had to evolve past ten color–screen prints. If I was going to mass-produce denim jeans and have them be recognized as Echo, what was I going to do? Put my best-selling T-shirt graphic on the crotch of a pair of jeans? (Not like I haven't tried that.)

Soon the rhino became recognized, and we transformed its meaning from just an "outdoorsy thing" into a banner for hip-hop, skate, and graffiti.

The rhino allowed me to "play designer" and paint outside the lines of my artwork. How? We put it on everything—in all our marketing and events materials—and established it as the flag of our brand. We sponsored the right club events and we shamelessly showcased the rhino. We hosted skating events and we showcased the rhino. Even when we just *attended* an event—street art, music, fashion—we showcased the rhino. We used some sales consultants in far-flung

 ## UNLIMITED
Since day one

When I started I used to call the business Echo Airbrushing. Then I noticed how so many companies used formal naming conventions like Cheshire *Ltd.*, which stood for Cheshire *Limited*. This was a naming taxonomy for businesses to express their partnership structures. LTD. was explicitly used in Wales and London. Ltd., LLC, S Corp—all of these formalities made no sense to me. Why would you *limit* yourself? I wanted a bigger playground, and my vision was growing larger than just airbrushing. So in 1993, we formally incorporated as Echo Unltd.

Unlimited.

For years we used that name, Echo Unlimited, as a sort of mission statement—a rallying cry—and made a conscious effort to push the limits, to expand instead of contract, to UnLabel our Label.

cities to expand our distribution, but we made all the core decisions ourselves.

Soon the rhino became recognized, and we transformed its meaning from just an "outdoorsy thing" into a banner for what was relevant in pop culture: hip-hop, skate, and graffiti. Now I could take the rhino, put it on a half-inch-by-half-inch damask woven label, and load an otherwise plain vanilla cargo pocket with a new meaning. It became an instant signifier of my brand's values.

I started applying my knack for illustration toward drawing proper fashion illustrations, or croquis. Using these sketches as templates, I then paid and directed third-party sample rooms throughout New York's garment district to create (expensive) prototypes.

The rhino logo, and all the ways I could deploy it onto fashion items, empowered me to expand my vision for the brand. I developed snowboard-inspired technical outerwear, cargo pants, and feature-rich DJ bags, unveiling these concepts—selling the "potential for them"—at trade shows and showcases.

Soon the buyers were saying, "Damn, this brand's more than T-shirts, and that kid can design." I whet the market's appetite. I had provoked a conversation where people would reimagine us as a new species of "fashion lifestyle" brand. A brand that was neither black nor white. Neither skate nor hip-hop. Neither pure outdoor nor pure street. It was unlimited.

This is *what we said*.

That's one side of the formula for infinite truth.

What about the other half: *what we'd do*?

Well, what I could *do* would be informed by *what I knew*—which, in the case of scaling apparel manufacturing, was almost nothing.

Color separation was Fisher-Price compared to the complexities of actually standing up all of those samples I'd hacked together into a business. I would need to secure a production facility, acquire heavy capital, take on inventory, and own every raw material.

Scary shit. Besides, at the time, I was only twenty-four years old. Opening up my own factory made about as much sense as, say, starting my own oil company.

This left me with two options that I understood at the time:

OPTION 1: ODMS

Original design manufacturers. These companies design and manufacture a product, and then you can brand that product with your own logo. This is sort of like how high school baseball teams get their uniforms and varsity jackets made. There's an array of product, and you have *some* (albeit limited) ability to customize it for resale. If "logo slapping" is your game, this is a perfectly suitable way to get something made with relatively low risk. But it's an expensive path for the consumer, as the item gets marked up at more times and in more places than if you just made it from soup to nuts.

This is a great way to "play house," but it wasn't allowing me to go as customized as I needed. I remember pulling clothes out of my closet to look at the labels with their notes of origin: Made in Hong Kong. I felt like I was a reading a *Where's Waldo?* book.

OPTION 2: CONTRACT MANUFACTURERS

I got turned on to the world of contract manufacturers, which allow you to customize to your heart's content. Basically, you bring your design to a CM, and it sizes up the task and quotes you a price that includes labor, parts, operations, and shipping. Contract manufacturers basically act as your factory.

This sounded like my speed. I could tweak and customize just like I did back in Lakewood, and they would handle every facet of production. But there was one problem: you need serious cash or credit. I would have to be prepared to own way more of the burden of risk. I lacked the capital to underwrite all those setup, tooling, and minimum costs.

My talk was slick. But I needed more *do*. And in the NYC fashion scene, who gets it done better than that special breed of doer known as the "the Garmento"? I needed a proper badass Garmento, a regular Mickey Fucking Drexler. (Now, 99.999 percent of consumers have never heard of Drexler, but as the man behind the scenes, without putting his name on a single label, the dude turned the Gap and J. Crew into a juggernaut. How's this for clout? He even sits on Apple's board of directors.) What I needed was a guy who was one part Mickey Drexler and one part Winston Wolfe, the one who cleans up the bodies in *Pulp Fiction*.

Baked into the not-so-sexy part of the New York fashion scene, far away from the spotlight and hand waving that you see at the end of a runway show, are these curious beasts with an endless stamina for making, merchandising, and importing fashion. These unrelenting Garmento types often have their own "gun for hire" brokerage shops, and they connect broke-ass start-ups, like mine, to manufacturers in those faraway places. All for "a fee."

Careful, though. Like their infamous reps, fucking with the wrong Garmento can be risky. And in typical middleman or agent fashion, they make their money by getting inside the "cost sandwich," puffing up the prices to get their take. It's easy to get scammed. Outside of giving equity to a new partner (which we *never* contemplated), this was the most viable option. At least it would allow me to get the ball rolling as I kept my eyes peeled for the more

The perfect fashion industry CEO would be one part Mickey Drexler and one part Winston Wolfe. They move in silence and execute relentlessly. Or alternatively, just Mickey Drexler. Legend.

ONE PART
MICKEY
DREXLER

The PERFECT CEO

ONE PART
WINSTON
WOLFE

optimal solution, which, in my mind, was someone as close as possible to the manufacturing and the *Do-it* part of the promise.

I FOUND OUR version of Mickey Drexler at the Jacob Javits Convention Center trade show for manufacturers. Whether by good fortune or by my insistence of wanting "to hear what I needed to hear," I found the secret weapon I was dreaming of: Wu.

Frustrated and sick of the clichéd middleman Garmento types with comb-overs and bad loafers—schelping their run-of-the-mill "buy-it-by-the-pound" manufacturing—I was hell-bent on finding someone with a clue.

On that day, the trade show was central casting for a self-hating Jewish character, the kind of guy typically reserved for Woody Allen movies. Then I saw this Taiwanese guy standing in front of a folding table. The table had racks of snowboarding jackets from SMP Clothing. The jackets were beautiful. Not North Face slick, but the needlework was crisp. Taped seams. Gore-Tex. Engineered to death.

"Which SMP do you like? *Surf More Pipes* or *Skate More Parks*?" asked the Taiwanese man. He was tall, slender, and well manicured. His gestures were silky smooth. And he didn't have a comb-over.

Smitten with his "Camper" brand shoes, which were unusually worldly for this shack of Garmentos, I replied, "Sex, Money, Power," and asked, "Did you make these?"

"Of course I made these," he said with an easy smile.

"Do you sell these?"

"Yes." He laughed. "I sell these."

"Where?!" I found myself getting excited. It was like Drew from Eighth Day all over again.

"I have a place in Hong Kong," he said.

He introduced himself. Wu. It turns out that he had heard of my brand, heard of me, and he was eager to connect with the brand.

"Can you make these?" I opened my bag and out spilled all the Echo prototypes: jackets, pants, vests.

He nodded, amused. "I can make anything you like."

"How much would this cost?" I held up a polar fleece jacket with reflective tape trim.

CAN MAKE

SMP

+

WEARS

=

GARMENTO

Wu closed one eye, did some quick math, and then opened his eye. "Seventeen dollars, FOB."

Freight on board. With my current agent, it would cost me $30. Holy shit. That changes the math. That changes everything. We talked more, and he proposed a deal that could finally crack our production, assortment, and capital problems all in one fell swoop. Since we didn't have enough capital to fund the manufacturing, and since he already had the relationships, the infrastructure, and the know-how, he would fund and oversee the manufacturing. I would handle the marketing. He would effectively own the formula's WHAT YOU DO, and I would own the WHAT YOU SAY.

"This is how we'll do it," Wu said. "I'll pay for the raw materials. We'll make them in Hong Kong. You'll have *almost zero* markup. We'll ship them out of our California warehouse. You guys fund the marketing from your cash flow. You'll set the price for wholesale."

"And what's your take?" I asked, skeptical.

"We'll both get paid out of a joint venture where we split the profit fifty-fifty between the landed cost goods and what we're selling at wholesale."

I tried to keep a poker face, but I was practically glowing. This was perfect. Now, at last, we had a legitimate way to move beyond T-shirts. We would have the capacity to make jackets, denim, and the entire scope of my new design portfolio. Finally, we could fulfill the promise we were making to the industry; at last we could *do* what we were *saying*.

I shook Wu's hand, left the convention center, and sped home to our tiny offices in Jersey. Marci was working on a Saturday, calculator in hand, trying to tackle our twelve different lines of credit (cards). I told her about the proposed deal.

"Sounds too good to be true," Marci said.

"We're making money. Wu's making money. It's square."

"So you're okay with just—" Marci waved her hands. "Relinquishing control of our entire company?"

"Relinquishing control!? Marci, all they're doing is manufacturing."

She laughed. "Oh *that's all*? Just creating our product?"

"Besides, we'll still handle the T-shirts and hats. We'll use them for everything else."

Marci was silent.

The Kabuki theater of teasing the market with samples we couldn't ship or produce at scale had to end. How else could we fulfill our promise to the market?

She came around grudgingly. Same with Seth. The company was finally "real." Now we were more than some mom-and-pop T-shirt shack. Those other street-wear guys at 432F were still schlepping away to pound out more T-shirts, but we'd do something game changing. They didn't have the vision to try to be a Polo or a Levi's. We did. Our direct competitors at the time seemed content being "cool" and running with the herd. That was not for me.

Besides, I didn't have any data that said my competitors *wouldn't* track this way, right? And how pissed would I be if *I* treaded water, limited myself to T-shirts, and then one of *them* stepped up with a broader assortment? We had to be the first.

Less than forty-eight hours after my Wu meeting, we invited him to our Jersey offices. He met Seth and Marci, we cobbled together a quickie contract, and then he boarded a flight back to Hong Kong. It was a shotgun wedding.

III. CHECK'S IN THE MAIL

OUR COMPANY WAS schizophrenic. We had two personalities: first, the shit-hot brand that threw great parties, dazzled the trade shows, and teased compelling designs that could maybe rival Tommy or Polo. Then there was the second personality—the one we kept locked in the attic: a company that couldn't pay its bills and was constantly behind on shipments.

Outwardly we looked good. We were no longer a ragtag crew, and we bought a new place on Martin Avenue, in South River, jumping from three thousand to thirty thousand square feet. Seth hired and managed a sales team, Marci oversaw production and the warehouse, and I hired and managed the design and marketing.

We spent so much money. We were so hell-bent on *investing in the brand* that we overindulged at every corner of margin. We dropped $100,000 on trade booths, we booked splashy ads in *Vibe* and the *Source*, and we threw party after party. We spent on street teams, "wild-posting" street campaigns, and all things slick talk.

HANDMADE HIGH FINANCE:
Buying Time by Any Means Necessary

You know how when you write a check, your bank numbers are printed at the bottom? If you lick your thumb and smudge those numbers, the check has to be processed manually, as those numbers are typically machine scanned. If the machine can't read them, this could inadvertently buy you another thirty days before the banks cash it. The banks have to reprocess the check the old-fashioned way. By hand. So we smudged every check before we sent it out. Wet as a Slurpee. Not bragging. Jus' sayin'. This is how desperate we were.

ECHO UNLIMITED, LLC.
1 Martin Ave.
South River, NJ 08882

1936

DATE

PAY TO THE
ORDER OF _____ $ _____

_____ DOLLARS

Security Features Details on back

FOR _____

Our brand building was on the surface. It was on the skin. We slapped on a cool Band-Aid. This let us avoid looking at the grisly, unromantic parts of the operation.

I maxed out my credit card, and then I maxed out a second credit card, and then a third, a fourth, and a fifth. So Marci volunteered her credit card—and then a second, a third, and a fourth. Seth had five credit cards. When our photographer was in the field, at one point we had no way to give her any petty cash.

"Tell her to use her personal credit card," Seth said.

"On her personal?" I felt queasy. This didn't feel right.

"We'll pay her back," Seth said. End of discussion.

So we asked her to use her own credit card, and an unintended line was crossed. We were all naive. Youth was no excuse. It was all just such new territory. Building on the promise. No one knew exactly what he or she was signing up for other than buying more time and keeping the dream alive.

When the next bill came, we asked another employee for their credit card, and then another, and then another. Soon we had an unofficial, unspoken policy that haunts me to this day: Those *Echo Unlimited employees who made over $50K were asked to donate their personal credit cards to the company.* We would pay them back. I knew that halfway across the globe, in Hong Kong, Wu was about to unleash the future of our company. Echo jackets, Echo denim, Echo polos. We just needed to hang on a little longer. We would pay them back. Somehow. Someday.

W E ONLY HAD $8 million in sales, but we spent like we were a $20 million company. We felt it was critical to establish the "theater of the brand," and we kept making promises that someday would need to be fulfilled. Perception is reality, right?

But reality came to roost when the lights went out in our offices. Complete darkness. Everyone panicked, and Seth grabbed my arm. "Dude, we're six months late on our PSEG bill."

WTF? Six months?

"Okay, what do we tell everyone?" I whispered to Seth.

"I'll handle it," he said. Then he addressed the company.

"Listen up, everyone. We just heard from the power company—PSEG. A cable truck ran over a power line, so the power's going to be off for a while."

$$\left(\begin{array}{c} \text{WHAT WE} \\ \text{SAID} \end{array} \right) > \left(\begin{array}{c} \text{WHAT WE} \\ \text{DID} \end{array} \right)$$

Our employees grumbled and bad-mouthed PSEG. I felt sick to my stomach. Then we cut a check—after smudging the bar code, of course—and sent a runner over to PSEG to pay it that afternoon.

I started dodging calls from advertisers. David Mays, the publisher and cofounder of the *Source* magazine, called me up and said bluntly, "You're one hundred eighty days late. I like you, but you are fucking up my money." This wasn't some accounts manager; we were so delinquent paying for past ads that the *publisher of the magazine* had to give me a personal smackdown.

Parties became awkward. I started running into more people—colleagues, vendors, friends—who had lent me money. They were lenient because they believed in the brand, believed in me, and we seemed like a good bet. Besides, even in the darkest hours, I knew that we'd turn it around. Those new shipments from Hong Kong . . .

IV. **BLACK TUESDAY: THE LETTER**

T HE DEBT KEPT growing, Wu was now months behind with our product, and even more distressing, the prices he was quoting now seemed high. The entire point of configuring the relationship the way we did was to help us price our goods in a way that could be competitive. He had promised essentially no markup (or at least a 3 or 5 percent reasonable one)—that was the whole point of using him. The warm and fuzzy was wearing off. Even though I had traveled to Hong Kong* to meet with him and his team, something seemed off. Funky. Garmento slick.

Exterior of South River office on Martin Avenue

Then came moving day. Most of the company had already moved to the new complex on Martin Avenue. It was the middle of summer and hot as hell, and I stood in the abandoned parking lot in a sea of black asphalt, surrounded by a barbed-wire fence. The only thing left was a single phone/fax line, my car, and a few boxes of sample Echo product.

I stood by myself, staring at the steaming asphalt and feeling like the sun was holding a grudge against me—maybe I owed the sun money too? Crazy how that pit-in-your-belly thing is all too often right. That day, I received two

---

* I traveled to Hong Kong with a girl I was dating at the time: Allison. And she eventually became my wife. *Wife?!* Yep. I'm now happily married (with kids) and have a family that I love. But that's a different book.

pieces of communication over the fax line. Either document, by itself, was enough to sink our company.

My Nokia flip phone rang. Seth. "Marc, did you get the fax?" he huffed, out of breath.

"Nah."

"Get it. *Read it*," Seth insisted.

Fine. It was a formal, wordy letter that used a bunch of legal language, and then I saw three words underlined: *Cease. And. Desist.*

"Cease and desist?"

"Who's this from?" I asked.

"Echo Design. We're infringing on their name."

"*I'm* Echo." I immediately thought back to that other graf artist "Echo," who had accused me of being a biter and putting the "dash" over the *o* in my name so as not to copy him. "That kid's a punk. I can't believe he lawyered up."

But it wasn't the graf artist Echo. And it wasn't the Amsterdam *Echo*, and it wasn't the Taiwanese woman author known as Echo. In fact, this had *nothing* to do with street handles and aka's. It was from a man who had nothing to do with graffiti or skate or hip-hop. As I soon learned, in 1923, on his wedding day, a man named Edgar C. Hyman started a clothing company. He sold scarves. The name Edgar C. Hyman doesn't really roll off the tongue, so he used the acronym Echo for *E*dgar *C*. *H*yman. I'm not sure where the *o* came from. To me, it stood for "*O*h shit, with this cease-and-desist letter, I'm fucked."

Edgar Hyman and his lovely wife, Theresa, had long since passed away, but his company, Echo Design Group, claimed that I was creating confusion in the marketplace. This struck me as hilarious. Their company was the maker of scarves, ties, home furnishings, and umbrellas. I was into graffiti and T-shirts.

"This is bullshit," I said to Seth.

"Not really. They have strong legal grounds. We have to deal with it," he said.

"We're not shutting down."

"They own the trademark," Seth said. "It's cut and dry."

"But I'm *the real* Echo!"

We called our lawyer, we brainstormed with Marci, and we tried to figure out something that would save our collective ass. I argued that since we had the *ō* in *Echō*, they didn't have a case, and my lawyer basically laughed. This

O

vs.

ō

came at the worst possible time. I had ads going to press that said *Echō*. And even though the pricing seemed high, our new, hotly anticipated shipments from Hong Kong were about to arrive. It felt like the equivalent of the studio tapes of Dr. Dre's *Chronic 2001*—and that line would be a cult classic. Now, finally, we were about to unleash our product; we were ready to deliver on our promise. And now we had to shut down? This would sink us. We'd be done, game over.

"If we are going to settle with them," our lawyer said, "you may want to consider legally changing your name."

I stared at him. Seriously?

"Change your name to Marc Echo," he said, pointing out the obvious.

I thought about this. Okay, maybe I could do that. After all, my friends had called me Echo for most of my life; why not make it official? Then again, my friends just called me Echo—one word, like Prince—never as a last name. "Marc Echo" felt so overly grown-up. Mr. Echo. Weird. But there was some precedent for this, as even Ralph Lauren was once named Ralph Lifshitz. (In an interview with Oprah, he famously said that part of the reason he changed it was because his last name literally contained the word *shit*.)

So I agreed to change my name, but even that wasn't enough. Since Edgar Hyman had held the trademark for over sixty years, we needed to change the name of the company too.

"One detail, change the *h* to a *k*," the lawyer suggested. "Eckō."

No way. That's not how I spell it.

"C'mon, dude," Seth said. "No one's even going to notice."

"Of course they will. It will look like some knockoff shit!" I was so disgusted.

"No one fucking cares," Seth said, and he made me redraw the *h* and the *k* again and again so that I could see how little difference there was. "Echo, Eckō; *h, k*. Who gives a shit? The brand already exists. The rhino is what counts."

So *Echo* became *Eckō*, and they were right: the change was almost invisible. We didn't have to destroy any existing inventory (we had a grace period), but we literally stopped the presses, pulling the levers and grinding the manufacturing to a halt. Then, one by one, we changed the logos on every piece of inventory, swapping an *h* for a *k*. I spent a week tediously changing all the artwork in our Photoshop files, .jpg by .jpg, serif by serif.

— **vs.** —

THE VIRUS OF A TRADEMARK:
Baby Ape Unlimited by Ralp Lauren

There's this place in Hong Kong called Women's Street. It's a night street market that sells souvenirs, teapots, fake watches, fake Louis Vuitton bags, fake Guess purses—the works—and folks buy them on the cheap. One night I walked through Women's Street and saw, amidst all the fake Puma sneakers and Sony batteries, a shirt with a rhino. My rhino.

It's an eerie and perverted thing to see, like looking into one of those distorted mirrors at a carnival. Over the years the fake Eckōs got bigger and stranger; they would mix and mash logos, breeding the rhino with other brands—like the popular Japanese street-wear brand A Bathing Ape, creating unholy hoodies that said "Baby Ape Unlimited."

At first this made me hot and bothered. But years later, I went to Hong Kong with Cindy Livingston, a former Timex exec who eventually became a partner of ours, and she said, "Marc, you'll get a lot angrier when you *don't* see any fake Eckō. It's a validation that your brand crossed the ocean. It crossed the language barrier. People are taking the time, the energy, and the resources to go do this. Now the challenge is, how do you get in the *legitimate* market to claim this piece of the pie?"

I agreed to change the brand name to a *k*, but as for my own personal name, my own identity, my own authenticity? No way was I going to a *k*. *I'm Echo. Marc Echo.* That was my authentic personal brand, right? I clung to this identity, which caused confusion at every corner. Articles in the press described "*Eckō* Unlimited" clothing designed by Marc *Echo*. Journalists called to double-check spellings, baffled. Customers were bewildered. On some of our advertisements, I wrote this little note at the bottom: "If you've noticed, the spelling in our name is going from *Echo* to *Eckō*, but we're still the same *Echo*."

"Marc, spell it with a *k*! It's bad enough that your first name is fucked up!" Seth said, exasperated.

That got a laugh from me. Fair point. *Marc* (with a *c*) had caused me trouble for years.

"So now your first name is fucked up, and your last name—Echo—doesn't even match the name of the product: Eckō. Just make it simple!"

Fine. Seth and Marci were right, and I submitted. So we changed the product to Eckō, and I legally changed my last name to Eckō.

To the credit of Echo Design Group, they were very reasonable, and now, having been on the other side of the table, I can appreciate their position. When you have your trademarks violated, it's an awful feeling. I've had my logos completely hijacked. There are people who "technically" claimed my logo in China, without my authorization, and actually to this day, there are fifty plus unauthorized Eckō Unlimited stores in China. We are still navigating to right that wrong.

After changing to Eckō, we could resume production, we could stagger forward, and we survived by the hair of our chinny-chin-chins. But all of this cost more money. All of this added to our debt: legal fees, change fees, and *rushed* shipping fees.

V. BLACK TUESDAY: THE SECOND FAX

O N   T H E   S A M E   day I received the fax from Echo Design Group, I received a second fax, from a subcontractor of Wu's. He was the manufacturer who actually assembled the goods. (Wu's role was to connect me with these end manufacturers, with minimal markup.) Here's the thing:

Me, Marci, and some of the better contractors we worked with over the years (notably, not Wu)

the fax I received *was addressed to Wu*, as if the vendor had sent it to me by mistake. And the fax, interestingly, showed prices that were *lower* than the ones Wu had quoted me. Lower by a lot.

The translation seemed clear to me: Wu was jacking me, and the vendor was doing me a favor by "accidentally" sending me the proof. (There's no way that was an accident. How could you accidentally fax the wrong number, especially when it includes international area codes?) Wu was marking up the goods far more than he'd promised, which made it impossible to price my products effectively in the marketplace. This sabotaged the entire process.

I showed the letter to Seth, and a vein appeared in his forehead and neck. That was never a good sign. "We're suing this fucker."

"Marci?"

She nodded. Even the Ghost of Reason wanted blood.

After I'd met Wu at the Jacobs Convention Center, we had drawn up some fairly simple contracts in our backyard. Even though they were simple, the language was crystal clear, and our lawyer agreed that we had a slam-dunk case.

But Wu had a nasty surprise waiting for us.

Wu represented, to us, that he "owned the factories and had the cash." But he didn't. In fact, it was clear that he was borrowing from "someone" to make the operation tick. But who?

Not only that, he marked up the cost of goods way beyond our agreed-upon terms. He lied to us. So what did we do? We rushed his warehouse, *Zero Dark Thirty*–style, and took our shit back. In the dark of night. We had a friendly insider who operated Wu's LA warehouse, and we told him that we had a "big order to fill." We went in late one night—with a U-Haul—and cleared the fucker out, effectively seizing the goods. *Our* goods.

Justice! Right? Courts didn't think so. Without getting into the legal weeds, here's what happened: instead of financing the operations and production himself (like he promised), he used a Vegas-based financier, and he secured that financing with collateral. And guess what Wu used as the collateral? Echo product. The very Echo product that we had seized and miraculously got back into our makeshift warehouse. We only found this out when this third-party financier swooped into the courthouse, out of nowhere, like the fucking Terminator.

It turned out these clever Vegas rollers got more than old-fashioned collateral; they exploited a legal loophole that involves the "Uniform Commercial Code," or UCC, which is designed to ensure fairness in state-to-state business. Even though the Echo product was ours in the first place, since Wu pledged it

to them as collateral—and they represented that we were partners—the Vegas guys claimed that we stole *their* merchandise. They demanded $2 mil or the courts would seize our warehouse. Checkmate.

You might ask the question, But wait, Wu lied—he can't pledge what he doesn't really own, product with the Echo name on it? He can't get away with that, right? Wrong. The answer to that is the truth, but it's not the law.

So we had two ugly lawsuits at precisely the same time. When you add it all up, here's a quick summary of where we stood on that day in 1997:

- Lawsuit with Edgar C. Hyman that could cripple us.
- Lawsuit with Wu and the Vegas financier that could cripple us.
- No ability to pay legal fees.
- New, larger offices that we can't afford.
- Confusion from having changed Echo to Eckō.
- A larger staff that we're having trouble paying.
- Thanks to Wu, we're late on shipments to the market.
- Thanks to Wu's markups, our prices are too high.
- Worse, with Wu out of the picture, we have *no ability to manufacture* ourselves. We have no plan B.
- The cherry on top: $6 million in debt.

Other than that, we were in good shape.

OUR LAWYER FILED the lawsuit, the Vegas guys countersued, and before we knew it, Seth, Marci, and I were in a courtroom in a proper Mexican standoff—legally speaking. Our lawyer had just advised us to cut our losses and settle.

"Settle?" I asked. That's what guilty people do. Is that authentic?

Wu's lawyers would ask us questions like, "At trade parties and trade shows, did you introduce Wu as your 'partner'?" Maybe I did—who knows?—but I used the word *partner* socially, as in, "Hey, this is my business partner." It was a synonym for colleague or associate. It didn't mean we were actual *equity partners*. This crazy lawsuit hinged on conversational hearsay, and clearly it would get ugly if we went down that path.

So, short on patience and long on experience, our lawyer pulled us into the hallways to address Seth, Marci, and me. "Sit down," he said.

The three of us partners—*real* partners—sat down on a bench, shoulder to shoulder, and he stood over us in a pressed navy suit, like an exasperated professor lecturing a class of imbeciles but trying to respect our intellectual challenges.

"Guys, I'm willing to fight," he said, looking each of us in the eye. "But it's going to cost a lot of money, and you haven't paid me in a long time."

He let that sink in for a second, pacing back and forth. Then he continued. "Maybe we could win. But we don't have enough data, and their legal team is very, very good, and they are willing to make this a long, distracting, bloody war."

He looked at me, hard. "Or . . . we could settle right here in these halls, today, and make this all go away."

Seth had his fists clenched, the vein came back, and I could tell that he wanted to fight. Me? I felt like I was going to drop the lower part of my bowels.

"Let's take a vote," I said. "Who wants to fight this?"

"Fuck 'em," Seth growled. "Let's fight."

"Marci?" I asked.

She let out a deep sigh. "I want to get back to work."

So did I. The vote was two to one. It doesn't matter if we were in the right, because at the end of the day, there's *truth* and there's *the law*. In hindsight, if I had known then what I know now, I'm 95 percent sure that we *would* have won the lawsuit, but at what cost? It was time to move forward.

We settled. Wu and his lawsuit went away. And we ended the honeymoon with a shotgun divorce.

WE HAD THIS choking debt and late product. But even if we could repay the debt, with Wu gone, we had no way to manufacture new product, which meant we were back to square one. I didn't sleep well, didn't eat well, didn't think well. The only thing we had going for us was the promise of the brand.

If I couldn't deliver this collection, I would go backward in establishing my UNIQUE VOICE. I was like the knife that James Brown sang about: "Like a dull knife that just ain't cuttin'. Just talkin' a lot and sayin' nothing." Moreover, the promise of my brand was being squandered, and *what we said* to the market would hold no juice. But that's only half of the INFINITE-TRUTH equation. How could I equalize this, how would we fulfill that promise and deliver? I needed a massive dosage of "the *Do*." But the last time I went on that hunt, I ended up with Wu: a fugazee Mickey Drexler. This time I needed a brand of "the *Do*" that had real gravitas.

There seemed to be only one fix: selling to a bigger company.

And as luck would have it, around this time, we started getting inbound calls from big brands as a possible acquisition target. Ralph Lauren, Nautica, a team from the former Bugle Boy, and Levi's. They knew we were operationally distressed (to put it mildly), but they saw value in the brand.

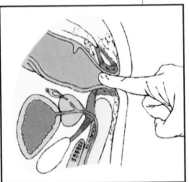

Due diligence

I met Ralph Lauren and agonized over what to wear. (I went with denim carpenter jeans—maybe that's why he didn't want to buy us?) Nautica flirted with us and then made an offer that it quickly yanked off the table. Seth had high hopes in Levi's. Back and forth to its headquarters in San Francisco we went. We tried to play all these suitors against one another, but we were amateurs, junior varsity, finally exposed as early twenties kids, and they were sharks intent on doing their due diligence.

Due diligence is like getting a rectal exam. You get naked, put on a hospital gown, stand over a mirror, and watch the floor as they poke every nook and crevice. Then they peel back your label and inspect. It almost feels like they're performing an autopsy on a still-warm body. They ignored our skin—(the "WHAT YOU SAY")—and they plunged their scalpel into the meat and the bones (the "WHAT YOU DO"). But instead of a scalpel, it felt like they were poking with a dull spoon. We had $16 million in revenue and $6 million in debt. Authenticity formulas aside, that's straight-up piss-poor math. So why *would* they want to buy us? What were we bringing to the table, besides the brand? They had no interest in our "executive team"; this all-star roster had just nose-dived into debt. The Levi's deal seemed to have legs, but the company's senior execs, like many people who'd negotiated with us before, found us—well, mostly Seth—abrasive. (In his defense, Seth was always cast as the bad cop.)

On the last day of negotiations, the Levi's team wanted to meet me, alone, at their hotel. No Seth. No Marci. Why did they want to meet me at their hotel and not at our offices in Jersey, where we had been negotiating up to that point?

"Do you know why we wanted to talk to you first, Marc?" the VP asked. He pointed to a tray of pastries and orange juice. "Want a danish?"

"I'm good. I'll wait to eat until Seth and Marci get here." I crossed my arms.

The VP sipped his espresso. "Marc, we're willing to make you an offer for the company. And to bring you on board."

"You mean Seth, Marci, and me," I said.

The VP frowned. "Just you."

I looked every executive in the eye. "This meeting is dead right now unless you understand one thing. These guys—Seth and Marci—took me to the party. No one's breaking us up. And we're going to *do* this, with or without you."

VI. **HAND HUGGER**

I WAS WORKING in our new office building on Martin Avenue, staring at all these luxuries we shouldn't have paid for: new computers, new folding tables, and fresh paint on an otherwise mildew-stained conference room wall. I wondered if we would have to undo it all—put it all on eBay, maybe? I thought about laying off employees, laying off my friends.

Then I heard a woman scream, "Seth's dead!"

I sprinted to Seth's office. The scream came from his assistant. He wasn't dead, but he had collapsed on the floor with a towel on his head. His eyes were red and bulging. "Levi's pulled out," Seth said, sweat dripping down his face.

"It's okay, man," I said.

"There's no deal!" Seth said.

"We'll figure something out." I sat down next to him on the floor.

"I fucked it up. It's all my fault," Seth said, crying. He wiped himself with the towel. I'll give Seth credit: he always claimed that everything was his fault. He was the brawler, the executive guy, the guy who ran the P&Ls. So whenever "material" transactions went south, Seth always threw his body on the grenade.

"Dude, we got here together," I said. "We're going to figure this out."

So we tried to figure it out.

Having a good brand wasn't enough, having a UNIQUE VOICE wasn't enough. That doesn't make you AUTHENTIC, and that alone doesn't make you successful. There's more to the equation.

We were going to have to deliver on what we said. We'd been promising shipments in September but not delivering until November. That had to stop. We'd been splurging on marketing and scrimping on operations. That had to stop. We had to simplify, we had to focus, and we had to be honest with the marketplace and with ourselves.

Having a good brand wasn't enough, having a UNIQUE VOICE ($^{Uni}_{V}$) wasn't enough. That doesn't make you AUTHENTIC (ΔWƷ!), and that alone doesn't make you successful. There's more to the equation.

But how would we get out of debt?

Seth pulled himself up, wiped his eyes with the towel, and straightened his back. "I got a guy," he said.

I smiled in spite of myself. Seth always had a guy. This guy was Alan Finkelman, who owned Scope Imports, a Texas-based clothing wholesale company. A proper *schmatta* guy. We had met several times at the trade shows.

I liked Alan. A six-foot-plus former athlete, he was colorful, folksy, charming, and famous for always making slightly off-color remarks. When he placed a hand on your shoulder, it was less a pat on the back and more like a hug. He was a hand hugger. He seemed like a straight shooter and the type of gambler who could see the upside in our company, but I saw him as, well, a *discounter*.

"Dude," I said to Seth. "Why would he give two shits about our brand?"

"Because we're related," Seth said.

"Really?"

"I don't know. Maybe. Third cousins?"

We had been courting A offers (Levi's, Polo) and B offers (Bugle Boy, Nautica). I viewed Finkelman as a D–. He had no sex appeal. It was like the Michael Bivins thing all over again. I was chasing the sizzle, but sometimes quiet and unassuming is what you need.

Alan had been friendly with Seth in the past—reviewing our spreadsheets, giving some advice on how to deal with costs—but Seth knew that this was an entirely different ask. This was a Hail Mary. You don't just ask your three-times-removed cousin for a $6 million loan.

But after Alan reviewed all our books, he came to a different conclusion than the other potential acquirers. He realized that of the $6 million in debt, only $1.5 million was due *immediately*. After Seth came back from a Shabbat where he brainstormed a model with Alan, he brought Marci and me to a table in his office. He started scribbling numbers, describing how it would work.

"One and a half million of the debt is due immediately. Alan will give us that right now. He will make the wolves go away." (And as part of this new arrangement, our silent Austrian partners would leave the picture.)

Done and done. We were saved.

"But there's one catch," Seth said. "He'll have 'debt collateral' of the majority of the company."

Wait, what?

"If we can't pay him back within three years, the debt turns to equity, and he'll own the company. If we can pay him back, the company is ours again."

The clock was ticking.

You hear these "early business war stories" a lot. Usually they're told with a brash nostalgia, as the billionaire CEO puffs a cigar, swirls his Scotch, and remembers the good 'ol days when he had to max out his credit cards. But here's what those cigar CEOs don't tell you: the truth is often ugly and exasperating.

Yes, I *survived*, but it's not something I look back upon fondly. I had to borrow money from employees on their credit cards, and that's not something I'm proud of. I had to tell some white lies and not-so-white lies to vendors, clients, and friends. That's not part of some "hero's journey"; that's just being untruthful, that's being inauthentic.

Yes, I *survived*, but we didn't have to endure so much pain. We were inauthentic, and it cost us. Authenticity isn't just some brand-speak nonsense. It's not just consumer facing. Inauthenticity can cost you millions. Inauthenticity can sink your brand, kneecap your company. If I had just focused on being truthful in the promise of my business—not just the promise of my brand—then we wouldn't have pushed it to the bleeding edge. You can't think about authenticity in your *brand* as separate from authenticity in your *business*. The two are one and the same.

$$\mathcal{T}^{\infty-1} = \text{INFINITE TRUTH} \geq \frac{\text{``\textit{What you Do}''}}{\text{``\textit{What you Say}''}}$$

Business

Brand

$$\tau^{-1}_{\infty}$$

INFINITE TRUTH

IV

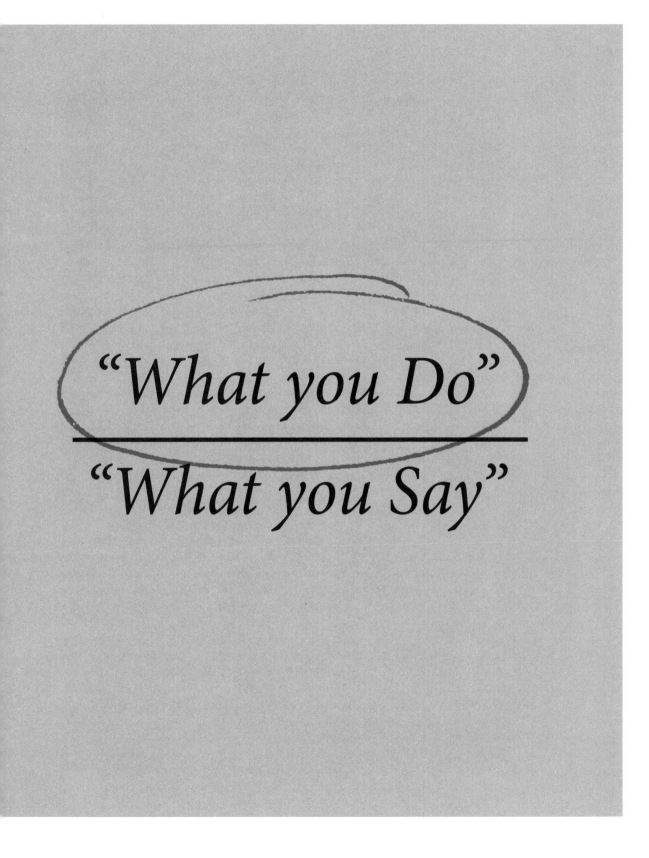

"Money, it's gotta be the shoes!"

—MARS BLACKMON
(SPIKE LEE),
She's Gotta Have It

"The way to get started is to quit talking and begin doing."

—WALT DISNEY

CHAPTER 6

WHAT YOU
DO

INFINITE TRUTH: WHAT YOU DO. *The most critical part of the INFINITE TRUTH ($\bar{T}$) variable, which governs the truthful nature of your personal brand, is the WHAT YOU DO. Nike didn't become a colossus just by talking about sneakers. Its motto is not "Just Say It." Results matter. Artful execution matters. When my company embraced this part of the INFINITE TRUTH ($\bar{T}$) formula, "the Do," we finally allowed the Eckō brand "to Be," AUTHENTIC (ΔWƎ!).*

I. THE QUIET

WE FINALLY HAD room to breathe, and, thanks to our unromantic flirtation with insolvency, we started to figure out what an actual "company" should look like. Alan Finkelman gave us more than just debt relief, he gave us space; proper "head space." After the past year of juggling Master-Cards, battling lawsuits, and dodging calls from creditors, now we had a Zen-like sense of quiet, and we could use that to focus.

We were lucky with Alan, if not straight-up blessed. Instead of some predatory vulture, he clearly had our best interests at heart, lending his experience and insights to help us turn around the business. Like a tough-love basketball coach, he gave each of us marching orders. "You," Alan said, pointing to Seth. "Go make the business stronger. Bolster up your sales arm and stop dicking around with the finances."

"You," Alan said to Marci. "You're going to stay with me in Houston, and I'm going to teach you everything I know about operations. Here's my Rolodex. This is every sourcing guy I know from Pakistan to China. Use it. Tell them you're working with Scope Imports and use my name."

Finally Alan turned to me. "And you're going to focus on product. Go make cool shit that we can sell. Quit distracting yourself with overproducing for a marketing campaign that doesn't fit our budget. You've been making more ads than sweatshirts."

If Alan was the coach (maybe the "interim" or "exec" coach), Seth was our power forward; he was the banger, the bruiser. Marci was our center: steady, reliable, played tough D. She gave us gravitas and anchored the team. Me? I ran the point.

We started to actually understand what a big-boy company should look like. Any time you try to sell your business, you meet all these corporate executives and gray-haired types. Learn from this experience. We kept getting handed business cards with job titles we had never heard of, like "VP of M.I.S." (management information systems) or "head of licensing." We stared at these exotic titles, puzzled, and we realized how little we knew about the guts of Big Fashion 101. It cued us in to our deficiencies.

We hired with more industry insight. During our failed negotiations with Polo, we met a guy named David Panitz, a young cat who was heading much of its systems innovation and a part of its biz-dev team. We had a good vibe, so we recruited him after the Finkelman deal, installing him as our new chief operating officer. Now we had instant pedigree. Adult supervision.

Most important, we started to focus on our *core competency*—two words I'd never heard of until my due-diligence exam with Lance Isham, also from Polo. One day, after listening to me spew a long rant about the Eckō brand and our assortment, Lance asked me, "But, Marc, what's your core?"

"'Core?' Well . . . at my core is creativity," I said, playing the designer.

"No. I mean your *core* competency? The building block. The anchor. From what I can see, it's this fleece hoodie." He held up the sleeve of a fleece hooded sweatshirt, which indeed became, and still is, one of our most foundational pieces.

Eureka! Polo's core was that cotton pique mesh short-sleeve shirt, the one that comes in every flavor in the rainbow, replete with the pony embroidered on the left chest. I soon realized that the hoodie, and that balance of rhino logo with applied type, could fuel the beast. If I did it right—in a commercially responsible and cost-conscious manner—every core hoodie could pull the weight of ten other disparate items, like sweaters or snowboard jackets. This was my first insight into the basics of merchandising, and I realized that prior to this, as a newb merchandiser, I'd had my head up my ass.

Core competency: our classic heather gray fleece hooded sweatshirt modeled by then "Mos Def"

Think of merchandising as "storytelling through product." The real art exists, like in any great film, in the "casting" of the characters and their performance. Let's say that your line is a theme of "expedition and adventure," and you have an assortment of twenty different styles. I would overthink it, overassort it, and overobsess about trying to make *each and every one* of those twenty styles a star. But the market doesn't want that. In an expedition theme— I'll simplify this to illustrate the point—what the market really wants is a pair of good cargo shorts, maybe an ecru linen military camp shirt, and a single safari-themed illustra-

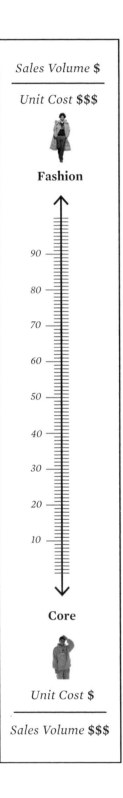

Sales Volume $

Unit Cost $$$

Fashion

90
80
70
60
50
40
30
20
10

Core

Unit Cost $

Sales Volume $$$

tion T-shirt, which helps to express the "high concept." The trick is to find your star.

If you're putting on a Broadway production of *Grease*, you've got your character actors (these are your fashion items), and then you have your star who plays the lead (the core-competency bangers). In the old days, I treated each and every actor equally. My new insight: you don't make *Grease* without John Fucking Travolta.

I realized that for every assortment, I needed to find my John Travolta, my Harrison Ford, my Denzel—and I needed to build the line around that star. In the past, I'd make thirty sweatshirts and be disappointed that twenty-nine of them wouldn't be as good as the thirtieth. Epiphany: I should be *proud and conscious* of that one darling of a thirtieth sweatshirt, make it the star, and I should build the collection around it.

Prior to this, I would just do pure themes, like *travel*! Or *space*! Or *splatter paint*! The new mind-set: core. Always core, core, core. Build the back and abs. The center. I redid my lines, and they took off.

II. **WHERE'S ECKŌ?**

MARCI, SETH, AND I huddled up in our South River conference room. "It's that time of the year again," my sister said.

"Already?" Seth buried his head in his hands, dead tired.

The Magic trade show in Vegas, version 1997. As per our new emphasis on the "Do" part of the formula—and our almost obsessive lust for quiet, focused "Winston Wolfe"–like execution—we knew we couldn't afford to do a lavish trade show like we had in the past. But we couldn't afford *not* to do a trade show. On one hand, trade shows had been good to us: we'd made our first mil at trade shows, we'd showcased our brand at trade shows, and we'd earned our bona fides at trade shows.

But they were also insanely indulgent. Gone were the days of Seth, me, a hammer, and a stack of wooden pallets. This was new to us: a *hard fiscal constraint*. No more playing make-believe. No more 117th credit card to scrounge up.

"We should just spend twenty bucks on a fucking folding table," Seth said, joking.

I hopped up from my seat, started pacing around the room. "Not bad. No shit."

"I was kidding."

"Not a folding table," I said, my mind suddenly laser focused. "But a pedestal. Right in the middle of an empty-ass booth. An Eckō sign and nothing else."

The room was electric with energy. Marci and Seth also stood up, and the three of us bounced around like balls in a pinball machine, pacing, lobbing ideas off one another. I don't remember who said what, but we had this flurry of collective brainstorming.

"We'll make a statement by doing *nothing*—"

"Let's put a red velvet rope around the damn thing, like you can't get in—into an empty plot of trade show real-estate!"

"The market already knows we're broke—"

"So let's just *own* that story, and flip it on them!"

"But if we're not there, how do we tell that story?"

"Street teams!"

"We'll bomb the place with stickers . . . "

"All over fucking Vegas."

"Let them ask, 'Where's Eckō?'"

The three of us had the same thought at the same time: *Where's Eckō?* The ads wrote themselves.

This sticker— in 11″ x 17″ and 6″ x 9″ forms— blanketed the streets of Vegas.

We placed ads in the trade magazine that just teased enigmatically, "Where's Eckō?" and then listed a phone number. We bombed the Vegas strip with thousands of stickers—literally thousands—we promoted it with the marketing version of hand-to-hand combat, in the streets, like how early Wu-Tang Clan would push a new album. If you were a tourist visiting Vegas that weekend, you would have thought it was the biggest draw in the city. (And it was.)

We were so intent on saving money, so determined to be frugal, that Seth, Marci, and I didn't even go to Vegas. We flew down our street team, our sales team, and that was it. Lean and mean. Instead of that $300K booth albatross, we sold our gear directly from a single hotel suite, which, for better or worse, was basically a huge *fuck you* to the cynics who prematurely printed our obituary.

"You think this will work?" Marci asked me.

I shrugged and tried to play it cool, but deep down I was embarrassed, anxious, and always on edge. The financial lifeline from Finkelman came with a catch: any false move, any hiccup, and we wouldn't be able to pay him back on the timetable, which meant that we could lose the company.

And if this didn't work? Would the trade community snicker? Would the gatekeepers thumb their noses? Would we have egg all over our faces?

A T THIS POINT, we were no longer chasing the adulation of insiders but, instead, chasing *the paper*. Orders. Receipts. Magic accounted for a huge chunk of our revenue each year, and the real magic wasn't what happened inside the convention center but, rather, what happened when you punched the calculator's "=" button at the end of the day. We needed it to work.

A few days before the Magic convention, the "Where's Eckō?" ads ran in the trade show rags, like *Women's Wear Daily* and *Sportswear International*. No reaction. On the first day of the show, I called our sales guy for an update.

"Nothing," he said. "But the street team killed it! Rhino's everywhere."

I tried to bottle up the disappointment, to push it down deep, and to focus on work. I remembered what Finkelman said: *You—focus on product, not marketing.* Besides, *It's only eleven in the morning in Vegas*, I reminded myself. *Chill*. Things would be different at the end of the day.

I called again that first night. "Still dead?"

The sales guy paused, and through the phone I could hear him choose his words very carefully. "We're doing okay," he said, his voice measured.

"What's *okay*?"

"Down seventy-five percent versus last year," he said.

I thanked him, tried not to freak out, and hung up the phone. Well, we gave it a shot. We tried something different, and different doesn't always work.

On Day Two, I was so disgusted that I didn't even call for a morning check-in. I just buried myself in work, work, work. Seth and Marci did the same. Maybe this is how politicians feel on Election Day: useless, stressed, impatient, waiting for the polls to be tallied. (Or maybe they feel that way just because they *are* useless, stressed, impatient, waiting for the polls to be tallied.)

Finally I broke down and called again.

"OLD SCHOOL" VIRAL:
Catching the Cold of Cool

Before there was YouTube, Twitter, or Facebook, "going viral" meant that you took it to the streets and made people catch your brand of the "cold." But not just the common cold. *The* cold. When done properly, street teaming, or any sort of great outdoor advertising, stops you cold, makes you think, and jars you from your routine. And whether you're a slick ad agency or an insurgent street artist, making a pedestrian *catch* that cold is no easy task in a world littered with transactional imagery.

This is the playing field that I've always embraced as my home turf. This has been my sandbox for years, ever since my "Vote for Marc for Class President" posters in the seventh grade. Street teaming, wheat pasting, stencils, and stickers were all born, partly, through the midnineties music marketing made famous by Loud Records, Rawkus, Delicious Vinyl, and, of course, the enigmatic Wu-Tang Clan. These tactics were simultaneously adopted by the street art and graf community, although many hard-core "aerosol traditionalists" loathe stencil art or postering as "inauthentic."

If your balls were big enough, it was easy to go for it. Mechanically speaking, you would sandwich two posters around a telephone pole and then staple the edges together. Voila. This method helped you avoid paying fines, because the telephone pole itself was left unscathed. Sanitation would simply rip down the poster—which, worst case, meant a fine for littering—versus the "permanent" method of spray-painting graffiti, which could mean a much higher fine for vandalizing. (Although "permanence" is a funny and relative thing; I still see Shepard Fairey posters in some parts of the world that are damn near fifteen years old.) This changed by the late nineties. Over time, street teamers started putting the signs higher and higher, using ladders to slap them twenty feet above the ground, which, inevitably, led to the cities cracking down and issuing more punishing fines.

From Day One, I was drawn to the power of street teaming, which is why the core image of my brand, the rhino, was created to be stencil friendly. Meaning: instead of drawing the legs of the rhino together, I drew them separate, so that you could easily razor blade and punch out the counters, leaving structure to the stencil and illustration. People often refer to the rhino logo as the "target," as they say the path around the rhino looks like a target from a hunter's rifle scope. It's not. Instead, those four lines, in the negative space of the path (at twelve, three, six, and nine o'clock), act as counters to hold the structure of a paper stencil in place. Simply put, it was designed to be sprayed. And we did. A lot.

At eighteen years old, I was putting the virus out there, stenciling my footprints all over Rutgers University.

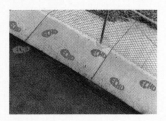

We put so many stencil rhinos and stickers around the world, people did their own send-ups. The virus mutated.

"How bad?" I asked.

"Marc . . . you might want to get a lawyer out here."

"Lawyers?" Oh God, it keeps getting worse. Visions of Wu and Edgar C. Hyman. "Lawyers, really?!"

"You need some lawyers, because the street team went *all city*."

Huh?

"The shit's blowing up!" the sales guy said, excited. "It's all anyone's talking about. Your stickers are all over the streets. Is it even legal? Are you sure you're not gonna get sued?"

It took me a minute to process what he was saying. It turns out that Day One was the calm before the storm, but now, on Day Two, the "Where's Eckō?" campaign was the talk of the trade show. Our hotel room buzzed with buyers, orders, and random people curious about the story. The Magic convention itself was pissed at us—they probably still are. Our fines were higher than expected, but far cheaper than a $300K shrine to ourselves.

In terms of gross receipts, that one "non–trade show" was, at that point, the biggest trade show in our company's history.

III. THE EXHIBIT

THAT VEGAS TRADE show gave us more range of EMOTIONAL IM-PACT, flipping a weakness (no budget) into a strength (a provocative viral campaign). And this time we could back it up: we could fulfill the orders, we could answer the market, we could deliver on the promise. The truth was starting to ring clear. WHAT WE DID > WHAT WE SAID.

Make no mistake, we owe this squarely to Marci. She was our "Governance."

MARCI HAD FLOWN to Houston, studied with Alan—the way I had studied with Drew—and emerged as a Sith Lord of operations. Marci threw herself into the ring, turning into a world-class sourcing, buying, and operations player. We all did our part to push it forward, but she led the turn-around on the sourcing and fulfillment side of the business.

BRAND BALANCE

Swagger

Governance ▰▰▰▰▰▰ *Brute Force*

Think of a brand as a triangle with three legs: Governance, Swagger, and Brute Force.
No single part is more relevant than the other. You control these parts, individually and collectively. If you ignore this balance, don't be surprised when you shit the bed.

GOV-ER-NANCE: influence, control, order (represented by Marci).

BRUTE FORCE: beastly or animallike strength or energy exerted, without constraint. (represented by Seth).

SWAG-GER: how one presents and carries him or herself to the world (represented by me).

Don't be afraid to seek out others who don't look like you or think like you; these are probably the other two legs of the triangle. And put mirrors in your office and home and bedroom—not so you can watch yourself screw, but metaphorically, so that you watch yourself and know your weaknesses. Then try to fix them. Seek brand balance. Internally and externally.

Marci always realized that we didn't need a Wu; her instincts were right all along. We didn't need any shortcuts. Instead, she worked with the vendors and factories directly, never surrendering, pounding the pavement to get us the best quality at the best price and the best value for our end customer. Now we also had a bit of scale; before, we offered the vendors only a plate of bones, and now we could offer them some meat: 3,500, 10,000, sometimes even 100,000 units of one style.

Plus, the world itself was changing. I'd rather drink a bucket of gasoline than bore you with the details of factory operations, but in a nutshell, we could take advantage of new markets. India, Pakistan, and China were more open and no longer looked at our genre of business as small time. The street-wear arena was now as relevant as the surf or branded-denim landscape. Instead of relying on hope* that our brand would be enough, we started relying on our own know-how. Marci sharpened our operations, and I helped sharpen our marketing. In the pre-Finkelman era, I had a willy-nilly method of advertising, doing whatever gratified my immediate emotions. Back then, if our photographer said, "Marc, we can get Celebrity X for $YK, should we do it?" Done and done, yes, let's do that, no matter what it costs. It's worth it.

* A hope method of production is about as effective as the hope method of birth control.

(Top) Jermaine Dupri;
(middle) Mike Shinoda
and Joe Hahn (from
Linkin Park); (bottom)
Too Short

We needed to break the pattern and step off the rat wheel of also-ran. We needed to challenge our LOYALTY TO NOSTALGIA. What could we do that was different? What could we do that better defined our brand? And what was it, exactly, that I wanted to express?

I realized that I needed to channel that very same thing that created a distinction for me in high school: my art. But this time, I'd have more organized resources, and a more strategic means to execute the brand and the business.

Once a year in the mail, I received this massive catalog featuring the work of illustrators from all across the world. Most people dismissed it as junk mail, but I used this giant, four-hundred-page collection to discover the best-in-class trends in the commercial art world. I was floored by this one photo illustration of a tech nerd, midthirties, white, wearing a button-down shirt, tie, and hands in his khakis. Behind him are three tapestries, each woven with a naive and (intentionally) poorly drawn version of him.

This image spoke to me for some reason. My "intuition glow" lit up, and I got that buzz you get when you have déjà vu, or a moment of self-induced clairvoyance. I realized that I wasn't looking at some random page, I was looking at the future. Picasso said it first: that line about borrowing versus stealing, and good artists versus great artists. I reflected on it for about three seconds. Then I said, "This is it."

Why? For starters, it was simple to produce. All I needed was a light kit, a white seamless backdrop, and a camera. I could easily hang unpainted canvases or frames on a wall, and then, in postproduction, complete the caricature. But that's the Xs and Os. More important, I saw the potential for the oohs and aahs, and for the fulfillment of expressing my brand's love for "art"—the kind that hangs on walls, blended seamlessly with a "model" (a celebrity) wearing my clothing. This moment was the makings of a "rinse and repeat" type of aesthetic that I could produce into our first truly organized advertising campaign. It had legs and the promise of being flexible and iterative. I could build on it.

Clearly, alignment with celebrity was good, but that alone wasn't enough. This new ad idea would get people to see celebrities *in our glow*; in our brand's energy. This new campaign, which we called "the Exhibit," would trim the risk of them just showing up, putting on a hat, and smiling for the camera. Without sacrificing their integrity, the celebrities could stand in the light of our brand's UNIQUE VOICE. And feel good about it.

I drew a mind-map on my bedroom wall, and I brainstormed which celebrities could be in each of these vignettes. My team of illustrators would do the illest paintings of each celebrity and elevate the "art" part of the conversation. Celebrities started to embrace the aesthetic, and many gave us a meaningful endorsement by being in the campaign. We brought in names like Jermaine Dupri, Prince Paul (the hip-hop producer), Method Man, the band Linkin Park, and Fred Durst from Limp Bizkit. The glow of our brand's light stayed on the page even after they were unplugged from the wall.

IV. **SPIKE LEE'S FORGOTTEN CLASSIC**

I N THE LATE 1990s, motocross and street bikes were an emerging trend, and we made proper riding gloves, replete with protective padding and reflective tape. In technical-designer-speak, they were the shit. Our ads for these gloves featured Method Man from Wu-Tang Clan, and they were one of our top sellers.

Spike Lee called our office, hoping to use the gloves in his new movie *Bamboozled*. I couldn't let the opportunity pass. I had always dreamed of doing *something* collaborative with him. I nervously pitched him on directing one of our fashion shows.

Ghostface Killah and Method Man from Wu-Tang Clan

"Bet," he said in signature steely-cool Spike Lee style. "Let's do it."

I was so excited. I had just been accepted to the CFDA, the Council of Fashion Designers of America, and when you do a runway show, you need to pull out the big guns. Spike deployed a team through Spike DDB, his agency, which was a subsidiary of the ad firm DDB Worldwide Communications Group. I tossed around a bunch of possible ideas, and I think Spike humored me a little (after I browbeat him), because the idea we finally adopted was, quite literally, something that belongs in the toilet.

Here's what we did. For the Bryant Park Fashion Show, I set up these six Plexiglas rectangles, each one taller than a person, which acted like giant door thresholds. We called these doorways, which were supposed to represent some sort of fashion portal, the "pods." We lined the runway with these pods, so that the openings were parallel to each other. From the viewpoint of the cameras at the end of the runway, it was pretty slick. The symmetry created an "infinity" mirror effect. The Plexiglas edges, laced with reds, refracted the light in a way that made them glow like neon.

House lights go dark, down lights go on. Each one illuminates just one of these empty portals. Not so bad so far, right? Wait.

Cue the video.

The video was, theoretically, a high-concept metastatement about where ideas come from in the fashion industry. Translation: Spike filmed a hypothetical array of back-to-back pitches that (supposedly) happened between me and my team. The short series of vignettes ranged from the sublime to the ridiculous.

"Let's do fur this season!" exclaims our assistant.

"I got it! Let's send the models in naked!" suggests Raphie Aronowitz, one of my senior marketing guys. He says this in front of me, balls-ass naked.

In this vignette, I reject each idea, a la the stereotypical visionary creative.

"Nah!" I bark.

"*Pssst.*"

"Fail."

"Go back to the woodshed!"

"Let's do synchronized floor dancing!" someone suggests. Cut to an overhead shot of my marketing staff doing synchronized floor dancing, like 1920s flappers. Random.

Exasperated, I stand up from my desk, clutching my aching head, and I walk toward the bathroom. Camera follows me down the hall. My hand on the Men door sign. Camera swings through with door. Cut to overhead shot. Me, like a zombie drone, lining the toilet seat with toilet tissue as I prepare to pop a squat.

Then suddenly, in an ecstatic moment of revelation, I reach out my hands as if to prop up the bathroom stall walls from falling in. I look up directly into the camera.

"I got it! That's it!"

Projection fades to black. Runway lights go up. Cue the music. Out walks the models. That part was sort of epic. With Spike on board, we managed to get a cast that included Rosario Dawson, Mos Def, and New York Jets quarterback Ray Lucas. Then, once all the models had taken two laps around the runway, they stood inside each individual threshold of the pods, striking a pose like a mannequin. And voila, each pod, in complete synch, starts to spin—as they were all on electric carousels.

Photo from the Marc Eckō Cut & Sew Catalog from 2006, when we did a twenty-year celebration of 40 Acres & a Mule

Those walls were a metaphor for not feeling boxed in. The bathroom walls and the pod walls were one and the same. It was intended as a superabstract joke; I was taking the piss (or the poop) out of how heady and indulgent runway shows could be, all by being too cerebral and indulgent myself.

I realize now that I pushed this idea down Spike's throat, and I'm guessing that when Spike ranks his personal top five films he directed, the list does not include *Marc Eckō on the Shitter*.

Idea aside, Spike did teach me one very important thing, and it had nothing to do with pods or toilets.

We filmed the video in December, on a day where a blizzard blanketed the city and the tristate area, shutting down most of the schools and offices. The roads were a mess. My employees started calling me at four thirty in the morning, asking when we had planned "the makeup day" due to the weather.

"There isn't a makeup day," I said.

"Spike cancelled?" they said.

"Nope. Spike's here." Spike had called me several times the night before, assuring me that he wouldn't slow down for anything, especially just weather. "The shoot is indoors."

BOW IN THE PRESENCE OF GREATNESS:
How to Collaborate with Domain Experts

1. Don't Toady. Bow
It's annoying to them if you're a fan-boy. It's distracting to them if you make them behave like a teacher rather than like a contractor.

2. Define Your Business Objectives
Ultimately you're working to execute a task. Your relationship is defined not by an amorphous "collaboration" but by the business milestones you agree upon mutually. Define the finish line.

3. Don't Expect a Curriculum
Yes, you want to learn from them, but this education should come organically. They are the master, you are the student, so create an environment that allows them to do what they're best at, and then learn through osmosis.

4. Don't Project Your Professional Crush onto Them
Just because you have love for them doesn't mean they have it for you.

5. Don't Brag About It
Never use it as social currency. The only currency should be the success of the final product that you did together. Otherwise you'll be perceived as some kind of professional star fucker. You did a job with them, great, but that's just one of many things that will grow the professional body of work that defines your brand. It doesn't give you a Boy Scout badge.

Spike didn't just show up, he showed up *early* to this damn thing. He was, and is, all pro. He could have easily cancelled or rescheduled the entire gig. Instead, he dove into every detail, headfirst and hands-on. He's not afraid to get his hands dirty, and he never begrudged the bad weather or the toilet humor.

That's important no matter where you are in life: who you are or how you may be perceived. It's part of the INFINITE-TRUTH aspect of the formula: Are you just saying it, or are you *doing* it, no matter the circumstances, or even if you're out of your comfort zone?

This also speaks to the idea of accountability.

In both creative circles and business projects, it's typical to do work "by committee." It's like that old cliché: "If everyone's responsible, then no one's responsible." Instead of operating by committee, give the artist the wheel. Let him drive.

Let him keep that hand on the wheel. When empowered, he's forced to be accountable.

Don't shout advice from the backseat. Don't try to put a second set of hands on that wheel. "Drive the car and get us home. If you crash that bitch, it's on you."

We gave Spike the courtesy of taking the wheel, and he repaid us with ultimate accountability.

As a leader, you should take the wheel. Wherever it takes you.

V. **LICENSE TO SHILL**

LICENSING GETS A bad rap. In the world of high fashion, or even medium fashion or gutter fashion, the word *licensing* is seen as taboo, schlocky, dirty. It's often viewed as the path brands take when they are on the downward cycle, looking to squeeze out whatever revenue they can get.

People warned me, "If you license your brand, they're just going to slap your logo on white underwear, and it will cheapen you."

If you're not careful, they're right, that can happen. But licensing can also crack open new worlds of possibility for your brand; it can expand your canvas; it can give you a dramatically broader range of EMOTIONAL IMPACT.

Before we got serious about licensing, Eckō Unlimited was pretty damn, well, Eckō *Limited*. We had lofty ambitions to be a lifestyle company, but if you're a lifestyle company, shouldn't you sell other stuff besides T-shirts? I looked at Polo. It's a lifestyle company, and it sells a lot more than clothes: Polo cologne, Polo watches, Polo sunglasses, Polo wallets, Polo paint.

We had been taking baby steps toward broadening ourselves, nudging from T-shirts to sweatshirts, and then to jackets, and then to sweaters and denim. But consumers didn't buy our hoodies because we had the best fabric or fit; they bought them because they preferred our brand. So couldn't, and shouldn't, that translate to a broader array of products?

Look at Nike, for instance. Its truth doesn't spawn merely from great product. Technically speaking, Nike is a sneaker manufacturer, right? You think they see themselves as in the business of selling shoes? *Psst*. Others make great shoes. It's never only about the *X*s and *O*s but, rather, the oohs and aahs. Nike synthesized a new religion out of "Just Do It." It makes and delivers the *truth*.

In the pre-Finkelman era, we had done some cheesy licensing deals with a few companies in Japan, but we had never been studious about doing it right. Back then, we had an employee who took these business trips to Tokyo to arrange licensing deals, and he would come back with these mysterious cigarette burns all over his arms and give us bags of cash. This was our "licensing model."

Now we would get serious. We started with footwear, ignoring our colleagues who said to us, "Footwear? *Licensing?* Isn't that what you do when you're dying?" Screw it. That's the same negativity I heard from Ben and my Rutgers friends. That's the same negativity I heard from the cool kids at 432F, calling me a sellout. Besides, why not sneakers? I always had a strong opinion on footwear, but I lacked the technical or financial wherewithal to do it on my own. Instead of losing focus on my core competency and retraining myself to be a shoemaker, why not harness the knowledge of others?

Seth, like a beast, took charge of tracking down licensing opportunities. We got into bed with some shoe companies that had huge distribution even if they had, let's say, questionable aesthetic choices. But that's where I came in. If they had a deficiency on the qualitative side, but we had a deficiency on the supply side, couldn't we combine that chocolate and peanut butter?

> I've made some really ugly shit. That's part of the process. If you're never making ugly shit, then you're never taking chances, and you're never pushing yourself to make the sublime.

You have to be willing to roll the dice. Some products will be dogs, and that's okay. I've made some really ugly shit. That's part of the process. If you're never making ugly shit, then you're never taking chances, and you're never pushing yourself to make the sublime.

One shoe that I felt strongly about was called "the Tongue." The tongue of the sneaker was made out of this bright, reflective material that would really catch the eye. In our ad for this shoe, we had a guy with his tongue sticking out, and then next to him sat the "Tongue" (our shoe).

My plan was for Fred Durst to wear the Tongue in the Exhibit campaign. We invited him for the shoot, and Fred showed up, looked at the shoes, looked at me, and said, "Look, I love Eckō, but I hate these shoes. Fuck that. I'm not wearing them in your ad."

I kept myself from getting pissy or defensive. My team huddled. "How do you feel about blowtorches?" we asked.

Instead of having Fred Durst wear the shoes, we photographed him torching the shoes—literally lighting them on fire—and that became part of the Exhibit campaign. That was a much more authentic expression of my brand's values than just another celeb hawking more "stuff."

Every creative director needs to keep perspective. As the author of your idea, you might love it and expect everyone to love it. But not everyone will, and that's okay. In retrospect, those shoes *were* kind of ugly. They weren't unwearable—I rocked them—but maybe they weren't my best work. So Fred Durst was sort of charmed that I wasn't fazed by his criticism. Ultimately he wasn't endorsing my *product*, he was endorsing our *philosophy*. He wasn't endorsing WHAT WE MADE, he was endorsing HOW WE MADE PEOPLE FEEL.

Fred Durst from
Limp Bizkit

SOME OF OUR first licensing partners were an eight out of ten on the schlock meter, but then, as we gained experience and scale, we courted progressively better brands. We went from Jeffrey Allen to Mountain Gear to Skechers, and our revenue—just from licensing footwear alone—grew well north of $50 million.

Seth went on a mission with watches. While traveling to Odessa, in the Ukraine, he saw this tiny duty-free shop in the airport. In the shop were displays of Montblanc pens, Smirnoff vodka, Toblerone chocolate, and a tower of watches by Guess, which had aligned itself with Timex. Seth called me from the airport.

LICENSING = CONSENSUAL SEX:
Know Who You're Getting Into Bed With

Licensing has been very good to Eckō, and it allowed us to deliver on the promise and *creation* of Eckō Unlimited. But you have to be careful. Lessons from licensing:

1. Get Over Your Fear
Too many people are afraid of licensing. (This goes back to the FEAR part of the formula.) Great, authentic brands have the capacity to flex and to stretch, and should have good elastic memory so as never to lose the form of the core. Licensing needn't be a dirty word. Is Gucci suddenly a schlocky brand because its eyewear is licensed by the Luxottica Group?

2. Take Your Time
Wait for a partner that's right for you. With Timex, it took us two years of courtship before we climbed into bed. It's worth the wait.

3. Don't Immediately Go to the Highest Bidder
It's easy to get seduced by a frothy forecast of royalties. If you have to choose between two partners:

Partner A: guarantees a higher royalty percentage, and has a lukewarm and outsider sense of your brand.

Partner B: gives you less favorable terms but understands your brand completely, internally, intimately, and in ways *even you* haven't considered.

Go with partner B ten times out of ten. We had plenty of higher bidders than Timex (and other great partners), and the "advisors" said we should go with the $$$. Instead, we went with a partner that knew us from our guts to the skin.

4. Let Them Take You to School
Good licensing partners are ones you can learn from. This is a free education—take advantage of it.

5. Pretend That *You're* Hiring *Them*
It's easy to shake hands with a partner and then walk away, thinking that you'll never really deal with him on a day-to-day basis. False. For a licensing partnership to truly work, you need to get in the trenches together, and that means you should actually *like* working with the dude. So when you make your decision, pretend that this is not just someone you'll be meeting with occasionally, but someone you'll see every day as if he's your employee and *can't* be fired. Would you still do it? If the answer is no, then walk.

"How the hell does *Guess* end up selling watches in the Ukraine?" he shouted into the phone.

"I don't know, man—"

"The Ukraine! Do you think the owner of Guess has ever been to the Ukraine?" Seth asked. "This is what we need to do. We need to get Timex."

That became our goal: to work our way up the licensing ladder and eventually get into bed with brands like Timex. After hounding the phones, Seth eventually convinced Timex execs to come out to our offices in South River.

We met Cindy Livingston and Gale, these two sweet, middle-aged ladies with really big jewelry and Ferragamo purses. We were so excited to meet them. It took another meeting, and then another month, and then another *year*, and finally, two years after we'd first stalked them, begged them, Timex agreed to a licensing deal. I knew that working with world-class partners like Timex would give us more than just a splashy headline: it would give us more learning, and it unlocked a greater range for the brand to create an EMOTIONAL IMPACT.

VI. A COMPLEX TIME

LICENSING INCREASED THE range of our brand, and, by extension, it allowed new products to make deeper EMOTIONAL IMPACT points. It fueled our growth, broadened how we viewed marketing, and helped our revenue almost double. All of this is what you'd expect from an ambitious fashion-lifestyle company, but in the back of my mind, I had a couple of other pet projects that would extend our range of EMOTIONAL IMPACT off the GPS.

I've always had a bit of attention-deficit disorder. And I've always had a tendency to self-medicate, but my "self-medication" isn't drugs or booze, it's usually working on something *other* than what's on my plate. Sometimes this can be fruitful, sometimes this can be indulgent, and sometimes it's a little of both. As self-medication—and because of my lust for "creation"—I usually explore a new outlet that can seem, on the surface, completely out of my wheelhouse and distracting.

One of these outlets seemed like a radical departure from everything we did: I wanted to start a magazine. On paper, this made no sense; I was just starting to come into my own as as a fashion designer; what business did I have going into publishing? That just wasn't done.

Two problems:

1. How does a fashion reseller create a business model dependent on the subsidy (ads) from other fashion resellers? He doesn't. Imag-

ine the bewildered looks I got when I asked marketing execs from Diesel and Nike to consider buying a full-page ad in *Marc Eckō's Complex Magazine*.

2. When a designer or celebrity starts a magazine, it's usually a vanity project that does little more than wax on his or her own brand. (See: *Trump* magazine. Oh wait, you can't. It folded.)

But I didn't want to create a self-serving *Eckō* magazine that would publish articles about the glory of Eckō hoodies and Eckō fleece. That wasn't the vibe. Instead, even in the darkest hours of our debt, I envisioned something that wouldn't be about my brand but would view the world through the values that created my brand. A world that's neither simply black or white, high or low, but *complex*.

I looked at my consumer, and I looked at the landscape of consumer publications. There were all these vertical platforms: *Rolling Stone*, all music; *Thrasher*, all skate; *Slam*, all basketball; the *Source*, all hip-hop. When traveling in Japan, I discovered this fashion magazine called *Hot Dog*, which had this obsessively detailed consumer guide that was curated with a fusion of style and street. That pearl had me asking, Why couldn't I do the same?

I had a name for this magazine: *Climate*. (Just like with "Cram," sometimes my first idea for a name doesn't stick.)

Years ago, I drew sketches in my black book and even whipped up a prototype. When we tried to sell the company to Polo, I even showed Ralph Lauren a rough cut. Ralph was lukewarm on the idea of purchasing Eckō Unltd., but when I handed him the prototype of *Climate*, his eyes widened.

"This . . ." Ralph said, flipping through the magazine, "is good."

"I'm going to separate church and state," I said. "We'll never promote Eckō apparel in a heavy-handed way. But we'll use the *values* of my brand as a lens for how the consumer can shop."

"I can't take this," Ralph said, giving it back to me.

"It's okay. No worries," I said.

He told me that he loved our idea, but he'd been running his own magazine, and he didn't want to ever be accused of stealing anything.

That gave me a jolt of confidence; I knew I was on to something. And as it turned out, Ralph's son started a magazine called *Swing*, which was similar in intent: attempting to be a lifestyle magazine for generation X, with a dash of nepotism for one specific brand (Polo). Despite big financing, it never stuck.

I knew the idea had legs, but I couldn't afford to scratch this itch when we were maxing out our credit cards. And once Finkelman gave us the lifeline, the new mantra was to focus, focus, focus, so that's what I did, tucking this idea into my hip pocket.

But once we had revenue again? I knew it was time to make the investment. I approached Seth and said, "I really want to develop this business."

To Seth's credit—and a testament to the fact that we had learned little—he was equally bullish.

"This can be good marketing for us."

"I thought it wouldn't promote our clothes?" he said.

"It's not, but Eckō Unlimited is *bigger* than clothes. We're going to be talking about street culture, video gaming, hip-hop, fashion. It's completely consistent with our brand."

"Just make sure there's plenty of Eckō product placement!" Seth said, wanting to make sure that there wasn't *too* much church, and that the state (Eckō) got some credit for being the parent.

> But like all failures, it made for a great practice run . . .

"Don't worry. Let's give her her space. Okay?"

Seth and Marci talked it over, and they agreed on a compromise: they would let me develop the idea, but by using just 10 percent of the creative team's time. They helped me mock up prototypes, storyboard, and bring the idea to life. Seth would get flush with energy and dip in as well. We brought in a trusted friend of ours, Alan Ket, who had launched a hip-hop and street-culture magazine called *Stress*.

We kicked off the concept by developing a mini CD-ROM prototype for *Climate*. "It won't be paper. All digital." That didn't work, and, frankly, the market wasn't ready for that kind of all-digital platform. But like all failures, it made for a great practice run on establishing the editorial needs and team structure. Alan cobbled together a skeleton team, bringing in the players that we would need to start a magazine.

Rather than the all digital, we pivoted and started with a print magazine. But we'd have to rethink the name. Despite loving the name *Climate*, we had learned our lesson from Edgar C. Hyman on trademarks, so upon our due diligence, we learned there was already a registered trademarked magazine named *Climate*.

What could a better name be? Back then we romantically referred to our South River offices as "the mind labs," or "the complex." The word *complex* became a part of our brand vernacular. In fact, at the dawn of the dot-com gold rush, everyone had to have a website—whether or not they knew what to do with it. I would market ours in ads by asking the viewer to visit "ecko.com*plex*." This caused confusion. In those early days of web browsers, people would actually type in "ecko.com*plex*" and receive error messages for "invalid domain." The *plex* part was an accessory.

Complex magazine it would be. But would our customers even give a shit? How could we gauge the market's appetite? We realized that we shipped two million T-shirts every year, so we leveraged that as a platform. We put hangtags on T-shirts, giving customers a *Complex* postcard. If they returned the card, we'd mail them the first issue for free. (You could argue that we jumped the gun: it would be another three years before we published our first issue. Nothing happens overnight.)

A few weeks after those T-shirt hangtags, Bernadette swung by my office. "Look, we got one!" She held up a postcard, amused. The next day we got another postcard. The next week we had about fifteen.

The next week?

A knock on our door. It was the USPS dude. He dropped off two of the white, oversized, industrial-strength crates that held thousands of letters, both overflowing with postcards. We would eventually receive two hundred thousand of them, and, finally, we were ready.

I looked at Seth—told you so.

NOW, FINALLY, EVERYTHING that we did helped assert the expression of AUTHENTICITY. With respect to the formula, it's not accurate to say we "maxed out" our score, because the equation isn't about a number, a solution, or a final product. The formula evaluates the vectors, data points, and variables along the axis; it doesn't output a score like "42."

Examples of Climate, *a digital mini-magazine made by us,* Ecko.com(plex)

My love of video games goes back to playing Donkey Kong, Q*Bert, early John Madden Football, and so many other titles with my best friend, Darren. In the mid-1990s, it was clear that video games were evolving into something more interesting, and I hit on the idea of mashing up gaming and graffiti. Something that could give our brand even more range of EMOTIONAL IMPACT. Make our audience *feel* beyond the borders of just the cuffs and the collars. This idea had one thing going both for and against it: it had never been done.

As another bit of self-medication, I spent hours late at night immersed in my black book, wide awake, scribbling story concepts for a fictional graffiti hero named Trane, short for Coltrane, which was a nod to both jazz saxophonist John Coltrane and the graffiti-tattooed trains that I fell in love with as a kid. I dreamed up this dystopian story idea where Trane had to save his city, New Radius, by using graffiti to incite a rebellion against a brutal, Orwellian regime. But I knew as much about making a video game as I did about how to perform neurosurgery, so how could I make this happen?

I tried to align myself with the best in the business. And just as with *Complex*, it wasn't an overnight process. In '97, I walked the Electronic Entertainment Expo (E3) trade show as a consumer, geeking

out, meeting the players in the industry, and getting a lay of the land. We hired a guy named Mike Lynch to help me biz-dev. Mike and I would meet the marketing heads from different gaming publishers, and I'd say something self-effacing, like, "I'd like to do some marketing collaborations with you," but what I really wanted to say was, "I have this crazy-ass idea in my head for a graffiti video game, and I want you to make it." But if I told them that, I would seem like every other outsider who pitched them crazy-ass ideas, so, instead, I started incrementally.

We met Glenn Chin, a senior marketing director at EA Sports, and I pitched Glenn on the idea of an Eckō team in Madden Football. The jerseys would be Eckō jerseys, and the players would be pop-culture celebrities.

"I love it," Glenn said. "We'll do it as an Easter egg."

The '99 Madden Football included a hidden Eckō team that you could unlock, featuring players such as Kevin Smith and Jason Mewes (Jay and Silent Bob), Jamie Foxx, Jermaine Dupri, and rapper Noreaga.

EA liked it, I liked it, and the consumers seemed to like it. This helped build up my bona fides in the gaming world. The next year we did it again, only this time it wasn't an Easter egg, it was just one of the teams you could play.

This was *huge* from an EMO-TIONAL IMPACT point of view. I loved the idea of my brand popping up where you wouldn't expect it, the way a Coca-Cola sign can appear suddenly in a jungle. Best of all? It was capital efficient and cheap to pull off. EA viewed this as a cool value-add for its consumer, and I viewed this as better marketing than a Super Bowl commercial.

The relationship with the people at EA was a good one, so they put me—not my brand, but *me*, the dude—as a boxer in Knockout Kings, and they also included actor Marlon Wayans and Q-Tip. At the time, I weighed 240 pounds, but I looked 180 in the game. The miracles of digitalization.

These were great platforms for the brand—almost *too* great. EA (and the game industry in general) eventually wised up and started charging for product placement, and at that point, I couldn't justify it from a cost perspective. But in addition to getting free commercials to an engaged audience—and the *right* audience—I had cut my teeth in the gaming world. It was time to think more seriously about my game, but would this just be an indulgent hobby, or could it make the company any real money?

Time would tell.

That said, the data points and variables were all in alignment, moving upward along a positive curve:

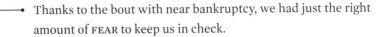

$$\int_{0}^{100} f(\text{FEAR})$$

$$\int_{0}^{100} f(\text{ACTION})$$

$$\left(\begin{smallmatrix} \textit{WHAT WE} \\ \textbf{SAID} \end{smallmatrix} \right) = \left(\begin{smallmatrix} \textit{WHAT WE} \\ \textbf{DID} \end{smallmatrix} \right)$$

$$\int_{0}^{100} f(\text{SELF})$$

- Thanks to the bout with near bankruptcy, we had just the right amount of FEAR to keep us in check.
- We were willing to take the ACTION we needed to take, no longer using the middle-men (Wus) of the world as a crutch but, instead, acting as our own agents to make our product.
- WHAT WE DID finally matched WHAT WE SAID.
- We had a strong (but not too grandiose) sense of SELF, as the Eckō brand became more self-referential, validating its place in the pop-culture ecosystem.

Thanks to the growth of our core, focused product licensing, and the expansion of our platform through the early seeds of *Complex* and the game Getting Up, we expanded our RANGE OF EMOTIONAL IMPACT (more on this later), reaching our customers in surprising ways. We started to learn that great brands don't put limits on themselves.

When you create an authentic brand that you believe in, you need to push yourself to think about what that brand *really means*, and that's not limited to a product or industry. Go deeper. Think about its values, think about how it can be tweaked, reframed, and spun into something more interesting.

This is what Apple did. Jobs realized that, at its heart, the Apple brand meant something more than just "computer" or "microprocessor." The values, intelligence, and ethos that went into that brand are what counts, and when you realize that, suddenly it's possible to create iPods, iPhones, iPads, and expand the range of EMOTIONAL IMPACT for the products you make.

Remember the deal with Alan Finkleman? In 1997 he gave us three years to pay him back, or else we'd lose the company. Thanks to this focus, we didn't pay him back in three years.

We paid him back in eighteen months.

The company was ours again.

But could we save it from the next challenge we would face: a man named Marc Eckō, the "designer"?

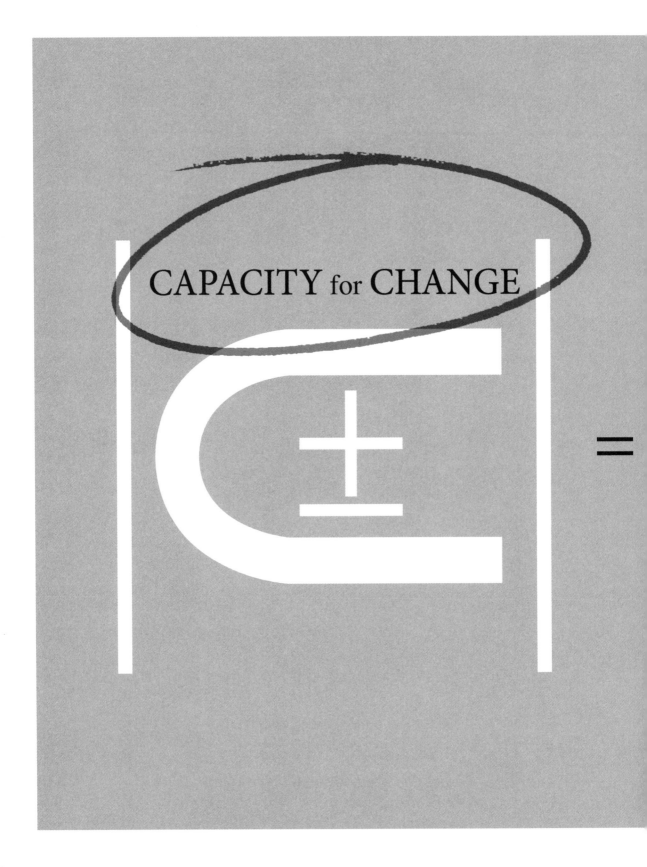

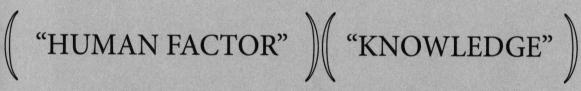

"I looked at the rap community like street kids wanting their own brand. But now I look at that period with the rappers in the nineties as a trend of the moment. What it taught me was never to follow a trend, because trends move on."

—TOMMY HILFIGER

"When it's time to change, you've got to rearrange."

—PETER BRADY
(CHRISTOPHER KNIGHT),
from the Brady Bunch *song*
"Time to Change"

CHAPTER 7

CAPACITY FOR

CHANGE

$$|\boxed{\pm}| = \text{CAPACITY for CHANGE}$$

CAPACITY FOR CHANGE: *This is the most complex part of the formula, because it expresses not a hard number but a fluid and differential calculus. It's a measure of your ability to change, grow, learn, and evolve through failing hard and failing fast, and then responding to that failure. Unlike other parts of the formula, this can be a positive or a negative. In a nutshell: this is how you deal with failure. It's not whether—or how often—you get knocked down. It's whether—and how often—you get up.*

You might ask, Okay, if failure is so important, why isn't "failure" a variable in the formula? Failure isn't a variable in the equation because failure transcends the formula. It's everywhere; it's in between the lines. Building authenticity isn't about the failures or successes. Those are a given: we all fail again and again, and those Ws and Ls are just blips on the radar. But how do you respond when you get your knees bloodied, your knuckles broken? This is the CAPACITY FOR CHANGE ($\boxed{\pm}$), and it's split into two parts:

$$\text{HUMAN FACTOR} \; = \; \int_{0}^{100} f(\text{HUMILITY})dx - \int_{0}^{100} f(\text{HUBRIS})dx$$

1. THE HUMAN FACTOR:
HUMILITY MINUS HUBRIS

This is trickier. It's one thing to have KNOWLEDGE, but do you have the ability to grasp that knowledge, to internalize it, to learn from it? We see examples all the time of people who clearly know something, but their HUBRIS gets in the way. Just look at the investment banks that leveraged their asses thirty to one and helped cause the 2008 financial crisis, and then, just a few years later, put their hands back in the cookie jar with Libor. Clearly, these banks know this is dirty pool, but their HUBRIS eclipses their HUMILITY.

Or if high finance isn't your thing, look no further than Mel Gibson. The dude must "know" that it's kind of uncool to make anti-Semitic rants and to call women "Sugar Tits," and he must "know" that acting like a douche has the power to submarine his career, but just like the I-banks, his HUBRIS trumped HUMILITY.

Businessman and investor Warren Buffett continues to show us that even having more money than God doesn't stop him from being humble enough to know what he doesn't know. He lives by the motto "Never invest in a business you can't understand." HUMILITY is one of the few variables in the formula that are okay to max out. Howard Schultz, the CEO of Starbucks, ate humble pie when he realized that his company had made mistakes by overexpanding, so he closed a thousand stores, slashed costs, and even shut down all stores for one day to retrain employees. The company roared back, and profits doubled.

$$\text{KNOWLEDGE} \; = \; \frac{\text{"What you Know."}}{\text{"What you DO NOT Know."}}$$

2. THE KNOWLEDGE FACTOR: WHAT YOU KNOW
DIVIDED BY WHAT YOU DO NOT KNOW

Straightforward enough. You can be the most humble person in the world, but eventually you need to couple that mind-set with some actual, real-world knowledge. And the best knowledge is the kind you get through experience.

THE CAPACITY FOR CHANGE
VERSUS "THE SECRET" TO CHANGE

Change isn't mystical. If you think my formula is wonky, check out the logic behind the best-selling self-help book The Secret. *Basically,* The Secret's *law of attraction says that if you think positive thoughts into the universe, this will metaphysically seek a "corresponding frequency," and then the universe, as a way of saying thank you, will give you positive results.* If you build it, they will come.

Look, I'm all for the idea of karma, and I'm not going to shit on the merits of optimism, but it's wrong, misleading, and counterproductive to assume that "If you think it, you will be it." Life doesn't work like that. There's a difference between doing *and* wishing. *Touchy-feely, warm-and-fuzzy lullabies like* The Secret *make you think that success is an out-of-body experience, and that dreamers are instantly doers.*

It's okay to have dreams. But how will you achieve them? How will you change? Will you embrace the HUMILITY to know WHAT YOU DO NOT KNOW?

This chapter on change—for me and my company, and for any entrepreneur on the cusp of massive success—is all about dreams and fulfillment. So let's start with an actual dream of mine.

I had a dream where I met Tommy Hilfiger.

In the dream, he invites me to his beach house in Nantucket, which is a Hilfiger catalog sprung to life. The lawn is green cashmere, the walls are embroidered with plaid, and the mailbox is a red, white, and blue Hilfiger logo. Woof! A dog, wearing a sweater vest and bow tie, nuzzles against my leg.

I knock on the tweed-coated door.

Tommy Hilfiger opens the door. He has gruff facial hair, he's wearing an open bathrobe, and he's smoking the biggest joint I've ever seen. He hands me the joint, and I take a pull. He looks and talks like "the Dude" from *The Big Lebowski.*

"Sloppy Joe?" Tommy asks, waving me inside.

"I'd love a Sloppy Joe," I say, transfixed.

We walk past the living room, which is filled with all-American college kids—his guests?—posing as mannequins: plastic, frozen, with creepy smiles on their faces. I feel their eyes follow me as Tommy escorts me into the kitchen, where he's cooking a steaming pot of Sloppy Joe. He scoops two portions onto a white bun.

"White buns, Marc, white buns," Tommy says. "Don't listen to that 'whole wheat' bullshit. It's a racket."

He hands me a sandwich. "This is delicious," I say, and I mean it. I devour my Sloppy Joe as the meat drips down my chin, spilling onto my T-shirt's rhinoceros logo.

"Nice rhino," Tommy says.

"You really like it?"

"Always have. It takes some balls to choose a logo like that. It's not what you'd expect for graffiti, but it sublimates other values."

"Yes! That's what I've always said!"

"Here. Have some milk." Tommy pours me some milk. "Milk and Sloppy Joe's, Marc. That's the shit. Let me show you: you gotta dunk the fucker in the milk, like this."

Tommy dunks the Sloppy Joe in the milk, and I do the same with mine, and he's right—it's incredible.

Suddenly he looks at me seriously. "You're about to be a designer now, Marc. You're

I. A PHYSICAL SCIENCE

I FORGET THE exact date that I dreamed of Sloppy Joe Tommy, but once the business turned around, I started to think of myself as a Designer. This meant that I needed to do all the things that Designers do. I had a dose of "Ralph Lauren–itis," and I thought I needed to check off the Serious Designer boxes:

- ☑ Join the CFDA.
- ☑ Do a Bryant Park runway show.
- ☐ Travel the world for "creative inspiration."
- ☐ Design a line that's so cutting edge, even your most trusted advisors shudder in curiosity.
- ☐ Loathe yourself.
- ☐ Loathe others.
- ☐ Listen to emo-Euro-trance music that is clearly digitally produced.
- ☐ Buy a glamorous corporate headquarters that's a shrine to your label.

RALPH LAUREN-ITIS

Ralph Lauren is one of the most authentic brands in America. *Ralph Lauren–itis*, however, is when other designers or creators, instead of creating their own authentic brands, are distracted by the pomp, trappings, and style of someone or something else. This causes emulation, inauthenticity, and can result in personal—and professional—failure.

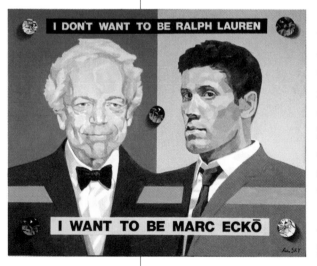

I Don't Want to Be Ralph Lauren, I Want to Be Marc Eckō *by Anton Kandinsky (oil on canvas, 2010)*

Clearly I had some work to do, so I started with the CFDA, or Council of Fashion Designers of America. Why did this group even matter? My theory: a proper designer becomes a member of the CFDA, and once you're a card-carrying member, you have more access. Right? People view you more credibly. So I checked off that box. (And yes, maybe it had to do with a certain amount of acceptance; of external validation. It's so easy to get seduced by this.)

Then it was time for travel. On the heels of that Spike Lee runway show, I traveled to Europe for "creative insight," in order to put my finger on the pulse. After all, I had sucked as much pulse as I could out of the Menlo Park Mall in Jersey. So I jetted to Paris to soak in Colette, hunted locations for early Banksy pieces on the streets of London, and canvassed the trends in Japan, Hong Kong, and Amsterdam.

As 1999 turned toward 2000, I became obsessed with our millennium collection, which I had obtusely titled "Rhetorical Distortion." In a radical departure from my core, I designed clothes that would have been appreciated by Neo from *The Matrix*: black nylon, fitted shirts, muted steel-gray parachute pants. (Trade secret: designers create clothes that they won't wear themselves.) I hired this amazing street-artist-turned-sophisto-painter, Doze Green, and said, "I'm just going to let him go off." To create this new line, I holed up in the dark war room with Doze and the other designers, listening to weepy electronic music like Portishead.

I even started to deconstruct the rhino logo, creating a shirt with the rhino split in two and sewed back together at an angle. It was so meta. One day Seth popped into the war room, saw the fractured logo, thought about it, and gave me a Seth Frown.

"You sure about this?"

"You either *get it* . . . or you don't," I said, ending the discussion.

Seth half nodded, looked at the rest of this steel gray, and then left the studio. He and Marci both knew that I had earned some creative breathing room. Remember the turnaround, right? Our revenue had eclipsed $100 million, I'm in the CFDA, and the Eckō brand was humming. With this veneer of success, it's easy to lose sight of WHAT YOU DO NOT KNOW.

In fact, our brand had so much heat, some guys from the NFL approached us about doing a licensing deal. We didn't approach them; *they approached us*. This was a couple of years before throwback jerseys took off, and they saw that one of our best sellers was a no. 72 Eckō football jersey, so they suggested a partnership.

My reaction?

Meh.

The NFL, really? I saw the NFL, frankly, as kind of lame.

"The NFL!" Seth said to me, excited.

"Dude. Do we really want a bunch of 'cheeseheads' and 'blue giants' wearing our brand and diluting the meaning of our Eckō jersey."

Omahyra Mota, modeling our Millennium Collection. This was her first runway show. The line was called "Rhetorical Distortion."

Why 72? That's the year I was born. Other best-in-class companies said things like "Established in 1954," but how lame would it look if, in 1999, we boasted, "Established in 1993"?

"It's the N. Fucking. F. L!"

"I like the Giants. *I get it*. But it's gotta be a different look," I said.

Suddenly I'm too good for the NFL. I took the meeting, and I flipped through their proposal, bored, not wanting to sully my good brand with such an obviously mainstream platform like the NFL, which was desperately seeking to turn around its licensed apparel business. Besides, Fubu, one of our biggest competitors at the time, had just signed a licensing deal with the NBA,

DJ Roni Size in Physical Science: thirteen years too early

and I didn't want to be perceived as cloning. As a gift, the NFL guys gave me a beautiful hardback book about football, and on the second page, in the introduction, it said, "The NFL: A Physical Science." That phrase stuck in my brain, and later I showed the book to Marci and Seth.

"A physical science," I said.

"Okay . . ." Marci said.

"Who gives a shit?" Seth said.

"A physical science," I said again. "Cool, right?"

They glanced at each other and were probably thinking, *Cooo kooo! Cooo kooo!*

"Instead of doing a licensing deal with the NFL, why don't we do something more interesting?" I said.

"Not following," said Marci.

"We'll make our own label. A new brand. We'll call it '*Phys. Sci.*' [pronounced *Fizz Sy*]. The new name will let us build something active but modern. Once we get it humming, then, maybe, if the NFL is lucky, we'll license the teams and incorporate them."

So we put the NFL on ice. What they wanted was simple and, in retrospect, hit the nail on the head. The rhino + the NFL. It wasn't that deep. And it probably would have worked just fine. But I wouldn't give it up. What I "knew" was somehow more relevant or real, however much it may have just been in my head. "Phys.Sci., that's whassup."

Phys.Sci. would take off and then, *maybe*, I'd let the NFL get a seat at the table.

One of the most frequent (and annoying) questions I hear from Fortune 500-type companies is "How do we connect with the youth? How do we make our brand seem cool?"

The first thing you should know about "youth" is that they would never use the word "youth." More substantively, we need to let go of the idea that teens are somehow so exotic, a different species. Companies try and manufacture or productize a conversation with teens as if they're this "other thing." Forty-year-old brand managers forget that they themselves were once teens.

Perhaps we need to remind ourselves, being a teenager represents everything that's hopeful about the future—but *fucking scary* as well. Parents aspire to relive those years (and they'll also parrot their teenage kids so they can seem "in the know" or "wid'it"); and teens' younger siblings look up to them for their independence, physical strength, and voice. Teens are the heart of the family. It makes sense that agencies want their attention. Just know that you can't capture cool any more than you can capture happiness. She's an elusive mistress . . . and hates to be described by name.

This generation, more than ever before, is deliberate and thoughtful about building their own personal brands. They recognize that cool is *earned*. It's a function of the respect they will pay someone or something for the performance, utility, or evidence of a unique skill or idea. It *only* comes from the inside out. The way that you become "cool" is by building your own personal brand, and by building it authentically. You must create the evidence through your actions to earn the currency of cool. Not to your "end customer" or to your "target demo." So scrap your PowerPoint presentations and think, instead, about fulfilling the deeper promise of your brand.

MEANWHILE, IT WAS time to showcase "Rhetorical Distortion: Spring 2000." First, it was market week and then the big runway show. This would be the line that cemented my status as a designer, not just a guy from Jersey who sold baggy sweatshirts. This would be respected by the critics; this would be blessed by the gatekeepers.

After the first day of market week to the buyers, Seth gave me the report. "We heard back from our top three accounts. They all unanimously hate it."

"They're wrong."

Seth tried to be diplomatic, and that was never his strong suit. "I spoke to them directly. They said they love the brand, and they love you, but these were their exact words: 'This line will be a *shit-show.*'"

"They're wrong."

JUST BECAUSE YOU SAY IT'S SO DOESN'T MAKE IT SO:
Don't Project. Build!!

For that Y2K line, I had lost sight of the HUMILITY component of the CAPACITY FOR CHANGE. I was so in my own head, so indulgent, that I forgot what had gotten me to the party. I had forgotten my core. It's fine to push the envelope, but you need to respect your brand and your customer. I realized later that my desire to dress up the brand and make "better" stuff wasn't a bad one, but instead of Frankenstein-ing or "projecting" this onto Eckō Unlimited, we later would launch a distinct brand that would cater to emerging trends: Marc Eckō Cut & Sew.

"They're our buyers!"

"That's just one opinion," I snapped. "Who else didn't like it?"

No one liked it. Even the cool mom-and-pops scratched their heads. They threw up all over it. You could hear the whispers: *Marc went off the deep end.*

"It's not too late to *fix* it," Seth said.

So I begrudgingly ate my humble pie. We halted the production, I went back to the war room with my designers, and I made some adjustments to bring it more in line with what was working commercially. For the first time in months, I even allowed the help of outside voices. Deb Medley, from merchandising, held up a sweatshirt and said, "This one sold really well. It's a winner. Given that, how would you remix it?" Ahhhh, the art of behaving commercially responsibly.

With those changes, we averted disaster.* There's an old Turkish proverb that says, "It's never too late to turn around if you're going in the wrong direction." Yes, it's good to have a strong point of view, but it can't be removed from some basic realities.

---

*Though I do believe, to this day, that collection had seeds of greatness, but they were never properly fertilized. A part of the innovation biz is to have baited lines out early enough to earn a seat at the table for the feast. (Or is that still the HUBRIS talking?)

FAILURE'S A BITCH:
Can't Live with Her,
Can't Live without Her

When you are successful, you will fail. And let's not fetishize it, deny it, or try to whitewash it. The ghost of failure haunts me every day. And he doesn't look anything like the grim reaper. In fact, it's a she. And she's hot. I envision her to look like Raquel Welch. She whispers in my ear, she wakes me up at night, she joins me on a morning jog. No matter how high I get, this mistress has her arm around me, seductive, teasing, just waiting for her chance.

Because that bitch knows that the forces of gravity are inevitable. What goes up will eventually come down—always—and she'll be there for me when it does, ready to smack the shit out of me. This is inevitable. So rather than avoid her, prepare for her, accept her, acknowledge her presence like an addict does his addiction.

The success-failure yo-yo *is* an addiction, and it follows the usual addiction cycle, and it's not one that can be slaked with nicotine patches or nonalcoholic beer. If you're like me, you're addicted to wanting to win, to be acknowledged for your ideas, your inventions, and the authentic brand you've created. Failure is the necessary hangover of success.

This is why there's no variable for failure in the authenticity formula. No curves. No predictive modeling tells the story properly. And the usual business "failure-to-success" graphs are wrong. Life doesn't work that neatly.

It's a given. It's like carbon or oxygen or water: it's just something that exists in the universe, and you'll be done with failure the day you're done breathing. Accept this as a condition of life, take your next step forward, let the mistress slap you, and then rinse and repeat.

TRUMP

Why does Donald Trump almost never talk about his failures? He's written thirty-seven books, each one about 250 pages, and each page contains about two hundred words, so, roughly, he's written over 1.8 million words, and almost nowhere in these 1.8 million words does he fail. Okay, so he gives a few quips, like "Sometimes by losing a battle, you will find a new way to win the war," but where does he really give us the gruesome details, instead of waxing on about his **W**s? Where are the **L**s diagnosed? Where are the ugly bits that contain the real pearls? Will someone show me? (There must be more to say about Trump Vodka, Trump Airlines, and President Trump. No?)

OH, AND AS for Phys.Sci.? The line bombed. The NFL eventually launched its own throwback jerseys, partnered with brands like Mitchell & Ness Nostalgia Co. and they crushed it. They hauled in millions, and when I couldn't do anything with Phys.Sci., I made the one play I knew instinctively from football: I threw a Hail Mary and managed to successfully license the brand to Target, sans NFL. Remember the Phys.Sci. socks? Don't worry—no one does.

Failure. You need it. You learn from it. And it is inevitable. Essential, really. And any business mogul who tells you differently is full of shit. And if they wax poetic on it, ask them to spill the details.

II. THE JUSTICE LEAGUE OF AMERICA

THE FASHION WORLD was buzzing about a bold new face. This new face came from street wear, had a brash energy, was nontraditional, and had his roots in hip-hop. He went by a single nickname: Puffy.*

He made it look so easy. This was the year he launched Sean John, presenting himself as a suave Mr. Armani who could seduce Anna Wintour with his blend of brashness and sartorial elegance. His fashion shows had the production values of the most high-end Bad Boy Records videos, earning him frequent coverage in media from *Entertainment Tonight* to splashy cover stories in the *New York Post*. The E! Style Network did a live two-hour simulcast of his launch. In a random coincidence, the very morning after his first celebrated runway show, both the Sean John team and the Eckō team were on the same flight, en route to Vegas for the Magic trade show.

I looked at Puffy's team, looked at my team, and I saw the difference between varsity and JV. And the entourage was led by none other than Spike Lee's old lieutenant, Jeff Tweedy (the same guy I had pitched back in the day). Where they glided, we *schlepped*. Tweedy carried barely any luggage, but I had my shabby-ass forty-pound backpack that dug into my shoulders. My team struggled awkwardly with its oversized Samsonites, bursting at the seams with product. Team Sean John had the latest slim mobile phones; I talked into

Who needs the Post *when I had Che?*

*So maybe he didn't go by a *single* nickname. See also: Puff Daddy, P. Diddy, Diddy, Sean Combs, Sean John Combs.

a brick. They sat first class, and I slinked into coach, avoiding eye contact with Tweedy, who showed the *New York Post*—with a photo of a grinning, triumphant Puffy—to his team, saying, "Front page, baby!"

I felt like a fashion wannabee, like a kid who still busted his ass at APSCO, learning color separations and watching cops get blow jobs. In my coach seat, I made a big show of taking out my book, a biography of the Cuban revolutionary Che Guevara, thinking immaturely, *Okay, maybe my team doesn't have matching sweatpants, but I'm a* real *designer, and I'm* deep, *I'm reading about Che.* What!?

There was no rumble between our two teams. There was no beef. I doubt they even noticed us. But this episode deepened my insecurities, this pricked my ego, and this fed my hunger to "play it" like a *real designer.* It was time to check another real designer box: get on the CFDA's board of directors.

I first went to the CFDA meetings with so much enthusiasm. I thought I would rub shoulders with Calvin and Ralph, we would swap stories and discuss best practices, and we'd all work together to improve the industry as a whole. I imagined it like the Justice League of America, where Superman, Batman, Wonder Woman, and all the DC Comics heroes convene in the Hall of Justice to rid the world of bad taste.

Ralph Lauren never showed up. Calvin? A no-show. For most of the meeting, the president of the CFDA, Stan Herman, merely told us about what happened at the last board of directors meeting. I felt like I was in an Amway meeting.

I was hoping to congregate with Wonder Woman, Batman, Calvin, and Ralph. Didn't happen.

The more that Stan, who was and is an awesome guy, talked about the board of directors, the more I realized that we, the *general dues-paying members,* were second-class citizens. (In truth, this wasn't at all the case, as my peers in the room included Michael Kors and John Varvatos—not chopped liver.) One day I couldn't stifle my boredom. I raised my hand and asked, "You've taken our attendance, right?"

"Yes," the custodian said.

"Of the general membership, what percentage of us has attended?"

He looked at his minutes. "Seventy-five percent."

"Okay," I said. "Can I get a recap of the board of directors attendance for the last three meetings?"

Nervous about where this was going, he reluctantly read off some names. I didn't hear Calvin's name, I didn't hear Ralph's name.

"Can I get a recap of the meeting prior to those? Maybe offline, if that's more appropriate?" I made my point. Right in front of the other members, like the problem child at school, I basically disassembled the board with a passive-aggressive game of gotcha. We'd all been coming to this CFDA meeting like Pavlov's dogs and for what?

$$(\; Hubris \;) \;\gg\; (\; Humility \;)$$

"How often do you vote on who's on the board?" I asked.

Some of the other designers gasped. I wasn't trying to shame anyone, but it occurred to me, *Who's this organization built for?* And why were we meeting in Condé Nast, which happened to be the publisher of *Vogue,* which happened to run advertisements for almost every designer in this room? I was just unfolding this origami of conflicted interests.

A few days later, one of the executives of the CFDA reached out to me and suggested that we have lunch. Uh-oh. Time for the slap on the wrist. Before they even served the iced tea, he said to me, "Marc, we'd like to nominate you to the board."

Reflecting on this now, I think the guy was genuinely trying to empower me, to include me, and to add a new, young voice to their governing body. At the time? I thought they were just trying to shut me up, and it gave me a chip on the shoulder.

At twenty-nine years old, I became the youngest member in the history of the CFDA's board.

Box checked.

But did it matter?

III. **BIG**

BETWEEN 2000 AND 2004, it felt like I spent twenty-three hours a day in taxicabs. The company kept growing, kept expanding, kept launching new subbrands, and every new business seemed to need a new office, and these were scattered throughout the city. We opened up Eckō Red, our women's line. Marc Eckō Cut & Sew, a brand focused on a more grown-up aesthetic and business casual. We bought the skate company Zoo York, deploying Marci to head it up and turn it around. We collaborated with 50 Cent on G-Unit, an overnight hit that seemed to grow at 1,000 percent every month. And then, of course, we had Eckō Unlimited (with a new showroom on Broadway and Thirty-seventh) and the early days of *Complex*. Oh, and one more ball to juggle: I spent half my time in California at the game development studio the Collective, focused on Getting Up—my video game published by Atari.

The big console video games are generally all franchises. There is very limited shelf space for new entrants. It's almost impossible to break into the industry as an independent content creator, particularly if your aspirations are to create long-format games for the megaconsoles. Grand Theft Auto, Halo, Call of Duty—you rarely see an original title make a splash, let alone get made. Even rarer? When someone from the nongaming world decides to make an original game. Even *rarer*? When someone from the world of fashion decides to do this. It's never happened.

After I cut my teeth with EA and the Madden Eckō Teams, I started to pitch my idea for Getting Up, featuring fifty graf-legends, including Futura, Cope2, Shepard Fairey (before the world knew him from the Obama "Hope" poster), and art from Banksy (before he became a household name).

At the launch of the game in Times Square. From left to right: RZA, Rakim, me

Trane, our lead character from the game Getting Up

The featured graf-legends of Getting Up. From left to right: Seen, T-Kid, Cope2, Sane Smith, Shepard Fairy (aka Obey), Futura

FASHION SHOWS ARE DEAD:
Don't Compete on Dollars. Compete on Ideas.

Fashion shows are dead. I say that with a fondness for fashion shows. But I also say that with experience on how dysfunctional they can be in delivering on the age-old business goal of "selling more shit."

When you go to fashion design school, you are *taught* to "present your collection." This means that you send model after model down a narrow, well-lit platform, sweating over the taxonomy of who sits in the front row and who sits in the back, spending $$$ to bewitch the all-mighty editorial gatekeepers.

I've spent up to $1 million for fifteen minutes and as little as $50K on fifteen minutes. On average, my fashion shows cost $500K. The process and the system are inherently overindulgent. Yes, of course, they are fun, and, indeed, there's a place in this world for the Karl Lagerfelds to put on a show—and I can respect that. But for the young fashion entrepreneur who's actually trying to launch a commercially responsible business, it's a financial loser. It's bad business. Find a new paradigm, a new medium, a more creative way to reach your audience. Showcasing is good. Theater and romance are

necessary. But don't compete on *dollars*. Compete on *ideas*. Maybe you have to do one or two runway shows to prove your chops—fine, get it off your chest—but then challenge yourself to grow outside the lines.

It's not the most obvious pitch, so to prove the concept, conventional wisdom says that I needed to invest $1M on a prototype. Instead, I hired an animation studio (Psyop in NYC) to effectively produce a 3-D animated storyboard, a sizzle reel—to close the deal and ensure that people got the true spirit of our protagonist, Trane, and the city of New Radius. To Atari's credit, it drank the Kool-Aid and went for it, and I spent several years on the game. (I first pitched the idea in '02, and the game came out in '06. Just like with *Complex*, nothing happens overnight.) Like so much of our business at the time, it was a big bet.

So whatever happened with the game? For a good chunk of my time, I went deep, deep into video game design and production mode. I spent hundreds of hours—hell, maybe thousands—in idea creation, biz-devving, game development, and marketing. We gambled with both cash and credibility. I even made some overly sensitive comments to the media venting my frustrations with the gaming industry (the model *is* broken, but that's a different book), but when the game finally launched, at the end of the PS2 lifecycle—where sales for new titles were at their weakest—we sold over eight hundred thousand units. This spells $30 million in revenue, and the game became a cult classic. Not too shabby for a T-shirt-peddling gaming outsider.

G ROWTH MEANS CHANGE. The CAPACITY FOR CHANGE can have a positive or negative effect on the quotient of your authenticity. And when change happens, it will occur at both a business level and an emotional level. As our company started to get more fractured, I started to get more unfocused. Or, more accurately, I was hyperfocused on many things at the same time. The huge growth that we were going through shielded me from having to look at my emotional state.

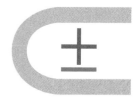

In the meantime, we kept trying to sell ads for *Complex*, and we kept getting shot down. It was never the easiest sell: *fashion designer asks other fashion labels to buy ads in competitor's publication.* We got a whole bucket of "no's." Some people understood the mag, and others didn't. An exec for one very well-known label, for instance, looked at our cover with Kanye West on it, frowned, and said, "Who's *Con-Eee West*?" (Which label was this? The exec happens to be the child of a famous designer of a brand that Kanye himself has publically lauded.) Eventually *Complex* grew, and eventually many of these nos turned to yeses. Persistence: you have to have it.

The time flashed by in a blink. Our higher revenue meant that we could get a massive line of credit, and that only made us want to go bigger, bigger, bigger. "Manifest destiny. We need our own retail stores," Seth said to me one day.

I was interested. I thought about how, years ago, I had played basketball in the driveway with my friend Cale Brock, and he dreamed about a duet with Mary J. Blige, and I dreamed of my own retail stores. *If you dream it, you will be it.* The law of attraction at work. Maybe *The Secret* works after all? Now it could happen. Even so, that sounded expensive, and I was still scarred by the pre–Alan Finkelman credit crisis. "Can we afford that?"

"We'll make it work," Seth assured me, eyes aglow. "But we have to put the flag in the ground. We need an anchor. Times Square?" This became Seth's crusade: a Times Square flagship store. He envisioned a thirty-thousand-square-foot monster that would anchor us in Midtown Manhattan, shining a beacon on the Eckō brand for all the world to see. I felt like my whole life was

Mock-up of our flagship store in Times Square. Big. Expensive.

VALUATION:
Size Matters

n. **val-u-a-tion**: The act of estimating or judging the nature or value of something or someone.

"Valuation" was one of those foreign words that Seth used when we first met in my garage. In a nutshell, it's putting a price tag on the company. There are gobs of different ways to measure a company's worth, and an I-bank (investment bank) churns through spreadsheet after spreadsheet to count up assets, liabilities, revenue streams, legal issues, comparables, and hundreds of other issues that will put you to sleep.

One way to do a valuation—on the quick-and-dirty side—is to take your gross revenue times the industry standard "multiple of trading." What's a multiple? It's an expression of how much comparable peer companies typically fetch on the market. So if the apparel industry has a multiple of 5x, that would mean that a company with $10 million in gross revenue, say, has a value in the neighborhood of $50 million. That's the starting point, and then, during the negotiation, other factors (leverage, competing offers, liabilities, and so on) come into play.

You know who else cares about valuation? Banks. When you have a higher valuation, banks will be more likely to extend you a bigger line of credit.

under construction. On top of new retail stores and the Times Square flagship, I was building a new home for my family in Somerset County, New Jersey.

These types of big-boy transactions—new buildings, new partnerships, new brands—compelled us to bring in an investment bank to do a proper "valuation" on our business and trademarks.

OUR FIRST REAL suitor was Liz Claiborne. At the time, in 2002, we had revenue of around $100 million, and judging by other industry transactions, we thought we could get as high as 3.5x that revenue in a deal. So a $350 million sale seemed like a real possibility—real enough to take a dinner with its CEO at the time, Paul Charron.

We met at a kosher restaurant, like always, so that Seth wouldn't have to eat out of a paper bag. Paul, who's right out of central casting for gray-haired, successful white businessman, showed up in a power suit; I rolled up in jeans. The waitress took our drink orders.

"Just some still water," Paul said, all business.

The CFDA board always viewed me as an outsider. A few years later, I challenged the board to create a new award that would recognize the sport and street design movement, from giants like Nike to undeniably influential brands like Supreme. I asked, what is "fashion" and who defines "what is in and out of bounds" of that definition? Why must the gatekeepers recognize only "high fashion"? Why not acknowledge these very real cultural forces, like James Jebbia and Supreme, and Tinker Hatfield for Nike? All of them are massive influencers on fashion, serving as catalysts who provoke traditional fashion houses to contemplate, and even mimic, their aesthetics. Somehow when Prada does a running shoe that's clearly derivative of Nike, it's deemed "fashion design," but when DC shoes does it, it's "industrial design." How does this make sense? I talked over the issue with Diane von Furstenberg, who loved the concept, and she suggested that I host a luncheon to present the idea.

As fate would have it, I hosted this meeting on October 6, 2008, which, coincidentally, was the first day that the stock markets were open after Congress passed the $700 billion TARP rescue plan for the banks. The CNNs and CNBCs of the world called it "Black Monday II," as panic on the Dow (an 800-point midday drop) triggered the dominos of hysteria that would haunt the economy. It was fitting. While I tried to impress them with a four-course lunch and a slick presentation, they pounded their BlackBerrys and counted their evaporating millions. At the end of the meeting, they said they loved the idea and would "form a committee" to look into it. *A committee.* So, of course, it never happened.

The important takeaway? The CAPACITY FOR CHANGE is a measure that's driven *internally.* It's not a measure of your ability to

change others. You—and only you—can control your HUMILITY, HUBRIS, WHAT YOU KNOW, and WHAT YOU DO NOT KNOW. But you can't assert those variables on anyone else.

The point is not that the CFDA is bad, because it's not. But *my* personal authentic brand, at times,

zigs and zags away from what's accepted by the gatekeepers. The solution isn't to change the gatekeepers but to play on your home turf. Instead of trying to *change* the system, I worked *outside* the system to *create* my own system by growing *Complex* as the authoritative voice on

fashion, as *we* see it. Through *Complex* (and its more than seven hundred million page views a month), we can talk directly to the end consumer, who's the only goalkeeper that matters.

Nas and Dominic Chianese (Junior from The Sopranos) *on the debut cover of* Complex *in 2002. Rosario Dawson was on the other side.*

"Mojitos!" I said. Mojitos were all the rage in 2002. "Have you tried the mojitos, Paul?"

"Just still water, thanks."

Paul buttered us up with tales of glory from Lucky Brand, which had been acquired by Liz in '99. It was a good story. The founders of Lucky, Gene Montesano and Barry Perlman, had made a cash bonanza when they sold the company to Liz, and then, even after the sale, the two were still given carte blanche to run Lucky "independently," with more financial incentives if they beat their plans.

"You guys could be the next Lucky." Paul sipped his still water. "You'll be the next Gene and Barry. And you'll still have creative control."

I slurped down the last of my mojito and waved over the waitress for another. "Have you seen the latest issue of *Complex*?"

Paul made a face like something smelled bad. "About *Complex*. Well, I feel you will need to forget about that for a while."

"*Forget* about it?" I said, laughing.

"Ice it."

"What about Getting Up?" I asked.

"Getting what?" Paul said, not quite using air quotes, but laughing a bit to himself. "No time for distractions now."

"And Zoo York?" Seth asked.

"Look. We want Eckō Unlimited. We want your core business, and we want you guys, the executive team, *focused*. Anything else, we can't justify in the deal."

Even before they served the entrée, I knew the deal wasn't going to happen. Seth, Marci, and I later said, "Fuck it. We don't need Liz Claiborne, we can get bigger on our own. We can expand our line of credit. We can grow *Complex*, Getting Up, Zoo York, G-Unit, Cut & Sew, and Eckō Red all on our own terms."

Here's the thing about banks: they don't really care about profits. They care that you're *profitable*, but they don't care if your margins are 10 percent or 20 percent or 50 percent. They just want you solvent. If the collateral is good enough—like, say, pledging ownership of your valuable Rhino trademarks in the event of default—you're good. I don't mean to oversimplify, because no doubt you *are* more attractive if your revenues are strong and growing. But the calculus that feeds your valuation, roughly speaking, is what helps kick up a big line of credit (at least, in the pre-2008 days). This gives a lot of entrepreneurs a false sense of success. The day you raise money is not a day that merits popping the champagne. This is not a moment of WHAT YOU DO; it's just another extension of WHAT YOU SAY.

So that's what we did: we continued to grow. We hired Rich Antoniello to oversee the *Complex* team, and under his leadership we launched the first issue in 2002, pairing the rap artist Nas on the cover with Uncle Junior from *The Sopranos*. (This goes back to my early paintings at Rutgers; waxing on race and what was black or white.) We opened the retail stores, and while they weren't lighting the world on fire, they proved it could be a viable business, and it made Seth salivate over Times Square. And thanks to Marci at the helm, Zoo York's sales rocketed from $5 million on its way to $45 million.

Zoo York came with a price: it meant that we saw less of Marci, and this meant, in turn, that we had less of our Governance. In the turnaround phase, after Finkelman's lifeline, we had the perfect balance of Governance (Marci), Brute Force (Seth), and Swagger (me). This is a stable foundation—like a delta, or a triangle—for your brand.

Now that delta started to wobble.

Seth, the Brute Force, had such a high capacity for pain and was willing to risk anything, so he wanted to belt home runs with *massive* projects. He was hell-bent on Times Square.

"I don't get it," Marci said. "The lease is two million dollars a year. It's going to take *five* years to open the store. It doesn't make sense."

"What doesn't make sense is how you don't see it!" Seth said intently. "Billabong just opened a store in Times Square, and they're killing it."

"Billabong had only six thousand square feet; you want thirty thousand."

"It's a *statement*, Marci. It's the right theater. It's the right perception."

The titanic store appealed to my narcissism, so I wasn't hard to convince. Marci was harder. She never fully embraced the idea, and it occasionally brought her to tears. She just didn't understand how we could justify the cost. (And as usual, she would prove to be right.)

Another Seth whammy: a gigantic new corporate headquarters. Seth had found a place on Twenty-third Street. Not really a place but more like a palace—all three hundred thousand square feet of it.

The old Stern's department store. Seth took me through a tour of the building, telling me, "You know they shot the movie *Big* here. Remember the toy company he worked for? This was the hallway!" He pointed down the long executive hallways.

Later I learned that the executive hallway was the same red hallway where, in the movie, Tom Hanks had his office. And it's perfect that the movie was *Big*—we were all about Big. "This looks expensive," I said.

In a full-throated expression of brute force, Seth just steamrolled ahead. "Do you know how much deal flow we're going to get from being in this building?" he said. "It's going to be like a self-fulfilling prophecy." I believed it.

I used to tell my employees, "Buy an expensive watch you can't really afford. This will make you hungry to grow into it, and soon you'll be able to afford five more just like it." (I didn't know it at the time, but I was channeling the theories of *The Secret*: thanks to the universe's law of attraction, if you dream big, you will become big.)

This new building was that watch on steroids; it was *The Secret* on steroids. Looking back, we should have noticed some early signs of trouble. Seth and I each took corner offices on the second floor, and we put our design team on the third and fourth floors. I was no longer in the trenches with my designers; suddenly I became an "executive."

We unintentionally reinforced this cultural gap, which started to feed my ego. For years I signed my emails with my initials, +*ME*. "We need to start calling you 'M.E.,'" Seth told me.

"That's wack," I said.

"No, it's badass," he insisted. In meetings with our employees, he'd say things like, "Okay, did you run that by M.E.?" or "Hey, M.E., did you need anything?" Proper Kabuki theater.

The new building, and the seductive new Times Square flagship were not something we could put on a credit card. This meant that we needed a giant infusion of cash. There are three ways to quickly get a mountain of cash: (1) more debt, (2) a sale, or (3) dealing hard drugs.

I don't think Seth was down for going all *Breaking Bad* and cooking meth, and, ideally, we didn't want more debt, so that meant we needed a sale. Since the Liz Claiborne possibility, we had flirted with potential deals, but it was just that: *flirting*. We had no intention of giving it up. It was a high-stakes game of speed dating, but speed dating is easy when you know you're never going to lift the skirt.

It gave us a false sense of achievement. Yes, the CEO of Liz Claiborne was meeting with me, but he was meeting with *everyone*. Yes, we were a potential "deal," but every day there are hundreds of *"potential deals."* You're just another deal in the cosmic stew of deals. Your relevance is about as relevant as the Earth is to the billions and billions of stars in the sky. But I saw myself as the *special star*.

Quickly we became hungry for a sale. Or at least we thought we did—we didn't know any better. When it came to changing from a lean, small business to a global corporation, from sitting on folding chairs to sitting on custom-made furniture, What We Know was dramatically inferior to What We Do Not Know, and so bigger meant better, right?

And then I got the call.

"You've built something that's real," Tommy Hilfiger said to me on the phone. "I want to congratulate you."

"Thanks."

"Your business represents a brand of growth that I think is important," he said. "Back in the day, your scene emerged and stole our thunder when Tommy Jeans was maturing."

$$\left(\begin{matrix} \textit{What you} \\ \textit{Know} \end{matrix} \right) <<< \left(\begin{matrix} \textit{What you} \\ \textit{DO NOT} \\ \textit{Know} \end{matrix} \right)$$

We had to take this call seriously. We had such big dreams: the store in Times Square, our new corporate headquarters, *Complex*, and a line of new retail stores that we wanted to own. We wanted to do all of that. The Hilfiger deal was a way to make it happen; it was the universe telling us, *Yes, the law of Attraction is real and has answered your prayers.*

We called in the investment bank that helped us during the Liz deal, and like a strike force, they stormed our offices to crunch the numbers and do a valuation. We felt confident. We'd already flirted with a $350 million offer, so we felt ready to run with the big boys.

After that first phone call, Seth worked with the president of Hilfiger, Dave Dyer, to see if the idea had legs, and it did. Tommy gave Marci, Seth, and me a tour through his showrooms. Tommy had his own private parking garage, his own private elevator, and his own private everything.

As we emerged into the showroom, I thought about my own showroom that I was trying to create for Cut & Sew: a meager three thousand square feet. I was so envious. His showroom wasn't a *room* but an entire multifloor complex, a retail palace with a children's floor, a women's floor, a fragrance floor—everything bespoke and oozing in proper men's fashion.

"Fucking crazy!" Seth whispered to me as Tommy led us through the tour.

"Shhh!" I said.

"This is why we need our own space," Seth said. "Look at the theater of it all." The perception. It always came back to perception. *If we dream it, we will be it.*

Tommy, Seth, and I had dinner—at a kosher restaurant, like always—in a private room, because Tommy was worried about being recognized. At the time, I thought this was vain, but now I realize that since Hilfiger is a publicly traded company, he didn't want any speculation about a deal.

The waiter came to take our orders. Tommy didn't order Sloppy Joes or milk, and he didn't have any facial hair or talk like the Dude from *The Big Lebowski. Real Tommy* was very different from *Dream Tommy*. A nice enough guy, but he kept saying things like, "Eckō's kind of like Rocawear, or Sean John: cool street-wear brands, but that genre needs to evolve."

"Fair enough. But how so?" I said, a little defensive.

"If it doesn't evolve, you'll never be like a Tommy Hilfiger, or a Hermès, or a Chanel."

Maybe I imagined it, but I smelled a whiff of classism. Who is he to judge? And should he really be putting himself in the company of a Hermès or a Chanel? He wasn't those things. Yes, I wanted to grow as a designer, but I wanted to grow into my own thing, and I knew that never, ever in my life would I say the phrase "like an Eckō, or a Hermès, or a Chanel."

I always believe that your brand is guilty by association. So it didn't bother me when he connected the dots to Sean John and Rocawear, but show me the department store that sells Tommy next to Chanel or Hermès.

Still, we needed this deal, or we needed another one like it. A few days after the dinner, just as I thought that we were nearing the solid terms of a LOA (letter of agreement), Seth grabbed my arm and said, "Pack your bags. We're going to Hong Kong."

IV. GENERATIONAL WEALTH (HUBRIS)

HONG KONG HELD another potential suitor. A Chinese exporting company, Li & Fung, had been a manufacturing partner of ours for years. And a great and generous partner at that. Li & Fung was a blue-chip company, worth billions, and it emerged as a real option. In many ways, this play made more sense than Tommy, as it would be about vertical integration: we'd be owned and operated by a company that did every facet of the ecosystem, except sales and marketing.

More important, Li & Fung could give us leverage. Classic Negotiating 101, right?

If Marci had been in the room, she might have said something like, "Shouldn't we stay focused on the deal in front of us? Shouldn't we just negotiate with Hilfiger in good faith? Don't all pigs get slaughtered?"

But Marci wasn't in the room. The Ghost of Reason was instead using her operations brilliance on Zoo York and leaving the children—Brute Force and Swagger—alone without any adult supervision.

Before leaving for Hong Kong, our number twos had already done the preliminaries with their number twos. We had swapped docs, and we knew the deal had legs. The first several Hong Kong meetings went well. They liked us. The real test was a final meeting with one of the richest men I'd ever met: Victor Fung, the billionaire co-owner of Li & Fung. I had met plenty of millionaires before, but this was my first time with a multibillionaire, a *multiple B*. Someone so rich that even trying to comprehend or calculate his assets makes you light-headed. At his

FIVE TIPS TO PRESERVE YOUR AUTHENTICITY WHILE CONTEMPLATING THE SALE OF YOUR BUSINESS

When your brand gets large enough, you will have suitors who will want to buy. Here's how to handle those meetings:

1. Have Sex with the Lights On

One reason that my marriage works so well—Allison, I hope you don't mind me sharing this—is that it doesn't matter if it's dark, if it's bright, if it's two o'clock in the morning or two o'clock in the afternoon, it's go time. When you have the right partner, you don't need the dark, and you don't need to be drunk. The same goes for businesses. When you first meet someone with a different company culture, it's tempting to *not show your true self*, maybe tweaking your presentation (what you wear), the way you communicate (suddenly becoming more formal), or changing your overall cultural vibe. Just be yourself. If you're meeting with a suit-wearing exec from BFC (Big Fucking Company), don't pretend that you're blue blood when you are not. Yes, be respectful, but you shouldn't change how you present your personal brand. If you and BFC are going to go into bed together, it's better to know early—*with the lights on*—if you still want to see each other naked.

2. Sleep

You need it for your mental health. Don't take sleep for granted; work at it like you would an exercise regimen. And if you aren't sleeping, talk to a professional—because you are not alone in twisting and turning. Sleep is crucial, so don't be a hero and bottle up shit that keeps you awake. Not kosher.

3. Design an Exit

If you've built and designed your home, it's your responsibility to have contemplated the backdoor exit, or the fire escape, or the double-swing glass doors that open to the veranda. What does that back door look like? Where does it take you in event of a fire, a flood, a sand storm, or maybe converting that back door into a new extension of the house? Even if you don't *want* to exit, having this back door will give you confidence when you meet with potential suitors. It's irresponsible to you, your loved ones, guests, and neighbors to build a house with only one way in and one way out.

4. Be Unemotional

Try to separate the emotions from what's best for you and your brand. You will feel anxious, threatened, and saddened even at the very *idea* of selling your business.

5. You Are the Goose, Not the Egg

A lot of entrepreneurs are worried that they have the ingredients to the secret sauce, or a "golden egg," and that if they meet with anyone to discuss a partnership or a sale, they'll somehow jeopardize their trade secrets. Unless you're an inventor wunderkind whose ass is sitting on some pharmaceutical cure, you, as the *idea creator*, are more important than the idea itself. Yes, there are golden eggs, but what matters isn't the egg itself, it's the goose. At this point in your brand's development, your secrets aren't as valuable as you. When you have your own personal brand, this is what the BFCs are after. So when I met with suitors like Hilfiger and Liz, I knew that I had what they didn't, wouldn't, couldn't have; I had the personal brand of Marc Eckō, and that's what they coveted. I didn't have any design schematics, I didn't have any magical tonic for how to build clothing. I had me, my voice, my brand.

suggestion, we met in a New York–style deli, which meant that I had traveled eight thousand miles to eat the same pastrami you get in Lakewood.

The billionaire wore a white short-sleeve button-down shirt tucked into unassuming pleated trousers, unassuming black shoes, and the most unassuming $10 digital wristwatch. I remember staring at that watch, utterly baffled. (Clearly, the dude had never heard of the "buy an expensive watch" theory, or *The Secret*.)

"So tell me about yourself," Victor Fung said, smiling.

He asked about my commute, my family, and my home. We had an incredibly grounded, bizarrely down-to-earth conversation. This man could have name-dropped, he could have bowled me over with stories of the industries he's conquered, he could have waxed on about his triumphs—this is what a Donald Trump would have done. When the talk rolled around to business, we reviewed the P&L, talked tactics, and walked through the plan. Smooth sailing.

Then he asked me one final question, and it's a question that, ever since, has been stuck in my head. It's a question that I ask whenever I consider a partnership, think about an acquisition, or make an investment. He asked, "But how will you mainstream yourself?"

I was completely thrown for a loop. How do we *mainstream* ourselves? Weren't we already mainstream? The old graffiti artists from 432F called me a sellout—weren't we as mainstream as they came? Hip-hop had been bleeding into the mainstream since the nineties; he didn't see that?

"Do you know Eminem?" I asked him.

He looked confused, as if I'd asked him "Do you know Star Sector 6 from the Zoltan system?" Clearly, he had never heard of Eminem.

"Mainstream? Eminem is the biggest thing in America right now," I said, and we changed the subject.

He smiled, polite as always, and we left the lunch on good terms. That night, in the piano bar of a Shangri-La high-rise hotel, as a lounge singer crooned Celine Dion, Seth and I looked out the windows at the Hong Kong skyline, soaked in the glittering lights, and raised our glasses.

"To generational wealth," I toasted.

"To generational wealth."

"I love that Victor Fung guy," I said.

"He's so unassuming."

"A Chinese Warren Buffett." I drank more champagne.

"Did you see his watch? I loved it. Ten bucks, tops."

"No way." Seth laughed. "They sell those in gumball machines for twenty-five cents."

We went to bed drunk and dizzy with ambition, but the next day, after we packed our bags and were on the way to the airport, Seth got a phone call, spoke for a few minutes, and then hung up the phone.

He turned to me. "The deal's not happening. He likes us a lot but doesn't see how we intend to mainstream the business around the world."

"Huh?"

"Marc, he doesn't know who Eminem is," Seth explained. "He thought you were talking about chocolate—about M&M's."

"Eminem?" I said. "He just didn't get us."

Here's what I didn't realize: Victor Fung wanted to know, tactically, how we would broaden our appeal. *Not* how we intended to cross over in the way that the rapper EPMD talked about on his 1992 hit "Crossover."

He wanted to really understand the storytelling in our PR strategy. The blocking. The tackling. He didn't want to hear about some "birthright" or "manifest destiny" because I was the kid that came from my garage. That was a feat, indeed—but it didn't express the next big move. When my mom's in a store and she sees a pony logo on a shirt, she recognizes that as Polo. When she sees the small Tommy flag, she knows that's Tommy Hilfiger. How do we get there? How does our brand play in China? How does the rhino become instantly recognizable, like Kleenex or Coke? That's what Victor Fung wanted to know, and we couldn't give him an answer.

"There's more bad news," Seth said.

"Yeah?"

"We also lost the Tommy deal."

What? I started to freak out. That was impossible. Right before we left for Asia, they were hot and heavy for us.

"Just fucking with you!" Seth grinned. "See? It's not all bad. You were about to be all depressed if Tommy fell through. Relax."

Okay. Game on. We spent the entire flight back from Hong Kong thinking about our earn out, counting our invisible stacks of millions—soon to be billions?—and wondering whether it would take two, four, or six years for us to become so big that we would buy out Tommy.

Back in New York, we finally nailed down the terms with Dave Dyer. Maybe our strategy using Li & Fung worked, as Hilfiger's terms were good—almost too good. With the earn out, the deal would be north of $500 million. This would make us instantly wealthy in a way that we had never dared contemplate.

Dave invited us onto his yacht. He poured us champagne, served us sesame-encrusted seared tuna, and showed us the letter of intent. On that yacht, I felt like king-of-the-world DiCaprio. Seth and I bullshitted about how we'd spend the money—maybe form a new company called B.O.T. for "Buy Out Tommy." There was only one thing left: for Dyer to get it approved by the board of directors, which he assured us would be strictly ceremonial.

"The board just wants to meet you," Dyer said. *Piece of cake.*

I walked into that meeting with my swagger at a 9.5. The board wasn't in some corporate cathedral like you see in *Wall Street*—the settings of high-stakes finance are, more often than not, more mundane than you see in the movies—but just a regular conference room, oval table, and six members of the board.

One of them, a woman with braces, asked me the only question that really seemed to concern them. "No offense," she began, "but we've seen this in business before; when founders become flush with cash, they lose their hunger. So to be blunt, when you get rich, how will you keep your hunger? How will we know you aren't done?"

No offense? One thing I've learned in life: when people start a sentence with "No offense," the next thing they say will offend you. How was this her business? How were my personal finances her business? I remember thinking, *Don't ask about my religion, don't ask who I'm screwing, and don't ask about my bank account.*

WHAT'S YOUR MAIN? STREAM?

What is mainstream?

By definition, it breaks into:

(a) Main—the "most important" or "most recognized."

(b) Stream—trend, course, or path.

It's fashionable to loathe the mainstream, but most people mistake the idea of mainstream as being familiar, safe, and unthreatening to the masses. Therefore, they resent it, deeming it artistically and aesthetically inferior.

Instead of pontificating on what is or is not mainstream, take a mirror, and ask yourself: What is your Main? What is your Stream?

Do you really loathe the mainstream, or are you scared that *creating* your own stream can be treacherous work? Isn't the creation of a stream the work of the divine? Making your own stream with the knife-edged rocks, the meandering currents, the savage roots. Oh my! Messy shit, right?

People get caught up in the anxiety of it all. They worry about building something that declares, "I am most important" or "I am 'main.'" Or being daring enough to say that their efforts can define the stream, the trend, the course. I say: don't overthink it. *Start by being the water.*

As we left the meeting, I turned to Seth and said, "I don't think this is happening."

And it didn't. The board members decided that the deal was "too cash rich," and they were probably right. Not because we would have lost our hunger but because it really could have bankrupted them—or certainly have had the Street vomit on their stock for having authorized the deal. Maybe we had bid up too high? What we saw as assets—the new Times Square flagship, the new offices, the burgeoning retail stores—they saw as baggage. They made a cold business decision.

"Fuck 'em," Seth said.

"Fuck 'em," I agreed.

"Don't need 'em. You know how we grow Marc Eckō Enterprises?" Seth didn't wait for me to answer. "We need to grow Marc Eckō, the man."

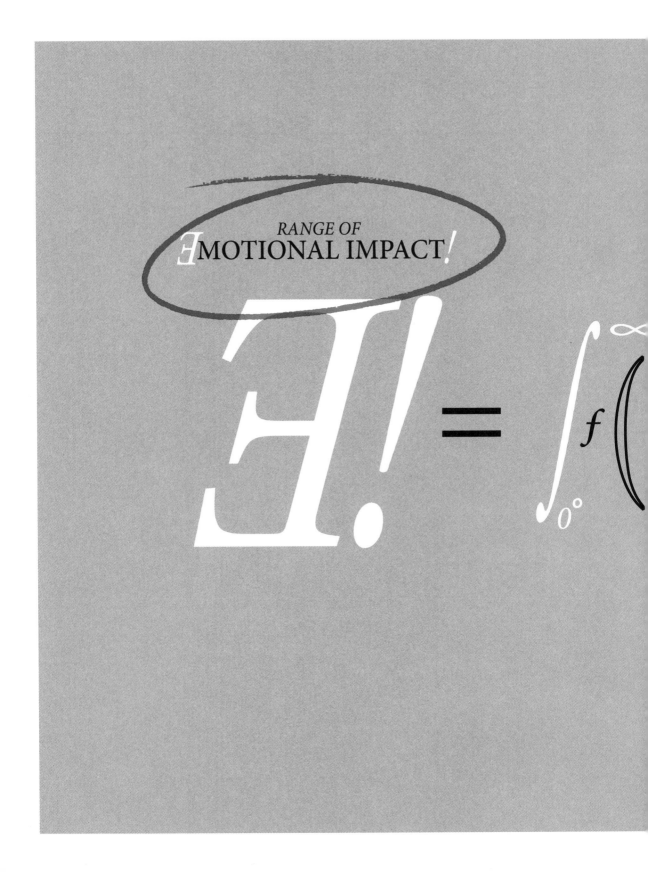

$$\left(\frac{\text{"How you make people FEEL."}}{\text{"What you MAKE."}} \right) dx$$

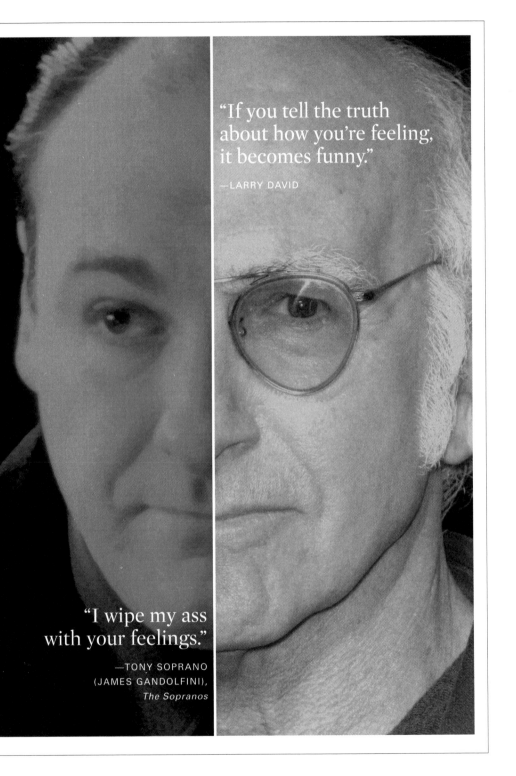

"If you tell the truth about how you're feeling, it becomes funny."

—LARRY DAVID

"I wipe my ass with your feelings."

—TONY SOPRANO (JAMES GANDOLFINI), *The Sopranos*

CHAPTER 8

EMOTIONAL

IMPACT

EMOTIONAL IMPACT: *In any business, at the most basic level, you're making stuff. But more important than what you make—whether it's a product or a service, physical or digital—is how that stuff makes people feel. Authentic brands seek to render an* EMOTIONAL IMPACT *(Ǝ!). This impact is measured not only in the force but also the range, or the spectrum, that it can travel.*

Think about your favorite music when you were in high school. Remember the best concert you attended? Whether it was a small hip-hop venue, a death metal show, or a stadium of fifty thousand rock fans, what the artist cared about wasn't the lyrics or his pitch, but the crowd swaying their lighters (or lighter app on their phones) back and forth, or maybe pumping their fists in unison. Artists don't make stuff. *They set out to make an* EMOTIONAL IMPACT *(Ǝ!), and the best brands do the same thing.*

I'll go even further: as a brand, caring about EMOTIONAL IMPACT *(Ǝ!) is your duty. This isn't always easy, but it's something you must contemplate. What are you making people feel? This sounds impossible, but it's not. Just look at McDonald's. Its "secret sauce" isn't at all secret: it's just catsup, mayonnaise, and relish. Actually, here's the recipe in full, courtesy of a seven-second Google search and About.com:*

¼ **cup salad dressing (like Miracle Whip)**

¼ **cup mayonnaise**

3 **tbsp French salad dressing**

½ **tbsp sweet pickle relish**

1 ½ **tbsp dill pickle relish**

1 **tsp sugar**

1 **tsp dried, minced onion**

1 **tsp white vinegar**

1 **tsp ketchup**

⅛ **tsp salt**

That's it. So, clearly, it's not what *McDonald's makes. It's how the fast-food chain's brand makes people feel. All* Super Size Me *jokes aside, it's the warm comfort of those Golden Arches; the somehow-not-too-creepy face of Ronald McDonald.*

But there's a flip side to EMOTIONAL IMPACT (포!).

In this journey of brand creation, you need to be mindful of not just the EMOTIONAL IMPACT (포!) to your audience, customers, or end users but also to your own EMOTIONAL IMPACT (포!). Yes, you are a brand, but no, you are not a factory. And in the full-contact sport of entrepreneurship, you will get dirty, bloody, angry, and depressed. It's silly to pretend that's not the case.

When you grow your own personal brand—the brand that's from your SKIN TO THE WORLD—if you're not careful, if you focus too much on checking the boxes, you can injure the brand that's from your GUTS TO THE SKIN.

When you leverage your brand to make people feel, it needs to come organically.

You can't just slap on a glossy brand Band-Aid to make it all better. You don't put a Superman Band-Aid on a sucking chest wound. This needs to be part of your brand's DNA. It's not something you can fake. It's not something you can parrot.

And if you try to fake it? If you distort your brand's reality to become something else? In the game of perception versus reality, it's easy to confuse the two in your own head. But in the end, reality is reality.

This has consequences.

I. MARC ECKŌ 2010

I N 2005, AFTER the Hilfiger deal buckled, and after we decided to go bigger on our own—more retail stores, more expansion—we knew that we had a branding problem. As Seth put it tactfully, "No one knows who the fuck Marc Eckō is."

We proved this with a video called *Who's Marc Eckō?* One of our marketing execs, Raphie Aronowitz, put together four head shots of Eckō employees who might or might not be Marc Eckō.

The four photos:

1. Me (chubby, wearing a Yankees hat)
2. Raphie (handsome, svelte)
3. A droopy-eyed, shaved-headed hipster named Matt
4. Coltrane Curtis (black guy with dreadlocks)

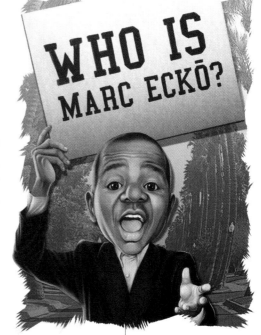

We pasted these photos on a huge poster board, and we asked actor Gary Coleman (rest in peace) to carry it around and help with the experiment. Cameras followed Gary Coleman walking into Los Angeles stores that sold Eckō product, and he asked people to look at the poster and guess "Who's Marc Eckō?" Gary quizzed random people off the street, customers buying Eckō clothes, store employees, and even people dipped head to ankles in Eckō apparel.

Only a handful of people got it right: the real "Eckō heads." Just about everyone else picked Coltrane, the black guy with dreads.

This had to be fixed. Fans of the product had clearly created their own history of where the brand came from, and we were missing a big opportunity to plug the man actually behind the rhino—me—into that history. I looked around the industry and thought about the great designers, like Calvin, Ralph, Tommy.

With these guys, the man himself comes out from behind the curtain. It's Fashion Designer 101. In the old days, this wasn't as crucial, because we had the rhino, and the rhino *did* have name recognition. But now we wanted to launch new brands outside the rhino's umbrella—Marc Eckō's Getting Up, Marc Eckō's *Complex*, Marc Eckō's Cut & Sew—so it'd be helpful if people actually knew who Marc Eckō was, right?

"We need to get you out there," Seth urged me.

"Out where?"

"*Everywhere*. You need to be on *Oprah*! You need to be seen at parties. You need to be seen."

"I dunno, man, I'm not the going-out type—"

"You are now. This needs to be your full-time job." Seth looked me up and down. He took stock of my appearance, judging, processing, thinking, and slowly shook his head. "But you're a fucking fat-ass."

"Thanks, dude."

"I'm serious. You look ridiculous. What size are those jeans? A forty-two waist? Fifty? If we're going to invest in making you presentable, take some fucking pride in yourself."

"Good talk." I thought that was the end of it, but he barreled ahead.

"Look at you. You walk in here with a Tabasco stain on your shirt." He dabbed the stain. "C'mon, man, you're a fucking mess."

He was right. I was fat. (And it was Tabasco.) I've always been up and down with my weight, and at the time, I weighed a deuce . . . a deuce and a half . . . actually 255. Seth kept needling me, and I kept ignoring him, but soon I would be defeated by, of all things, a waterslide. Marci and I flew out the entire family to the Bahamas, bringing our parents, nieces, nephews, and in-laws to the Atlantis resort.

Atlantis has a water park, and I took my nine-year-old niece on one of the waterslides. She sat on my lap as we slid down the tube, and I used my arms to push us around the corners. At one point in the slide, you get to this drop where they scare you; you get stuck, and then the water gushes down the slide and pushes you down.

So we get stuck in the slide for a second, the water comes—and we didn't budge.

"What's wrong?" my niece asked me.

"Nothing, baby, we're fine."

The water came again to flush us, and we still didn't budge. I'm too fat.

The water came a third time. Still nothing.

So I used my arms to push off the sides of the tube, fighting panic, pushing, pushing.

"Are you okay?"

"*Yes!* We're fine!" I kept pushing, pushing, pushing, and then *pop!* My left shoulder dislocated out of its socket.

We finally slid down the slide, and then, in the Atlantis medical center, I accepted that Seth was right. It wasn't even about looks or vanity; it was about health and quality of life.

Besides, since my new job was to get in the public eye, if I weighed 255, how could I be credible with a renewed focus on how I could "make people feel" when I felt like shit myself?

It was time to get serious.

I HIRED A trainer. I ordered calorie-customized food: meals came to my office in ziplock heated bags, and I tracked every calorie. I counted everything. I knew that if I was going out partying, then I couldn't eat all day. My calories would be whiskey. I strapped thirty-pound weighted vests to my chest and ran five miles. I also seized more control over my diet. As anyone with weight idiosyncrasies knows, so much of how you eat has to do with how you deal with emotions. When I was an awkward kid with little control over my emotions, I chubbed up. Now, I became more self-aware, took control, got in shape.

Still, at a gut level, I resisted the whole "become a celebrity" angle. *I'm an artist, a designer, a creator—I'm not a disposable celebrity!* Seth kept pushing it, though, and one day he slapped a PowerPoint presentation on my desk. "Read this."

The document was called "Marc Eckō in 2010." He and the marketing team listed all the objectives that he wanted Marc Eckō, the person, to accomplish by the year 2010. This manifesto was intended to create the momentum for a self-fulfilling prophecy, with my own personal fame serving as a halo for the

The M.E. Diet

Nutrition Facts	
Calories	78
Protein	0g
Carbohydrate	0%
Total Fat	0%
Dietary Fiber	0%
Alcohol	11.1%

35mL

brand. It was another (unintentional) version of *The Secret*: *If you dream it, you will be it.*

I read his document and laughed. "C'mon, Seth. Nobel Peace Prize?"

"Bono's being nominated for a Nobel Peace Prize; you can too. Just save enough rhinos from extinction."

"Dude, that's not the vibe. Here's what we need to do." I started working on the doc, and Seth smirked as I fell right into his trap. This was a common tactic of Seth's: he got me off my butt by intentionally doing something half-assed, knowing that I, as a perfectionist, would jump in and do it myself.

So I worked on this "Marc Eckō in 2010" doc. We nixed the Nobel Peace Prize, but we still had these overly ambitious and ambiguous goals, like:

- I have to get on the list of *Time*'s 100 Most Influential People in the World.
- I will own a soccer team or football team.
- I will be photographed with XYZ celebrities.

I T WAS A self-improvement project on steroids, but one that carried the weight of a company north of $500 million in revenue. (Thanks to the explosive growth of G-Unit, Eckō Red, and Cut & Sew, our revenue had doubled from the $250 million circa the Liz Claiborne deal.) Despite the diet working, and shedding my physical weight—somehow I became more conscious of size on an entirely different level: my company's size. Eckō Unltd., now called Marc Eckō Enterprises (another nod to propagating that SKIN-TO-THE-WORLD personal brand), would soon have 1,500 employees, and most of them had dependents, so I had thousands of mouths that depended on me (or the "collective me"). That takes a toll.

And the toll was getting heavier. Seth and I had convinced ourselves that it was *good* that we didn't get the Tommy deal, because now we had complete freedom to chase the glory on our own. So in lieu of Hilfiger, we leveraged every asset we had to get more credit. We pledged personal guarantees (PGs), as well as our company's inventory, our trademarks—*everything*. We pushed it to the bleeding edge, and we used this credit to go on a shopping spree: Times Square, the Twenty-third Street offices, our retail stores. This left zero cushion, so we'd be exposed if anything unexpected went south, like, say, an economic collapse.

CIT, our primary creditor, was happy to give us more cash. They were delighted! (At least, that is how I remember it.) They saw a megamillion-dollar retail company with growth, growth, growth. Risk? *Pffft*. That was America circa 2005, after all.

What did the Ghost of Reason say about all this credit?

Marci was leaving the company. It was time. Seth and I were hell-bent on this growth, but we knew that Marci had less appetite for risk. And now, thanks to our sudden influx of credit from CIT, we had the resources to buy out Marci's equity. This was just one more item on our shopping spree, and with no *real* board of directors to challenge us, we never contemplated a buffer for the future.

"Marci, it might make a lot of sense to take some chips off the table," I told her as we sat in a car in Lakewood, eerily echoing the conversation we had fifteen years prior, also in Lakewood. "You're about to have another kid. The timing's kind of perfect."

She was torn, and she hated to separate what she called the "Three Musketeers." But she knew it was time. She saw that Seth and I were going in a different direction.

Governance had left the building.

From then on out, it would just be Swagger and Brute Force.

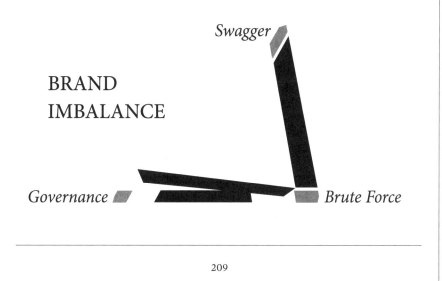

Swagger

BRAND IMBALANCE

Governance *Brute Force*

II. **THE JEDI: KING COMBS**

HOW, EXACTLY, DO you become a household name? What's the road map? Who are the benchmarks? Who's the best at influencing *how people are made to feel?*

I came up from within the hip-hop and pop-culture scenes, and, clearly, I had lusted after the power brokers and social engineers that seemed to magically steer and influence others into action. I studied them. I imagined what magical powers they may have. How do I get to the other side? Is it like joining some secret society of magic? Is it a club? Who runs that club? Illuminati?

I needed a friend with "connects." No, strike that—I needed a teacher. A mentor. So I looked to the enigmatic ringleader of this scene, a man who I had once seen in a white linen suit at the Michael Bivins birthday party, way back when in 1994: Puffy. I was fascinated by how he controlled every aspect of his environment, the way he could own a room.

MY TIME WAS dominated with polishing the final production for Getting Up, and the music and score was important to me. I went for the haymaker, and used this as an excuse to reach out to Puffy. Who better to produce the game's soundtrack? I wanted the music of Getting Up to win an MTV Video Music Award, and with Puff's access and insight, maybe we could. But my creative ambitions with him didn't stop at the soundtrack. I had the video game bug, and I wanted to make a second game, starring Puffy himself, called Hire Ground. Puffy would play Robert Ground, a sort of black James Bond. I wanted to kill two birds with one stone: Getting Up and Hire Ground. I called him to make a pitch, and I went all in.

"Video game??" Puffy said. "We gotta go to LA. That shit's a franchise! That's a movie!!!" He was in.

I knew I could learn so much from him. It's not a one-to-one comparison, but his skill set didn't fit neatly into a box—rapper/businessman/designer/producer—and I didn't fit neatly into a box either. Puffy could become yet

What, exactly, are "friends," and how do they fit in the framework of brands, labels, and authenticity?

You have hundreds of "friends" on Facebook. You have a handful of lifelong friends for whom you would take a bullet. And then you have a range of people in between.

The roots of the word go back to the Old English *frēond*, which was a riff on *frēon*, which meant "to love."

Why does this matter? At every level of the game of perception, people like to toss around the word *friend* so that they will, in turn, benefit, whether it's a B-lister who wants to be "friends" with Oprah or someone who says to the club doorman, "I know I'm not on the guest list, but I'm friends with the DJ."

Friendships should be treasured. Friendships shouldn't be used. When I talk about this phase of my journey and drop names like dandruff, I do this not to talk about my friends, but to share an instructional warning, of sorts.

another unlikely mentor, a Yoda, like Drew (the stoner from Eighth Day), Alan Finkelman, and Dean Colaizzi from Rutgers.

Puffy came out to my new office on Twenty-third Street, which was now tricked out with an indoor basketball court, fully stocked bar, and swinging chairs that dangled from fifty-foot ceilings. Puffy and I clicked. I told him straight up that I respected the way he shrewdly finessed the media, the way he cultivated his own personal brand, the way his power impacted the way people FEEL.

"I want to learn from you," I said, not caring how it sounded. "I want to study with you and learn."

We connected beyond the mechanical checklist (soundtrack, score, music licensing), and went deeper as entrepreneurs who both had ambitions in the

"ANALOG" SOCIAL NETWORKING 101

Not digital, but real-world social networking. If your goal is to grow your personal brand into a public persona, the subtle, mysterious stranger approach is most often not going to cut it. There are only so many people that can pull off the J. D. Salinger route of becoming famous for not being seen. The easier (though more painful) route is to hire a publicist—more explicitly, hire *yourself**—and will yourself to want to impress the red-carpeted world of celebrities, CEOs, and Twitter famous. I can't hold your hand at the events, but here are ten tips for surviving them:

1. Value Quality over Quantity

Your publicist will give you a social calendar that's jammed with events, insisting that you "need to be" at all of them. This is false. Separate the "need to attends" from the "nice to attends," and this will serve you better in the long run. Chasing the second tier of events will exhaust you and overexpose you, and you'll burn out faster than yesterday's news.

2. Don't Overtly Parrot

Most of the management books tell you to parrot the person you're trying to impress, suggesting that you nod when she nods, touch your left nostril when she touches her left nostril, and then if she says, "I love Lady Gaga!" you say, "Oh my God, I love Lady Gaga too!!!!" The world does not need more parroting, and it's okay to *not* love Lady Gaga.

3. Use Mints

If, at any point in the day, your mouth has been open and if you've consumed food, chances are that your breath stinks. Do yourself a favor and freshen up your face.

4. Don't Name-Drop

It's transparent and obnoxious. When I met George Lucas, even though at heart I was a starstruck fan boy, I would never say, "I saw Harrison Ford last week!" or "I just played golf with Steven Spielberg!" Lame. If you *do* want to slip in a name, it's better to use one that's more mundane, more grounded, like the celebrity's lawyer that you might happen to know.

5. Never Ask for a Card

You can (and should) give out *your* business card, but never ask for one in return. If people want to give you a card, they'll give you their goddamn card.

6. Respect the Handler

The notable might have a handler (assistant, publicist, manager, associate) standing with him or her at the party. When you meet the notable, also introduce yourself to the sidekick, and when you give the notable a card, give the sidekick a card too. Treat handlers with respect. Not only is this the right thing to do, but this could be the hand of the king—and they'll later whisper into the king's ear.

7. Drink Water

This is work, it's not a party.

8. Don't Try to Speak to Everyone

When Barry Sanders scored a touchdown, he would casually toss the football back to the ref, shrugging, and living by the credo "Act like you've been there before." Just chill out. Don't try to meet every celebrity and shake every hand. If you are conducting and managing your personal brand well, part of your brand will be to spend more time in this mildly toxic environment. You'll be at these events again in the future, so let things happen more organically.

9. It's Not About Being a "Closer"

Lower your expectations about imagining that you may magically seal any deals. These events aren't the right forum for giving someone the hard sell, for overt pitching, or to become someone's best friend.

10. Know That They're Working Too

Even famous people don't like getting dressed up and making a fuss about how they look. Even if they have a giant dick or won the Most Beautiful Woman in the World award, the chances are that they still had anxiety about getting dressed up and going to this event. It's work for them too. Take comfort in this.

---

*Be Your Own Publicist: The best publicist that you can hire is yourself. Publicists and PR agents are useful: they're concierges who can make introductions to people that might be outside of your network. But they can't replace the need for you to be your own bullhorn. It has to start with you.

media. Me in gaming, and him as an actor. We connected on how our dreams *made us feel*, and then, in turn, on how our own ambitions could *make others feel*. This is why I respected him, and, I suspect, this shared interest in EMOTIONAL IMPACT is what made him give me the time of day.

Puff helped with the Getting Up soundtrack, he gave me some advice on PR agents, he helped me sign George Hamilton to do voice acting ("Fuck yeah, I'll get George Hamilton, I just had breakfast with fucking George Hamilton!"), and the two of us went to LA to pitch Hire Ground as a movie.

For two days, we pitched the studios together. On the first day, we bounced from studio to studio, and at each meeting, I pitched Puffy as being not only talented but *funny*. This is a side of him that most people hadn't yet seen. I told the studio execs, "I think he could play a physical, serious James Bond–type character, but then also do some funny Chris Tucker shit."

As soon as I said Chris Tucker's name, Puffy got up from his chair, jumped on a table, did the crane kick from *The Karate Kid*, and said, "I'll do some *Karate Kid* shit!" I loved that about the guy; he didn't hold back. He wanted it. And watching someone with so much already be willing to work so hard to get it was humbling.

Puffy's a machine. In between our pitch meetings, I could hear him barking into his cell phone, chewing out a producer at ABC-TV.

"The motherfuckers don't want to let me on the red carpet next week at the Oscars." Puffy waved his phone.

"Isn't that something your PR person does?"

"Nah, man. You got to do that shit yourself."

The next week, he was at the Oscars, on the red carpet. Old. Fashioned. Schlepping. Puffy wasn't too big to do his own dirty work.

On the second day of pitches, we held the meetings in Puffy's bungalow at the Beverly Hills Hotel. With candles burning everywhere, talking to execs from studio after studio, we created a bidding war for Hire Ground. We weren't trying just to make a movie or even a game, for that matter, we wanted to create a black James Bond that would break through, inspire, and entertain. I was in a master's class of *how you make people feel*. Puffy controlled every variable of his environment so effortlessly. When he spreads twenty suits on his bed in the hotel room, carefully picking and choosing, it's not for vanity, it's for *purpose*. Atmosphere. Control.

After the meetings, Puffy asked, "What are you doing tonight?"

"Whatever you're doing."

Puffy gave me a once-over—still a little overweight, still no match for his three-piece suit—shrugged, and said, "You look like a downtown hipster. You're 'aight."

We rolled out of the bungalow and headed to a surprise birthday party for Chris Rock. It was supposed to start at 9:00 but we got there at 9:10.

"Fuck, we missed it!" Puffy said as we rode up the elevator.

The elevator arrived at the top floor, the doors opened, and the crowd yelled, "*Surprise!!!*"

"No, no, no!" Puffy laughed.

The entire crowd—expecting Chris Rock to emerge—took in the sight of Puffy and this unknown grimy hipster standing next to him. Oprah, Eddie Murphy, Reverend Run from Run-D.M.C. (I think), Jerry Seinfeld—all staring at me, wondering who I was and how I knew Chris.

It turns out there wasn't even room at the party for me—figuratively and literally—so I shuffled back into the elevator with the least notable person in the crowd besides me: Tim Meadows, formerly of *Saturday Night Live*. Awkward silence on our way back to the ground floor. I guess he wasn't invited either.

Still, it was my first real taste. I wanted more.

III. BLOCK PARTY

Nas, Fat Joe, Kanye, and me

"**H**AVE YOU SEEN the 'Gold Digger' video yet?" Kanye asked me about his latest record.

"Not yet."

"Hype Williams directed. That shit's gonna be huge." Kanye and I were backstage in Toronto for a music festival I had produced to promote Getting Up. He was about to go onstage. We had some big guns for that show: Busta Rhymes, Mos Def, Talib Kweli, and our headliner, Nas. (How crazy is that? Kanye *opened* for Nas.)

"I'm going to be on *Oprah*. I have my own version of Tupac's 'Dear Mama'— I dedicate a song to my mom."

We built three-inch-deep aluminum facades, like you're viewing the train from the side.

My phone rang. "Sorry, I gotta take this." I wanted to bullshit with Kanye, but I couldn't concentrate, as my phone was blowing up with problems from New York.

"The permits." The voice was panicked. "They're fucking us."

"Slow down. What's wrong?"

"They're revoking our permits."

The permits in question were for our graffiti block party, yet another promotion for Getting Up and another way to create an EMOTIONAL IMPACT. When you challenge yourself to move beyond simple billboards, suddenly the range of EMOTIONAL IMPACT goes further, hits harder. I had built scale replicas of R-10 subway cars. We planned an outdoor event on Manhattan's Eighteenth Street and Tenth Avenue, where graffiti legends would paint on these subway car facades like they used to in the early 1980s. No public property would be defaced. No vandalism would occur. Just commissioned art.

We got the permits a year in advance. The city approved it. Out of nowhere, this Queens city councilman, Peter Vallone Jr., caught wind of the event, and he thought that I was going to trigger a firestorm of graffiti around the city, sending it up in flames. He warned the press, "This is going to be an exposition of how to pickpocket."

But we had the permits, right? What could he do to stop it?

At least one person was convinced by Vallone: Mayor Michael Bloomberg. The mayor went on the radio to say, "Graffiti is just one of those things that destroys our quality of life, and why anybody thinks that it's funny or cute to encourage kids to go do that, I don't know. We have talked to them and asked them to not have a subway car motif to write graffiti. This is not really art or expression, this is—let's be honest about what it is—it's trying to encourage people to do something that's not in anybody's interest."

So they revoked the permits.

I called my lawyer, and he said, "You know, we might have a First Amendment case."

When you dig deeper into Bloomy's rationale, he said that theoretically we *could* paint in public "on a canvas," but if we painted on these replica subways—*my* replica subways, by the way, that weren't cheap—it would be forbidden. How does this make sense? How is a *canvas* different from a *fake subway*? We knew we had a case, so we hired Ron Kuby, the New York civil rights lawyer famous for defending flag burners, alleged murderers, suspected terrorists, and now, graffiti artists.

We called a press conference. It was one of my first times addressing the media, and I felt confident. As the cameras flashed, video rolled, and the reporters shoved microphones in my face, *it felt good*. It was an echo of my high school performance as B-boy Toto in the musical *The Wiz*. Up until now, I had been the wizard behind the curtain. Now I stepped out in front.

After that press conference, we took it to the courts: *Eckō Unltd. vs. Mayor Bloomberg and the City of New York*. I liked the sound of that.

And the verdict?

The court backed my First Amendment rights and even showed a sense of humor. Straight from the pen of Jed S. Rakoff, the US district judge: "By the same token, presumably, a street performance of *Hamlet* would be tantamount to encouraging revenge murder. Or, in a different vein, a street performance of rap music might well include the singing of lyrics that could be viewed as encouraging sexual assault. As for a street performance of *Oedipus Rex*, don't even think about it."

So we do the block party, and guess what happens? Thanks to this controversy, MTV covered it, along with far more media outlets than would have

FIND YOUR FOIL

Peter Vallone, stodgy, prudish, nay-saying, was a great nemesis. He's the kind of adult that kids love to hate. ("Get off my lawn!") When you have a good foil, you connect with your consumer on a more emotional level. What is a foil? It can be anything or anyone that serves, by contrast, to call attention to your own merits, like Batman and the Joker.

With "nemesis marketing" or "foil marketing," you and your consumers suddenly become compatriots—coconspirators in righting a wrong. And if you don't have a good foil? Invent one. Look at arguably the most famous ad of all time: in Apple's "1984" spot, a fictional Orwellian dictator symbolizes IBM, suggesting that if you hate evil dictators or the status quo, you should buy a Mac.

---

otherwise. We had three Boy Scout troops, a public school, a host of notable old-school NYC fixtures of the rap community, and many others. The effect of the scope of our EMOTIONAL IMPACT? We quadrupled our planned attendance.

It taught me something important: find the foil.

IV. **AIR FORCE ONE**

THE BATTLE WITH Bloomberg was my gateway drug. I wanted another hit. A bigger hit. Seth and I both craved another splash in the media, and we wanted to do it on a grander scale.

"You should tag Mount Rushmore!" Seth suggested.

"The White House!"

"The New York Stock Exchange?"

We hired a blue-chip film, TV, video, and commercial production company called Smuggler to lead the charge on our next target. They brought in a hotshot named David Droga, who looked a little like Bono's lost brother. He came to our first meeting with a picture of Andrews Air Force Base, in Maryland, as seen on Google Earth.

$$\left(FEEL \right) >>> \left(MAKE \right)$$

"Gents," David said in his brash Australian accent, pointing, "this is the home of Air Force One."

Tag the president's plane? The idea had such an allure. And what better nemesis could we have than George W. Bush? The well-past-9/11, sloppy, overreaching, "mission-accomplished" George Bush. He had an approval rating of something like 3 percent. We would tag it with "Still Free," which, on a literal level, was the name of the lead character's graffiti crew in Getting Up, but it clearly had broader and deeper resonance.

Just looking at that image gave me goose bumps.

"There's a golf course next to the base." Droga pointed to the map, like a general in combat. "The weakness is on the perimeter. That's our entrance."

Our lawyer was in the room, and his face went ashen. "This could get you thrown in jail."

"It's just a hoax," I said.

"Marc, they *shoot* people for 'hoaxes.' Look at the Patriot Act. This is a bad idea."

Top:
*Andrews Air
Force Base*

My PR guy, Ken Sunshine, said, "I'm going to sit this one out."

It's too bad, because they missed a fun ride. My lawyer was only partially relieved that we weren't *actually* painting Air Force One—we faked it. We found a private airport that flew freight 747s out of San Bernardino, California. So we rented a 747 and painted one side of it to look like Air Force One; the other half still had "Joe's Freight" or whatever on it. We filmed actual footage of the perimeter in Maryland, we filmed us approaching the freeway, and then we filmed the rest of the footage in San Bernardino.

For a split second, we thought about tagging the actual Air Force One, but we knew that would be impossible. You can't do it. The real Air Force One has a rope on the runway that encircles the plane, and if you cross that rope, you get shot. We debated whether to include that detail in our video.

"The cops should be shooting at you!"

"And then you return fire!"

"That's not the vibe," I said, laughing, knowing that if we had Schwarzenegger-type gunfire, it would look corny at best and like a terrorist video at worst. Besides, almost no one knew about the rope.

We did everything under a veil of secrecy, swearing our crew to silence. The entire thing felt rebellious, wrong, and intoxicating. On the night of the stunt, in

The media bought it.

$$\int_{0^\circ}^{\infty} f\left(\frac{\text{"How you make people FEEL."}}{\text{"What you MAKE."}}\right) dx \cdot$$

3 DENIALS FROM THE PENTAGON

Between Wolf Blitzer and Anderson Cooper, it paid off

the middle of production, as we shot the scene where we cut through the chain-link fence, a police chopper suddenly flew overhead.

Oh shit. The chopper flew circles in the darkness and then shined a spotlight on "Air FARCE One." Soon another chopper appeared; they probably thought that Air Force One had been grounded, and that it was a national emergency. The whole night had the thrill of danger.

Staring at the choppers, I reached quickly for my phone, dialing the owners of the runway. "You need to call the police!" I yelled. "Tell them that this is part of a movie production!"

Soon the choppers floated away. (Since we were only an hour from Hollywood, they bought the whole movie thing.) We filmed until dawn, my team did some digital voodoo in postproduction, and we actually worked hard to make the video look *cheaper*, grittier. Thanks to Google Earth, we had a perfect rendering of the Andrews base hanger, so we used computer-generated imagery to overlay it onto our video. That's why when the video went viral, most of the experts thought it was real—they recognized the hanger.

CNN had Wolf Blitzer reporting on the story. The US Air Force even thought that the plane might have been compromised, as Lieutenant Colonel Bruce Alexander, a spokesman for the Air Mobility Command's Eighty-Ninth Airlift Wing, told the press, "We're looking into it." And soon, once the media traced it to me, my name popped up on news show after news show—starting to fulfill the promise of "Marc Eckō in 2010."

We got lucky with the timing. YouTube 2006 was a different pre-Google creature from YouTube today. Back then, most of the videos were either overly produced ad agency stuff, or user-generated content, like dancing kittens. Viral videos were still an immature medium, and we exploited that.

More important, more than any hoodie or T-shirt, or big splashy outdoor advertising, for that matter, this helped *make people feel* something. It was the right time, the right place, the right nemesis, the right conversation. It wasn't about Getting Up or Marc Eckō, it was about something much deeper. "Still free." A message that was both subversive and, at the same time, fundamentally American.

V. **FORCING IT**

IN 2003-ISH, I bought tickets to a fund-raising dinner that was honoring George Lucas. I'm (obviously) a huge fan, so I bought an entire table, thinking that, at the very least, I'd be in the same room with the dude, and maybe I'd even get a photo next to him. At the eleventh hour, something came up, and I couldn't go.

But that didn't stop me from introducing my personal brand to Lucas. Years before, in Tokyo, I had bought a rare twelve-inch action figure of George himself. When I couldn't go to the fund-raiser, I asked my marketing director, who was to join Coltrane Curtis at the table, to take this action figure and have it sit in my place.

I asked him to get a photo with real George holding little George, and to tell him that this toy is from Marc Eckō, who regrets his absence, and it's very important to Marc that he gets this photo. I had Coltrane deliver this message, like Christopher Walken delivering the watch in *Pulp Fiction*, with solemn gravitas, telling Lucas that he had been carrying around this doll for years (maybe not up his ass), and that it's his life's mission to get the photo. Lucas

Coltrane Curtis, little George, big George

laughed—it turns out this twelve-inch doll was a one of a kind; he hadn't seen it before—and posed for the photo. Then he handed little George to Martin Scorsese, and pretty soon the entire dinner was posing for pictures with little George. As far as making someone feel something, the doll in that setting created an impression at the event. But it was just a dotted line back to me. Right?

Fast-forward to 2006. Spike Lee threw a fund-raiser to honor the twenty-year anniversary of his production company, 40 Acres & a Mule. It was a nautical-themed party on a Carnival cruise ship. Guess who else was on the cruise? There he was, George Lucas, dapper as a motherfucker in a mayonnaise-colored double-breasted linen suit. I had to speak to him.

At the time, I used to carry a customized BlackBerry I had designed. It was painted candy apple red with an etching of Yoda in it. On the cruise, Lucas was talking with some schmuck executive from Kodak who kept giving him shit about the prequels.

"George, your films just look so *fake* compared to the original trilogy, you know?" the exec said, his voice a nasally whine.

"They just look so cold. I'm sorry, but digital is not as warm." The Kodak guy kept droning on and on. I stood about five feet away, respectfully just outside their social circle, and I made eye contact with Lucas's assistant, holding up one finger in the universal language of "I'm next," like I was at a deli counter and my number had been called. The assistant nodded.

When the Kodak douche finally left, George turned to me. Without an introduction, I made a light-saber noise, pantomimed taking a saber from my belt, and said, "I was ready to exact revenge and cut his treasonous head off, my lord."

George laughed.

"Just say the word, Master Lucas." I tried keeping a straight face. "I'm not kidding."

We both laughed. I introduced myself and then showed him my geeked-out-Yoda BlackBerry.

"I haven't seen this case before." Lucas flipped the phone in his hand, curious.

If you read this sentence in a press release, it doesn't work: "Science-fiction megabrand (targeting boys aged 8–15) aligns itself with edgy streetwear brand (targeting men aged 17–29)." Maybe that's one of the reasons it worked: sometimes you can't tell "synergy" from the surface. You have to look deeper. I'm proud of those *Star Wars* collabs.

This whole encounter speaks to the tactile power of *objects*. Without my little George action figure, we never would have met. And looking back even further, as a kid, if Darren and I had never played with those Han Solo figures, Tauntauns, and rhino figurines, I never would have created my rhino logo. Physical objects tell a story under the surface, they connect the dots, they work deep in our subconscious.

Parents might look at their kids playing with toys and think they are wasting time. (In fact, my father once told me that his mother threw away his comic books because they were a "waste of time" . . . The comics happened to be *Spider-Man* number

1 and *Superman* number 1.) These objects fuel your creativity and your passion in ways that you can't understand as a kid. Thanks to those toys, I eventually learned more from studying George Lucas—and how he built and licensed his brand—than I did from fashion designers like Calvin or Ralph.

NOTE: *While I shamelessly used a* Star Wars *toy to endear myself to George Lucas, this does* not *mean that I want you to meet me at a party, show me an original Echo T-shirt, and then unzip your jeans and tell me that you have a rhino tattooed on your left testicle. Thank you.*

"That's because they don't exist." I told him about how I'd custom-made it. "This is a shot in the dark, but do you remember, a few years ago, a fund-raising dinner with a toy George Lucas action figure?"

Lucas thought for a second and then snapped his fingers. "Yeah, with Marty! I do!" He couldn't remember what the dinner was for, but he remembered the doll.

"Yeah, that was me—I mean, he was mine," I said, and we instantly had a good vibe.

That was enough to make the connect, and pretty soon I went out to Skywalker Ranch, stayed at an apartment on the complex called the Akira Kurosawa home, and worked with his team to license *Star Wars* for Eckō. It was a massive professional honor. I don't like to name-drop, and, frankly, part of me hates sharing these kinds of anecdotes, as I don't like being "that guy," but the Lucas encounter was truly a moment of creating a meaningful emotional impact that lasted. And it all happened by showcasing my authentic personal brand. The little George, the Yoda phone, waving my imaginary light saber—that was my playful provocation at work. This wasn't scripted or forced; it flowed naturally from deep in my muscle memory.

VI. ECKŌ IN WONDERLAND

THE WHOLE COMPANY knew about the "Marc Eckō in 2010" mandate. Part of my staff had been converted from people who make things—denim, hoodies, magazines—into a team with a mission to make me (and the brand) a star. When I went out at night, I had an entire crew who prepped the venue, talked to the doorman, and ensured that I could beeline straight from my car to bottle service.

Everyone knows that a good party has three ingredients: (1) alcohol, (2) good music, and (3) hot female models. So one of my employees, who looked sort of like Prince (circa *Purple Rain*)—and, in fact, his name was Prince Peter—made sure I always had models in tow.

"Russians! Brazilians! Badass women, Marc! All the time!" Prince Peter hooked me up with not just *models*, but the kind of exotic models that *Complex* featured: Dutch, African, Czechoslovakian, five foot eleven, six foot one, killer cheekbones, beautiful. I was role-playing. It felt like an RPG (role-playing game): go to a red-carpet event, hit a club like GoldBar, and, if all goes well, be in the room with someone like DiCaprio.

$\left(\text{ Humilty } \right) >>> \left(\text{ Hubris } \right)$

Me, my sheepskin coat, Nick Cannon, and two really nice models/photographers. If you want me to be authentic, honestly, I don't really remember their names, but one's Russian and one's Brazilian. (Pro tip: If you need to take photographs in hard-to-access places, give the cameras to 6-foot 2-inch-tall models.)

That wad of cash was a camera magnet: 0.02 seconds before Puff was merely doing an accounting. Camera comes out, voilà—a gem of a picture. Only Puff.

"SUNDANCE," **MY TRIAGE** unit of publicists urged me. "That's all you, Marc."

Upon the prescription from my growing PR team, I took the "Marc Eckō in 2010" show on the road, bringing a good chunk of my staff with me to Park City, Utah, for the 2006 Sundance Film Festival. *Complex* magazine threw a daytime party with Ken Block, the founder of DC Shoes, and somehow this became *the place.* Actor-comedian Nick Cannon was our DJ, and afterward he told me, "Yo, I'm DJ'ing at this other party tonight; wanna come?"

Thrust into the nightlife vortex, I headed to the 5WPR PR agency house party, which had DJ AM, Kim Kardashian, Chamillionaire, Reggie Bush, and, of course, the cheshire cat himself, Puffy.

Puffy took in my new vibe—I was wearing a sheepskin coat, looking svelte, herding models like Moses did sheep—and he gave me a knowing nod. I got his ear for a second and asked him, "Puff, how do you know when you've *arrived*?"

"Marc, you know how when you're in high school?" Puffy leaned in closer. "And you're walking through the halls, going from third to fourth period, and you're the kid everyone's talking to, saying 'What's up? What's up, Sean?' 'Yo! Sean! What's up?'"

Yeah, I guess I knew that feeling.

"That's what it feels like. That's when you know you're good."

"So how do you do that?"

He looked around this party, took in the models and the notables. Someone yelled, "Justin's coming!" And then moments later: "Josh Hartnett's here!" Puffy looked back at me. "Here's what you need to do: you need to make them WANT YOU like the dope man." And then Puff took out this huge wad of cash effortlessly, as if he was checking for singles to tip the doorman—it must have been $20K—and he starts counting it at the party. Reason number 4,726 that Puff is successful: only he can pull off a stunt like this without looking like a cartoon. This was Puff in all his authentic Gatsby glory; he oozes this charisma from every pore. He can do this. Others can't. When he drops pearls, or perplexes you with a question, it's important to listen, glean, and adapt—but never parrot.

I laughed, and then one of my PR soldiers appeared out of nowhere, grabbed my arm, and said, "Jamie Kennedy wants to interview you! Come on!"

I looked at my watch: two thirty in the morning. I just wanted to go to bed, but they ushered me into a room, the cameras were rolling, and there was Jamie Kennedy, who you might (or might not) know as the comic actor from *Son of the Mask* and *Scream*. He was doing a series of interviews on Sundance nightlife.

We got off on the wrong foot. For whatever reason, drunk on my own Kool-Aid, I decided that it was kick Jamie Kennedy time. He interviewed me, and I slipped into this fake persona, this wannabee cool guy, and I acted like a total dick to Jamie. I figured that's what you have to do, right? This is another box to check. This is the ultimate RPG. This is how you level up: you need to punk Jamie Kennedy.

I went to party after party, I trimmed down, I filmed fashion shoots of me sprawled out on a bed with half-naked models, and I even fleetingly breathed the same air with the gods of celebrity.

VII. EMOTIONAL IMPACT: HOW YOU MAKE ~~PEOPLE~~ <u>YOU</u> FEEL

E VERY ACTION HAS an equal and opposite reaction. When you aspire to create an EMOTIONAL IMPACT with your brand that's from your SKIN TO THE WORLD, you just might feel a recoil, a kickback, a yin to the yang, and this recoil is the EMOTIONAL IMPACT to your brand that's from the GUTS TO THE SKIN.

This chapter is about both of these twin forces. It's about how I tried to MAKE PEOPLE FEEL on a grand stage, and then, on the flip side, it's about how the high-wire act made *me* feel.

Cheshire Tableau

Opposite:
Alice Limits Tableau

The Donald Trumps, the business schools, and the marketing books of the world focus only on the external forces. But the stuff that's under the hood is just as important. Taking stock of your emotions isn't "indulgent" or "weak"—it's critical. Even when it's ugly. Even when it's confusing. Even when it seems like a waste of time.

We all have different ways of channeling and expressing our EMOTIONAL IMPACT. I'm an artist. For me, the clearest insight into my own emotional state—and how this impacts the business of me—is my art.

So at the risk of looking like a madman, I'm going to share how my art evolved during this phase of my journey in MAKING PEOPLE FEEL. This is what's going on beneath the hood. This isn't something from my career you can find from *Wikipedia*, and it's not part of a simple equation on A + B = Brand.

My trip down the celebrity rabbit hole reminded me more and more of *Alice in Wonderland*. My life had become Eckō in Wonderland. All of these characters from my life seemed like characters in *Alice*. Ken Sunshine and all the PR agents? They were the Brer Rabbits who were never on time but always telling *you* to be on time. The Caterpillar was the Svengali artist-photographer who could get you to do anything on camera—like a Steve Klein. The paparazzi

Opposite:
Alice's Regret

Left:
Humpty Tableau

were Tweedledee and Tweedledum. And then there was the Cheshire Cat, with his ability to seem to be everywhere at once, asking perplexing questions, and who sometimes helped Alice, and then darted in and out of her journey. For me, that was Puffy.

I happened to buy a children's book called *The Lion's Cavalcade*, by Alan Aldridge, and I loved the symmetry and color of those illustrations. So I repeated my old habits from way back when with graffiti, and started sampling and merging. I painted my own *Alice* portraits, sampling from the characters of Lewis Carroll, the styles of Alan Aldridge, and my own adventures in this chase for fame.

And they got *big*.

They started as normal-sized, and then they grew into six-foot-tall paintings, and then twenty-foot wide, until they became entire walls. I hired painters to help me. First one, and then two, and then soon I had an entire mini painting and art production factory right next to my office at work. Bigger, bigger, more, more. And when my factory couldn't keep up with my frenzied visions or volume, I orchestrated parts of my works' production to artists in

Below Left:
Alice Drops
Off a Venti

Below Right:
Humpty Suicide:
Marc Loves
Lindsay,
*Humpty suicide
triptych*

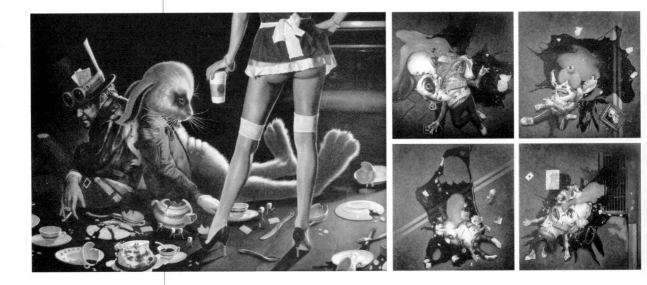

Russia and even China. Productionism, baby. I created a movement, but the movement was only in my head.

These began as simple illustrations, and they soon evolved into something darker.

What do these say about my EMOTIONAL IMPACT? What did they say about how my own personal brand was affected by—and *was affecting*—the external brand of Marc Eckō Enterprises?

We'd soon find out.

Opposite:
Humpty Suicide

Me and Adrian Grenier

*Kim Kardashian blows
kisses to the paparazzi*

VIII. ECKŌ IN WONDERLAND (CON'T)

WE THREW A party at the Twenty-third Street offices—the building
that Seth predicted would "get so much deal flow"—and I unveiled
the *Alice* pieces. I hired an androgynous rock band to perform, and they
painted their faces with Kiss-like makeup. The paparazzi wall of Tweedledee
and Tweedledum greeted the guests when they entered. It was some weird
shit. I had dialed up the avant-garde factor; I was making it more dangerous.

We drew the right crowd, as my guests included people like actress Malin
Akerman, actor Diego Luna, Puffy, the singer Ne-Yo, rapper Lil'Kim, and the
gossip columnist Baird Jones, who was an eccentric NYC nightlife promoter
and a Warhol-scene alum. Baird saw Puffy and me talking, and he interrupted
us, busting out his signature tape recorder for an interview.

Baird, a notorious fame seeker in his own right, asked Puff, "Can you talk
about *Any Given Sunday*?" *Any Given Sunday* had come out years before. What
was this dude talking about?

"Huh?" Puff leaned in closer, confused.

A Diego Luna and meselfie

"Are you mad that you didn't get the part that Jamie Foxx got in *Any Given Sunday?*"

I interrupted Baird and apologized to Puff. (But I had just checked another box: throw a party that attracts gossip columnists who annoy the guests.)

It was starting to work.

But I knew I needed to take it up a notch. What could really kick-start a conversation; what could *make people feel?*

I mulled this over as I had lunch in my office with Swizz Beatz and Terry George, the director of *Hotel Rwanda*. I heard Seth knock awkwardly on the door.

"You have a minute?" Seth loosened his tie, unbuttoned the top button.

"Look at you, all suited up!" I said. "Wedding or a funeral?"

"Bank meeting. We need to talk." Seth nodded at my guests.

I told Terry and Swizz I'd be right back, and Seth and I huddled up by the indoor basketball court.

"So, we made a mistake," Seth started. "*I* made a mistake. An inventory mistake."

Inventory mistake. *Booooooorrrrriiiiing.*

"It's gonna cause some headaches, but don't worry, it's not a big deal. It might cut into our marketing budget, but don't worry."

I slapped his knee. "Dude. We're good."

I didn't give it another thought, and I went back to my lunch, and my tireless RPG to become "Marc Eckō in 2010."

There was one brewing news story that grabbed my attention: Barry Bonds was in the news 24-7. He was on the cusp of breaking Hank Aaron's career home run record—some call it the most hallowed record in sports—and it seemed clear-cut that he was on the juice. People were so passionate about this issue and they either condemned Bonds, apologized for him, praised him, blamed Commissioner Bud Selig, or blamed the game.

One of our employees, Josh Rochlin, a recovering lawyer and a very creative guy who was an interim COO at the time, suggested, "Wouldn't it be great if we could do something with that Barry debate?"

Interesting.

"He's eventually going to break the record," Josh said. "And that home run ball, it might go on auction." He smiled knowingly.

Sure enough, Barry broke the record on August 7, 2007. I watched the coverage at a bar with friends, captivated, debating what it all meant. All ESPN could talk about was what should be done with the ball.

"They should just blow it up," one of my buddies said.

"Nah, it should go in the Hall of Fame," said another.

"They should just give it back to Barry," said someone else.

I slammed down my tequila. "I'll tell you what's going to happen."

They all looked at me. Dead silence.

"I'm going to buy it. I'm going to buy that fucking ball."

IX. $752,467

LESS THAN TWENTY-FOUR hours later, while having dinner with my wife, I got the text from my lawyer: "We got the ball. It cost seven fifty."

Seven hundred fifty dollars is a lot of money to spend on a baseball. But he didn't mean seven hundred fifty dollars. He meant seven hundred fifty *thousand* dollars. Of course, this wasn't any ordinary baseball. Barry Bonds smacked that ball out of San Francisco's AT&T Park for his 756th career home run, breaking Hank Aaron's career home run mark.

The ball was bigger than Barry Bonds, bigger than steroids, bigger than baseball. The ball was controversial, sacred, tainted, glorious. A proper enigma. I knew I had to have it.

I had authorized my lawyer to represent me at the Sotheby's auction in September (anonymously) and to spend up to a million bucks.

That text—"We got the ball"—kicked off a whirlwind that would follow me for years. I had the ball, but what would I *do* with the damn thing?

VOTE756.COM
FOR THE RECORD...
Decide the fate of Barry Bonds' famous 756th home run ball
Vote Now ▶
A) Bestow It
B) Brand It *
C) Banish It
by MARC ECKŌ

"Blow it up! Blow it up!" urged Seth.

"Nah, dude. It's bigger than that."

"What, then?"

I already had a plan. I would let the people decide. I would go all Simon Cowell on that ass. I wanted to put this ball up for a vote: *American Idol* meets hard news.

The night I bought the ball, I had my team working around the clock on building this website—Vote756.com—where people could vote on the ball's destiny. I gave them three options:

> Option 1: Send it to the Hall of Fame (as is).
> Option 2: Send it to the Hall of Fame (with an asterisk branded on it).
> Option 3: Put it on a rocket and blast the fucker into space.*

Even before I bought the ball, my people had been secretly negotiating with the producers of the *Today* show—keeping my identity anonymous—asking if they were interested in an exclusive interview with the new owner of the Barry Bonds ball. Of course, they were on board; for the *Today* show, this was catnip.

I went on the *Today* show the next morning, sleep deprived, a little hung over, but hopped up on a *doppio* espresso and righteous adrenaline.

"Why'd you do it?" host Matt Lauer asked me.

"I wanted to democratize the ball and to give the ball to the people; to give the ball to America." That's not just a platitude. I meant it.

Matt Lauer leaned forward, and he asked me what would turn out to be a prescient question: "If you brand the ball, would Cooperstown want it?"

"I don't know if they'll take it," I agreed.

As the segment ended, I slipped in a plug for the website—"Go to Vote756 .com"—and then *boom*! Two hours later, the site crashed from so much traffic. It felt like the beginning of the film *The Social Network*, where suddenly Facebook just takes off. I knew I had tapped into something.

But here's what you didn't see on the *Today* show.

On the way home that night, I drove past our flagship Times Square store, which was still vacant, still expensive, still bleeding our cash. I drove past some Eckō billboards we did with the *High School Musical* stars Ashley Tisdale and Vanessa Hudgens. I looked at that campaign and I realized . . . it sucked. It was so saccharine, even corny.

---

*That option 3 wasn't a joke, by the way. I actually had satellite-launching companies crunching numbers and figuring out how to do it. (Quick tip: if you ever find yourself needing to rocket something into outer space, it'll run you about $75K.)

Who the fuck made this ad? Who's responsible for this? I was. I was responsible, but I hadn't been to a proper marketing meeting in months. *Who's approving this shit?* I was so distracted with my painting factory, chasing fame, and burning 3,000 calories a day. And now I had my newest distraction: the Barry Bonds ball.

Here's something else you didn't see on the *Today* show. Remember that "no big deal" that Seth had mentioned, the inventory problem? It turned out that we carried some *0*s in our inventory system, and instead of ordering 10,000 units, we accidentally ordered *1,000,000*. That's a shitload of fleece. Worse, this didn't happen to just some peripheral fashion product, this happened to our core, which fed 60 percent of our entire season, which had a domino effect on the rest of our line. When you flub the inventory for your core—especially in a dramatic, 100x fashion—you have a problem that cannibalizes your other products, your inventory costs skyrocket, and you even botch the schedule for *next season*. This "no big deal" became a massive crack in the foundation of our business.

Here's yet something else you didn't see. When we created "Marc Eckō in 2010," we had cordoned off a marketing budget that I ran myself. This budget was its own thing. No one had a problem with that because, frankly, our pound for pound return on investment (ROI) was pretty damn high. On the surface, it seemed indulgent—$1,000 for Grey Goose here; $7,000 for a Vegas trip there—but at the end of the day, I was generating more media than I could get from conventional advertising. It was cost-effective, and all of us knew it, especially Seth. So I focused on my little fiefdom and stayed oblivious to the rest of our budgets. But in the background, my Spidey sense could tell that other parts of the company were getting trimmed, slashed, pared to the bone.

"Hey, man," I said to Seth one day. "Do we need to talk about my budget?"

"You just do what you do," Seth said. "You're the most capital efficient. Don't worry, don't worry."

I didn't worry. The buzz was fading, but I kept going out, being "seen," kept counting calories, kept painting, and kept pushing the Barry Bonds baseball show.

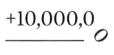

Why
Zeros
Matter

$$+10,000,0$$

X. TEN MILLION

PEOPLE COULDN'T GET enough of the Barry Bonds ball. Barry Bonds made people feel something. Maybe positive, maybe negative, but people had a damn opinion. It was a "sensation." And, as the word says, it creates "senses"—good, bad, and otherwise. Suddenly I became popular, like a math nerd in high school who somehow becomes the starting quarterback. This must be what Puff had talked about. This must be how I know I've "arrived."

When I walked the streets, random dudes would come up to me and say, "Hey, Marc, good job, screw that Barry Bonds!" or, more articulately, "Barry Bonds is a cocksucker!" I knew I had touched a nerve when I was in bed one night, flipped on the news, and saw on the crawl, "Barry Bonds calls Marc Eckō a 'jerk.'"

I almost always had the ball on me, like Frodo and the ring. I'd play catch with it in Times Square, under the shadow of my still-empty store. It felt like I was everyone's new best friend. Even Ken Sunshine took a newfound interest in me and dragged me to an impromptu cocktail party, which was filled with New York's highbrow elite. You had the Maureen Dowd–type intellectual crowd along with the requisite T&A celebrities. Each person in the room probably had an average of 5.2 graduate degrees, 2 croquet sets, and 1 stack of the *Economist* that he or she had never read.

I left the ball in the car with my driver, but Sunshine encouraged me. "Go ahead, get the ball!"

"You want me to bring the baseball? To the party?"

"Sure! Why not?"

So I brought the baseball to the party, and it became the chatter of the event. I just stood there like a proper tool, holding the ball, as people either frowned or fawned.

Sunshine nudged me. "Marc, meet the governor!"

And lo and behold, I turned to see New York's finest, Governor Eliot Spitzer!*

"Governor, this is Marc Eckō; he just bought the Barry Bonds ball."

*Pre-scandal Eliot Spitzer.

Eliot Spitzer sized me up. I held out the ball and asked if he wanted to hold it, but he grimaced and shook his head. Up close, he looked kind of like the handsome side of Two-Face from *Batman*. His eyebrows got all intense, and he stared me in the eye and said, "Marc, have you ever stood down a ninety-six-mile-per-hour fastball?"

"No, sir."

"Do you know how scary it is to stare down a fastball? I *played* baseball." The eyebrows were about to leap from his head and attack me. "Nice to meet you," he said, and then he turned and walked away.

Oh shit, I just got ethered by Eliot Spitzer!

After the party, I checked the stats on Vote756.com: ten million. Holy shit. Ten million? I knew this would be big, but *ten million*?

T HE VERDICT WAS in. The people voted to brand it with an asterisk and send it to the Hall of Fame. But only one problem: I had no idea if Cooperstown would even accept it. How phony—how inauthentic—would I look if I made this promise to ten million people and then couldn't back it up? (Back to INFINITE TRUTH: my WHAT YOU DO needed to match my WHAT YOU SAY.)

It was time for me to go back on the *Today* show and announce the verdict. I'm in the studio getting made up. I have the ball on my lap (like Frodo again), and it's right before a commercial, and I can hear them setting up our segment. "Up next, see the verdict. How did America vote? Find out the fate of the Barry Bonds ball."

As soon as the camera flicks off—not knowing I'm right there—cohost Hoda Kotb, who is also in makeup, making small talk, says, "What kind of jackass would buy this ball?"

Well, that kind of jackass slinks down a little farther in his seat. And then he slinks even lower when he sees that our segment is to include a second guest, Mr. Dale Petroskey, the president of the Major League Baseball Hall of Fame. Uh-oh. How's he gonna play it? Will he get all pious on my ass?

Mr. Dale Petroskey seems like a nice enough guy. And who am I to caste aspersions? I know that he once worked in the Reagan administration. Okay, fair enough. And I know that he once cancelled an anniversary screening of the movie *Bull Durham* because he didn't approve of star Tim Robbins's liberal political views. So for all I knew, maybe he hated my graffiti-ass guts.

As I sit next to Matt Lauer and the segment begins, Dale Petroskey appears on the TV monitor via satellite. He gives a big smile.

"Dale, will the Hall accept this ball?" Matt Lauer asks him. Holding my breath . . . wait . . . wait . . .

"You bet we're happy to get it," he says. "This ball wouldn't be coming to Cooperstown without Marc Eckō buying it."

You can tell it's killing poor Dale Petroskey to say these words. He looks like a hostage being forced at gunpoint to say to the camera, "I'm okay! Tell my family I love them! They're treating me well!" At least that's how I perceived it.

And say what you want about Matt Lauer, but give him credit: he even pushes Dale Petroskey a little bit and asks the real question. "By accepting it with the brand, do you think the Hall in some way endorses the idea that Barry Bonds used steroids?"

A pause. A very long pause. I don't know if Dale was expecting that one.

"No," Petroskey says. "I think what this is . . . is an intersection of a couple of deeply held American values. First of all, innocent until proven guilty, and the other one is fair play. People want to know that this record was gotten on a level playing field."

Huh. Seven years later, and I *still* don't know what the hell he said. The man really should run for Congress.

After the show, I got a call saying that Dale Petroskey wanted me to travel to the Hall of Fame and meet the museum's curator. By this point, I was ready just to be *done* with the whole damn thing. Maybe it was Eliot Spitzer, maybe it was the *Today* show, maybe it was the gnawing sense that my company was in trouble, but I *was* starting to feel like an asshole, and I *was* sick of being known as the "Barry Bonds Ball Guy." The ring was getting heavier.

Below:
In one of my marble carving "productionism" studios in China

XI. **JACK OF THE LANTERN**

I STARTED TO sense trouble when my employees began wearing suits. We seemed to have more lawyers and more finance guys buzzing around the office, working late, staring at spreadsheets. "Dude, is there a problem?" I asked Seth.

He rubbed the sleep from his eyes. "We're okay. The banks are just killing us. They are up our ass for numbers."

"What numbers?"

All the numbers, it turned out. The "no big deal" inventory problem was now a multimillion-dollar shit-show that threatened our solvency, and since we were on the hook for a huge-credit facility that was dangerously overdrawn, they gave us oral surgery through the back of our skulls. The banks investigated every transaction. The banks questioned our operations. They peeled back the label, and they probed around.

Soon even my "Marc Eckō in 2010" budget—which had been sacrosanct—started being probed. Seth didn't say it to my face, but I'd hear from my staff that he'd wonder aloud. "Do we *really* need to keep paying for PR? Can't we do this a little cheaper?"

I missed Marci. I missed the Ghost of Reason. Yes, maybe we had protective layers like CFOs and lawyers and auditors, but that's no substitute for the governance that's *in your bones*. Marci, Seth, and I had a familial, instinctive relationship. That was gone.

Four-Way Split (Homage to George Lois). *Clockwise from top left: a young Bob Dylan, Malcolm X, JFK, and Fidel Castro*

I may not have had Marci, but I still had the ball. Every day in my office, I tossed it from hand to hand, juggling it, staring at it, hating it. I couldn't wait to get rid of it, but I still needed to actually bring it to the Hall of Fame.

In the meantime, I kept throwing (quieter) parties and painting. I was inspired by an image created by George Lois who, in the sixties did a cover for

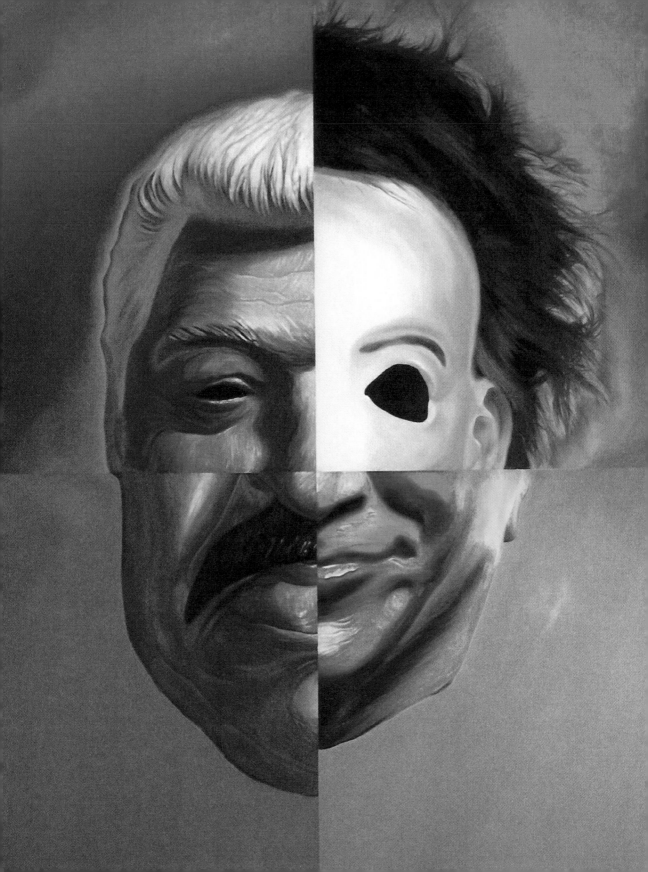

Opposite:
Horrorshow, *clockwise from top left: Bill Clinton, Michael Myers, from* Halloween *c. 1978, Dick Cheney, Saddam Hussein*

Left:
Clockwise from top left: Guy Fawkes, Mr. Bill, Grouthco, naked face

Below:
Sage, my daughter, was my first and only happy jack-o'-lantern painting. It hangs proudly in my home.

Esquire that split a face into four quadrants. As a homage to this photo, I did a productionism replica of the image in the painting, and Lois eventually visited my office and gushed, "I love it!"

"Do you mind if I use this split-face technique more?"

I developed an infatuation for masks, and soon I started to work more with sculptures, flying out to marble foundries to oversee their production. But all of this paled next to my new obsession: jack-o'-lanterns. I had lunch with a well-known socialite who also happened to be an avid art collector. She noticed an oil painting I did hanging in my office, which depicted my daughter, Sage, at age two, dressed up for Halloween, as a jack-o'-lantern.

"I love that you are doing jack-o'-lanterns," she said. "You really should do more of them."

"Skulls are the new happy face," I volleyed back. There's something more haunting about jacks, right?"

"You know the story 'Jack of the Lantern'?" she asked.

She told me the basics of the story, and then I would geek out and learn much more on my own. The story stems from an Irish folktale about "Stingy Jack," who once invited the Devil to have a drink with him. (Because why not, right?) Stingy Jack is sort of a dick, and, by all rights, he should go to hell. But Stingy Jack somehow tricks the Devil (in some versions, he turns the Devil into a coin, in some versions, he traps him in a tree—it doesn't really matter), and he makes the Devil promise him that he will never go to hell. The Devil agrees.

Later, when Stingy Jack dies, he gets to the gates of heaven, but he can't enter. Jack goes to the Devil all pissed, saying that a promise is a promise, but the Devil says something like, "I promised that you wouldn't go to hell. But I never promised that you'd get to heaven,

Purgatory Can Be Self-Indulgent:
Study No. 1 Blue

either." Jack, stuck in purgatory, complains to the Devil that he has no way to see where he is going. The Devil gives him a burning ember from the depths of hell, which Jack carries around in his lantern for eternity.

That story haunted me. The more I thought about it, the more I felt like my pursuit of fame was like making a deal with the Devil, and that I, like Stingy Jack, was in a state of purgatory. Not famous, not not-famous, just wandering around the world and carrying my "perceived" brand—my branded lantern— my rhino logo to light the way. Neither here. Nor there.

The pumpkins kept getting *bigger*. Just like I was trying to get bigger, just as the company was trying to get bigger, my lines of credit, just as Barry Bonds's head was getting bigger. (Note: nowhere in the authenticity formula do you see the variable *big*.)

> *"People will do anything, no matter how absurd, in order to avoid facing their own soul."*
>
> —CARL JUNG

But I do know this: they were telling me that something wasn't right. Marc Fernandez, one of my closest friends and also an employee, saw these paintings and said, "Do you think you should see someone, like a therapist?" *These paintings were my therapy*, even if I didn't know it. They were somehow cathartic. And they gave insight into my own EMOTIONAL IMPACT. Despite how it made others feel, I didn't like how I felt.

Seth entered the painting studio one day—he never did this—dressed up in a suit, and it looked like he hadn't slept in a week.

"We need to get out of Times Square," he told me. The banks said it was nonnegotiable. It was untenable.

Leaving Times Square? That had been Seth's baby, his vision, his holy grail. His pumpkin painting. We had built an entire scale model of the flagship store, we put the model in our showroom, and we cockily showed it off as the crown jewel of our empire. We walked international distributors through the empty

Jack-o'-lantern
Smashed to Bits

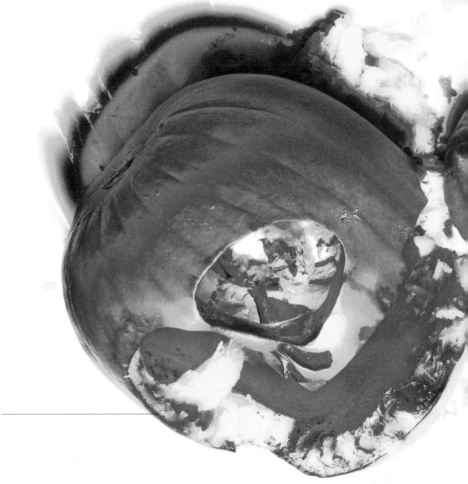

DEALING WITH YOUR OWN EMOTIONAL IMPACT

Right or wrong, these paintings were therapy. And I've learned that you can't ignore the consequences that brand creation has on your own EMOTIONAL IMPACT. Here are five ways to deal with this that are more practical than painting a hundred jack-o'-lanterns:

1. Know Your Emotions by Name

Write them down. Are you happy, are you angry, are you jealous? Are you suspicious? Identify these emotions and tack them back to reality. What in your real life is making you feel that way?

2. Take an Emotional Inventory

Either you're defined by the things you love, or you're defined by the things you hate. Draw a line down the middle of a sheet of paper. On one side write *Love* and on the other, *Hate*. Be honest and write down what's motivating you, and why. I'm not saying you should be all Dalai Lama and shit, and a bit of revenge can be a great motivator, but if you have too much negative energy, that can come back and bite you.

3. Don't Be the Round Peg in the Square Hole

With my trip down the celebrity rabbit hole, I was trying to be something I'm not. It wasn't who I am from the GUTS TO THE SKIN. Be honest about who you are and what you bring to the table.

4. Go Easy on Using the Word "Movement"

A lot of creators invest too much emotion into what they imagine as a "movement." Sorry to bum you out, but the only movements you're going to make are bowel movements. Instead of measuring yourself by crossing the finish line of that movement, measure yourself by one rung of the ladder at a time. Real movements congeal more naturally, organically. They sort themselves out in ways you can't plan or strategize. So be easy, Machiavelli!

5. Talk to Someone Besides Yourself

It's okay if it's a shrink, if it's your spouse, a best friend, or a loved one. Cherish that pillow talk. And if you're not getting pillow talk or the feedback of pillow talk at least once a week, something's not right. Don't be one of those people who are too proud to say that they're going to the doctor. And, no offense, even your relationship to God alone is not enough. You need someone who can talk back to you, give you perspective, and provide a feedback loop that's outside your own head. Shrink, wifey, or priest. Talk to a person!

store, dazzling them with possibility. Seth giving up on Times Square was . . . like Thomas Edison giving up on lightbulbs. For the first time, I knew we were truly fucked.

"You good here?" Seth asked, looking around at the deformed and violent images.

"Yeah. I'm good."

He left.

I stared at these paintings, and the room started spinning, spinning, spinning. I saw myself in the third person, lost in this vortex of splattered pumpkin. It's a cliché to say "out-of-body experience," but it was an out-of-body experience. The room finally stopped spinning. For the first time, I saw these paintings with clear, lucid eyes.

I finally understood them for what they were: a vomited-out therapy session to a shrink. But they were no longer therapeutic. I had tumbled to the bottom of the hole, and now I saw it was time to claw myself back into reality. Now the only therapy I needed was to fix my business.

XII. **THE HALL**

TO FULLY EMERGE from the rabbit hole, I had to get closure on the Barry Bonds ball. I wanted to just forget it, but I couldn't. I had made a promise. Steroids had become the biggest elephant in the room with regard to our generation of baseball, and you have all these suits in Major League Baseball pretending that nothing's going on. Bullshit. The asterisk was a blow against hypocrisy, it needed to be public, it needed to be displayed. I knew that if I didn't personally insist on an honest-to-God authentic display, they'd just bury the ball in a crate in some warehouse, like at the end of *Raiders of the Lost Ark*.

When I arrived at Cooperstown, I soaked in the complex. It was my first time at the Hall. And I'll admit: the first time, it gets you. As a fan, you can appreciate all the sport's traditions and pomp and circumstance, but it doesn't feel *real* until you're in these hallowed walls of bronze busts, plaques, artifacts.

But at the same time, there's this kind of weird hypocrisy that made me feel vindicated. Yeah, you have a whole wing devoted to Babe Ruth's nose hair, but what about the modern era? What about all the great modern moments? The Hall itself hasn't moved along. It is stuck in the past, like a grandpa who just tells old stories. How are they going to deal with the realities of our cream-and-the Clear era? They haven't had to make any decisions like that. Until right now.

I MET THE curator. Classic tweed jacket, suede elbow patches, and corduroy pants. Full-on professorial vibe. Certainly pleasant and warm.

"Right this way, Marc." He gave me an extended tour of the Hall, showing me possible areas of display. Meanwhile, I start to feel dizzy and even nauseous.

He pointed to a blank wall. "How about we put it here?"

I looked around. Huh? We were in this satellite area that wasn't even in the building, but kind of off to one side—just storage, really—an area that's *technically* in the Hall of Fame in the same way that Guam is technically part of the United States. Why not "display" it in the janitor's closet? Why not "display" it up Bud Selig's ass?

"Here?" I asked him.

"Maybe we should break for lunch?" He smile-frowned.

We had an insanely awkward lunch, joined by Dale Petroskey and a few other execs from the Hall. What could we even talk about? Even the most harmless subject—baseball—was an explosive topic. What was I going to lead with, "Gee, how 'bout that Barry Bonds!"

One of them said, "Marc, so . . . you make T-shirts?"

Another: "Marc . . . how was your drive up?"

"Marc . . . how's your chicken?"

They didn't trust me. I could tell. I was committed to giving them the ball, but not if it was going to rest at the end of some dark hallway.

After lunch, they showed me more of the Hall. I didn't feel right. My hands felt clammy, my body heated up, and my underarms trickled sweat even though the Hall was freezing with AC. I was having a panic attack, Tony Soprano style. Jesus, what was wrong with me?

I dashed to the bathroom and locked the door. I splashed cold water on my face. I looked in the mirror and saw bloodshot eyes and a strange version of myself.

What the hell am I doing here? Why aren't I in my office managing my business? I'm supposed to be running a billion-dollar company, and instead, I'm wandering around the hallways of the National Baseball Hall of Fame.

"We need to leave," I told my team.

The van pulled away from Cooperstown, and we headed back to New York. I realized that nothing was settled, that this was a pain in the ass, and the negotiations would drag on for months.

A few weeks later, while at my office, I felt dizzy again—and I blacked out. The next thing I knew, I was in Beth Israel Medical Center. I was so weak that I called my assistant Katie to help me fill out the forms; I couldn't even hold a pen.

The hospital had a huge line the way hospitals usually do. The nurse held her clipboard and asked for my name.

"Marc Eckō."

The nurse looked at her supervisor, he nodded, and they ushered me past the line to get treatment. When I walked out six hours later, hydrated, I saw the same people still waiting in line, still in pain. *Is this "Marc Eckō in 2010"? Is this the payoff of name recognition? To cut in front of people who are needier?*

The blackouts kept happening. I knew that part of it was just dehydration: I'd wake up after only four hours' sleep, pound some coffee from the French press, run five miles in the hills wearing a thirty-pound weighted vest, all after lathering my body in Albolene moisturizer to make me sweat.

I could explain some of it as a simple lack of electrolytes, but I knew there was something deeper, something darker, something more troubling. My body was starting to revolt; it had partnered with my art—the jack-o'lanterns—to tell me to wake the fuck up. My GUTS-TO-THE-SKIN brand was losing its way.

I was feeling the comedown, the crash after the high. All of the distractions were catching up to me. My "limitless" pill was not working anymore.

After I got back from the hospital, a guy stopped me in the street and said, "Yo, Marc, when are you gonna open the Times Square store?"

I looked at him. What I wanted to say to him—but didn't—was this: "I can't afford to."

The media smelled blood in the water. Someone from the Hall of Fame signaled to the press (I'm paraphrasing here), "Marc Eckō is full of shit; he's not giving us the ball."

SO WHAT HAPPENED WITH THE BALL?

My driver drove the ball to Cooperstown, and I felt immediate relief. And to the credit of good 'ol Dale Petroskey, it did go on display two days later, and it was and is displayed properly.

It turns out that not everyone was happy with that. Dale Petroskey soon "resigned" from the Hall of Fame. I can't imagine the ball helped him among the old-timers. A statement from Cooperstown referred mysteriously to Dale's "business judgments that were not in the best interest of the National Baseball Hall of Fame and Museum."

In the end, was buying the ball worth it? Seven hundred fifty thousand dollars for a baseball, performace art, panic attacks?

Yes and no. Yes—on a pure cash return on investment SKIN-TO-WORLD basis. But no—on mental health GUTS-TO-SKIN grounds.

I would do it again. It came at a huge cost, but it firmly established me as a voice of rebelliousness, irreverence, and insurgency in the face of authority. A T-shirt with the slogan "Stand Up to Authority"? C'mon. That doesn't have any EMOTIONAL IMPACT. That doesn't make people feel. The war of marketing isn't won with money, it's won with ideas.

I do have two addendums to "Was it worth it?"

1. "How you make people feel" also needs to include how *you* feel. I lost sight of that. And it took me to a dark place. In the brand that's to my GUTS TO SKIN, I'm not *authentically* a pop star, or a celebrity. I function best when I'm the creative director behind the curtain, not when I'm on the stage in front of it. I was trying too hard to fit the square peg into the round hole, and my guts-to-the-skin brand suffered. You lose your perspective and authenticity.

2. You can't be *so* focused on how you make people feel that you lose sight of *what you make*. The two need balance. And for this journey down the rabbit hole, I became so obsessed with the soft stuff—the *feel*—that I skimped on the harder stuff. I had forgotten about the cash register, the presentation of the product, the advertising, the merchandising. And if the banks had their way, we were about to be shut down permanently.

And at the same time, the parallel media story was, "Marc Eckō is an asshole who could afford to buy a $750,000 ball, but he can't afford to pay rent in Times Square." I wasn't too eager to see that headline.

Of course, this was ridiculous. I had always intended to give the ball to the Hall; my tax attorney had even finalized all the paperwork. I just didn't want to see the ball get buried.

But screw it. I needed to end the stalemate with the Hall; I needed to move on, I needed to start letting go of my nostalgia for the past.

I gave the ball to my driver. "Get this out of here."

IMAGINE FACTOR $=$ *delta of*

"I'm OG'ing the lane,
gotti in the league
So how the fuck
you gonna coach me
in your league?"

—WARREN G.,
"Still in Love"

"Statesmen . . . , standing
so completely within
the institution, never
distinctly and nakedly
behold it. They speak of
moving society, but have
no resting-place without
it. They may be men of
a certain experience and
discrimination . . . ; but all
their wit and usefulness
lie within certain not very
wide limits."

—HENRY DAVID THOREAU,
On the Duty of Civil Disobedience (abridged)

CHAPTER 9

LOYALTY

TO NOSTALGIA

LOYALTY TO NOSTALGIA: *The* IMAGINE FACTOR (⌾) *is a function of three connected forces:* VISION FOR THE FUTURE, LOYALTY TO NOSTALGIA, *and the* DELTA OF NOW (N∇W). *The future needn't involve flying cars or a Willy Wonka chocolate factory; the future is in five minutes. One definition of the future is simply "the time yet to come." That's it. The future can be your next cup of coffee.*

And there's no way to envision the future without the knowledge of where you are right now, this second. It's critical that you have the mental space, consciousness, and sobriety to fully inhabit the N∇W. Consciousness is underrated. Entrepreneurs can be so focused on the blinking lights of Tomorrow-Land that they overlook the reality of today.

Neither the FUTURE *nor the* N∇W *can be contemplated until you've cleared away your* LOYALTY TO NOSTALGIA, *and all the baggage of comfort that may come with it. It's important to respect history—learn from it, leverage it—but if you get too comfortable, this same history can blind you and trap you. Only when you've pruned and purged your emotional baggage can you see the horizon. The baggage of nostalgia comes in many different forms: your parents' nostalgia, your industry's nostalgia, and your culture's nostalgia. But the most dangerous nostalgia is your own.*

I. FAILED ENTREPRENEUR

EVER SINCE CHILDHOOD, I've been up against the gatekeepers. There have been so many: the break-dancing crowd led by Supreme Mathematics, the fraternity at Rutgers, the hard-core graf artists, the trade show circuit, the Council of Fashion Designers of America, the Baseball Hall of Fame. On every level of that video game, the gatekeeper gets a little tougher, a little craftier, a little harder to vanquish.

I've learned to ignore these gatekeepers or find a way around them. But in 2011, after nearly twenty years of working outside the system, I was about to be blessed by one of the holiest gatekeepers of corporate America: the accounting firm Ernst & Young.

Someone from the Entrepreneur of the Year committee reached out to me and suggested that I should be a nominee for New York's "Entrepreneur of the Year." A representative called me up and said, "Marc, you're a shoo-in for the New York award. Not for nothing, but I think your story's great. The fact that you turned things around and landed on your feet in this economy . . ."

"You really think so?" I was skeptical.

"We love your story. I'll interview you, you'll fill out some paperwork, and then you'll meet some of our sponsors. There's only one formal interview process. Not to worry."

"You know the last few years have been a bumpy ride . . ."

"Marc, trust me. Just fill out the paperwork."

The gates were opening. The gatekeepers were letting me in. Even after I had plenty of money, success, and was lucky enough to work at what I loved, still, even after all this time, the gatekeepers could be so seductive.

So I had my assistant Katie fill out some forms, connected the dots for the Ernst & Young guy, and I signed a few docs. Granted, I probably skimped a little on the paperwork—but they reached out to me. Shoo-in, right?

If the early gatekeepers (Rutgers, Michael Bivins) were a level 1 or level 2 boss, then Ernst & Young was the fire-breathing dragon, the ultimate Bowser. And I was about to defeat the game.

Months went by. Then it came time for that one "formal" meet and greet with the selection committee. I was honored, flattered, and I'll admit it: excited. This was a corporate coronation.

At the meeting, I wore my nonthreatening taupe blazer and jean getup. I had a pep to my step, and I shook everyone's hand warmly. The room was filled with rich old white guys. As I settled into my seat, a burly man in his midsixties, wearing glasses, introduced himself as Tim Zagat, the cofounder and CEO of Zagat Survey (the restaurant and hospitality review service). He crossed his arms and said, "So I think we have a mutual friend."

He named someone I didn't recognize.

Tim Zagat smirked. "From CIT."

CIT. The bank group. *Oy veh*. These are the guys who once featured me in their media campaigns (that ran in men's lifestyle and travel magazines) as a poster boy for success—a shining example of why you, too, should take out loans—and who then, when things got hairy, gave us a rectal exam for the next three years. Uh-oh. If that's the first thing that Tim Zagat wants to talk about, this is a bad, bad sign.

Another of the suits said, "You know, your paperwork is incomplete."

"We found your financials . . . vague," said another.

"You've had quite a run of bad press," said a third.

"And with the Times Square closing . . ." said a fourth.

"We're not sure you're in compliance," said another.

"Plus, there's your bankruptcy . . ."

Wait, whoa, what?! Bankruptcy? I never went bankrupt. In a frozen credit market, we found a way to *save* our company from bankruptcy, a nontrivial detail that the press seemed to overlook. The press pronounced us dead well before the funeral.

"Look," I said, trying to remain calm. "If my paperwork is the standard by which you guys measure, and if that paperwork is insufficient, then maybe I shouldn't be here, and I apologize." And I was genuinely sorry. "But I didn't ask for this award, you guys reached out to me, and I gave you access to my CFO. There was full transparency. I think there might be a misunderstanding."

Tim Zagat took off his glasses, leaned forward, looked me dead in the eyes, and said something that I will take with me to the grave: "Marc, we're not in the habit of celebrating . . . failed entrepreneurs."

Failed entrepreneur?

Failed entrepreneur. His words looped through my brain in slow motion, loud, his lips moving slowly as I visualized them again and again, the camera focused tight on his mouth. Failed entrepreneur. *Failed* entrepreneur.

Feeling myself get defensive, I blurted out the first thing that came into my head: "How can I be a 'failed entrepreneur' when I spent over twenty million building my home?"

They looked at me. Frowned.

As the words tumbled out of my mouth, I realized how defensive, how stupid they sounded. I had a Kanye tantrum. I had fallen into their trap. I was playing by the rules of their game, not mine.

But was it true? *Failed entrepreneur?*

II. TRAPPED

THE "FAILURE" THEY talked about was rooted in 2008, during a time when we were suffocating. We were imprisoned by twin forces, one of them legal and one of them philosophical, and both of them stubbornly real. These two forces were:

1. The noose of debt, which slithered around my neck and grew tighter every day, every hour, every tick of the clock.

2. The ivory tower of my own nostalgia. The concept of debt is easy enough to understand, but it's this second force—the seductive and poisonous power of nostalgia—that can kill you in the end.

During 2007 and 2008, we used our shiny new credit lines to scale up to more than one hundred retail stores (up from about sixty locations the year prior) at a pace that was very difficult to sustain. The stores were expensive. Think of it like having a baby: the costs don't end at the hospital. Well, Seth and I had a litter of babies, and every new store meant more inventory, more furniture, more fixtures, more employees, and always more, more, more. Then layer on our little inventory fiasco, and, needless to say, we were getting crushed.

To boot, we were dealing with the whipsaw of having so much hypergrowth from 2006 to 2008, which stretched our "elastic waistband" to the point where it lost its memory. We had stretched too far too fast. Not only with our retail but also with brands like G-Unit, a massive hit that went from 0 to 100 in eighteen months and then collapsed even faster. G-Unit, and the idea of diversification, was one of the reasons we moved to Twenty-third Street, and now, with that brand losing steam, we had an entire wing of our office barren; a sprawling cubicle wasteland.

There was also the supersized Times Square albatross that never made us a nickel. On top of the punishing lease payments, the building meant fees after fees to pay architects, permits, and consultants. In hindsight, we should have at least set up a folding table and a cash register and sold a few hoodies.

We had bought a company called Avirex to help us with the lower end of the market, but we quickly learned that wasn't an effective model. The margins were razor thin. A proper old-school grind, and we were not operationally fit to run that play. We were still spending cash on Zoo York, which, while successful and showing upside, wasn't the sort of beast that the Eckō brands were. Like Zoo, *Complex* too was growing, and it was still in reinvestment mode.

Then the real kicker: the market shit the bed. Like so much of America, we had spent and spent and spent from 2006 to 2008, putting more chips on the table and betting on continued growth. As any craps player knows, this is a damn good feeling until the shooter rolls 11. The market dried up at the worst possible time. Imagine having every penny you own in the stock market during the Great Depression. On a macro level, we all watched as consumer demand weakened, credit became an endangered species, and the banks made it a daily job to play ping-pong with my balls.

THE MARKET SHIT THE BED.

THE NOSTALGIA

NOSTALGIA

INSTITUTIONS

Loyalty to Nostalgia: Are you judging its institution on the ACTION and IMPACT, or merely celebrating its pomp and ceremony?

THE DEBT IS what's on the surface. That's what you can read about in *Harvard Business Review*. It's not unimportant, but it's not, ultimately, what will make or break you.

Artists, salesmen, and CEOs all have one thing in common: we get proud. When we grow our brand, we cling to it, we nurture it, and we often take that brand and use it to create an entire *institution*—sometimes losing sight of the original pearl. We grow mentally flabby. These institutions can be corporations, legal structures, or, more broadly, even mental frameworks of how our worlds should be configured. We get comfortable with these institutions. We swaddle ourselves with them like a warm blanket.

We have a certain nostalgia for these institutions, and this nostalgia can blind us to the future. Even more damaging, it can make us lose sight of the NOW. This is the formula's great equalizer. You could have a strong UNIQUE VOICE, be truthful, and exert a powerful EMOTIONAL IMPACT, but if you can't even see the NOW, much less the FUTURE, you're dead.

That was me in 2008. I had cocooned myself in this blanket of how Seth and I had configured the business. I had lost sight of the *anatomy* of what was beneath the company's skin. The world changed all around me, but I couldn't see it, wouldn't see it. Part of this nostalgia is something that might seem overly abstract and *boardroomy*, but it's a deadly serious issue that every entrepreneur should think about from Day One: the way your company is configured.

I had always been an equity hoarder. Instead of cashing out equity, I just leveraged it—and everything else along the way: my inventory, trademarks, and myself, for that matter. It was as if I were listening to the bizzaro version of Kenny Roger's song "The Gambler": "You gotta know when to hold 'em / Know when to fold 'em." Hold 'em, hold 'em, hold 'em. I had no other strategies. I was a holder—especially of a monster line of credit. The banks would collateralize this credit in one of two ways:

1. IP. THE INTELLECTUAL PROPERTIES.

All those expensive and defendable trademarks that had been meticulously registered and filed throughout the world.

2. PERSONAL GUARANTEES (PGS).

I had my big-boy pants on when I signed PGs, but I was working off decades of history that said that the market would act a certain way. Then came 2008 and the credit crisis. Suddenly PGs went from being this abstract concept to a cellophane bag that wrapped around my head and mouth. No oxygen. *They can take my home. They can force bankruptcy.*

Most entrepreneurs don't realize this when they start out. It's a common psychology: "I want to own my baby. I *must* own my baby." Seth loved to say, "I'd rather have a big piece of something small than a small piece of something big." Cute saying, but does it make sense? He was willing to grind the business down to a $1 million nub as long as *he owned it*. You don't need to tolerate that kind of pain. There are other ways. People confuse "selling equity" with "selling out." As long as you retain adequate control and along the way create value by liquidating some chips, who gives a shit about how much equity you own?

The perception is "I must own it all!" This is the reality: it's best to distribute the risk of the stakeholders into classes that best serve the needs of the company. It's like building your starting five in basketball. You don't recruit all forwards or all centers.

Neither Seth nor I was rigorous with high finance, and the company probably would have been better served if someone with those chops had some skin in the game. You have mouths to feed: not just yours but also your employees' and their kids'. It's unhealthy to not contemplate distributing the equity across smart and capable stakeholders with skins you may not have. When one sole proprietor loses his shit, breaks down, or gets caught with his pants down, it's a nice design to have other parties.

In fact, almost immediately after the inception of a plan for a business, you should be ready to ask yourself, "What about the exit?" A fire escape, an alternative egress, is not only valuable in the event of a fire or an emergency but exhibits responsible, preemptive thinking and is valuable to whoever may

"I will gladly pay you Tuesday for a hamburger today."

consider purchasing you. Even if you aren't looking to sell, it shapes how the Street may look at you in the event you go public. It's not about selling out. It's about optionality and understanding. When I tell this to young hustlers, they look at me confused and offended. What they don't realize is that it's one of the most responsible things they can do. "I may never exit," they declare. But they miss the point. Would you build a house without a back door? A fire escape? Knowing the exit scenario informs the way you may best grow a plan, while mitigating the downside. It makes you better understand the market on a macro scale. Some folks eat, others get eaten. Are you a viable acquisition target? To who? To just one company? Many? Why? Prove it? This is what I mean by saying "back door."

This LOYALTY TO NOSTALGIA was just as choking as any note of debt. And it was about to squeeze me on all sides and flatten my skull.

Another layer of nostalgia was that "Marc Eckō in 2010" document, which turned out to have some unintended consequences. I was getting plenty of media attention, as the *New York Post* called me a "flamboyant flameout" and a "debt-ridden designer." Gawker called me a "free-spending, once-cool designer," and then wagged its finger at me and said, "You lost all your money."

The media gobbled up this story. A guy who, seemingly overnight, went from throwing Sundance parties to questioning how I'd pay my rent. A guy who rose fast and fell faster. (For the record, almost no one rises "fast." It takes years of gradual growth, batting practice, and iterative improvement before you pop on the radar.) A guy who went from buying Barry Bonds's home run ball to closing down his Times Square store. (For the record, well, that's true.)

That's the dark side of entrepreneurship. The parts that Trump never seems to write or lecture about. When athletes compete, they bang their knees, they bang their shoulders, and it's physically traumatic. But entrepreneurs? It's a full-contact sport for them, too. They bang their emotions and egos, and that informs the very cadence of their walks. If a deal goes south, if your stock tumbles, if your brand loses its shine, suddenly you hunch over, you slouch, and you don't feel like yourself. It fucking sucks.

Another heavy bag of nostalgia I was carrying was the painting factory. One day Seth dropped by my office, which was strewn with paintings stacked five deep against the walls. "Marc, I've been doing my best to cut costs where I can, but we're getting down to the bone. It would mean a lot to me if you were more focused."

Never begrudge the concept of an exit plan. Yes, your company (idea) is precious. But like caring for a child, a company needs a contingency plan in the event of unforseen circumstances. It's never too early to think about it.

He left unspoken what "more focused" meant: the painting factory. I took one more look at these jack-o'-lanterns, and I saw that they were oddly clairvoyant. They foreshadowed the state of our company and our world: too big, too overstuffed, too inauthentic. Part of me *needed* to paint these paintings, as they were therapeutic, like some sort of emotional colonic.

But I needed to stop "playing make-believe Warhol." I needed to stop parroting some imagined "Marc Eckō in 2010" and start being Marc Eckō *now*. I had confused my personal brand with my company's brand, and it was time to set that straight.

I picked up a half-finished jack-o'-lantern painting. Instead of grabbing a paintbrush, I reached for a box cutter. I sliced the bitch in the middle. Then I got my packing tape and packed up the finished ones one stack at a time. Then another. And another. (NVW)

III. **MOMMY AND DADDY**

S INCE WE COULDN'T concentrate or focus on the now, Seth and I started fighting. Our employees could tell that "Mommy and Daddy" no longer got along. As the debt choked our company, we unleashed our frustrations on each other, bickering, sniping, fighting. It got ugly. We started raising our voices, and then we took to yelling, and pretty soon we had explosive fights that sent our staffs scurrying away anxiously. Every phone call ended with one of us hanging up on the other.

"Don't talk to Seth!" I'd bark at an employee. "Talk to me! This marketing budget—this budget needs to go through *me* now, do you understand?"

The pressure of doom can do funny things to how you treat people. My friend, my partner, my compatriot for almost twenty years suddenly brought out the worst in me, and I did the same to him. Seth was a high school and college wrestler, so he always used BRUTE FORCE and came out swinging.

Still, underneath it all, it wasn't as bad as people thought. We were mostly just mad at the situation, not at each other. Even in the darkest times, Seth and I had a fundamental and deep level of respect. Privately, we laughed about the fighting and even toyed with the idea of a hoax.

EMOTIONAL RESCUE:
I Hate Myself for Loving You

To some extent, a certain amount of fighting is natural. Human beings are emotional creatures. Despite all the guidelines of rigor and compliance, math and science, we have to work really hard to "act" rational. Bill Gates, Stephen Hawking, Elon Musk—all emotional little bitches. Doubt me? It's in our nature. So it'd be foolish and unrealistic of me to counsel you to never have emotional arguments, as that'd be like saying, "Never drink water" or "Never shit." We're humans. This is what we do. But what you *can* control is how public it is. Keep those emotional arguments in private.

We were so trapped by our own nostalgia. We couldn't see any options besides *pain*. The pressure was breaking us. Instead of working on what the fixes could be, we were trapped in the firefight of just-in-time crises. We had already abandoned Times Square, we started to shed Twenty-third Street by subletting space, we gutted our marketing budget, and now we faced the inevitable: layoffs. We worked with our board and did it George Steinbrenner–style, saying, "Okay, let's say you had to fire everyone. Now, who would you keep?" This is the ugly side of cutting your nostalgia to the past. It's easy to shuck away your hometown nostalgia, your industry's nostalgia, or the world's nostalgia. The hard part is letting go of *your own*.

The banks saw only one fix: bankruptcy. To them, it was simple: they had our intellectual properties as collateral, and in a fire sale, that IP would cover the nut we owed.

Advisors, lawyers, colleagues—*everyone* wanted us to declare bankruptcy. "It won't be that bad." "You have a lot to be proud of." "It happens to the best of them." "Wipe your hands and be done with it."

But what about the brand? What about my personal brand? What about the good work that I knew our company was still doing? Hidden underneath this muddy layer of debt, Seth and I could clearly see flickers of growth and innovation: the retail stores were alive and well, Cut & Sew was taking off, and *Complex* was firing on all cylinders (even though the banks *hated* it). Moreover, we had labored hard to create this platform that had been so good to us and that we still believed in. How could we just abandon it?

"Let's pretend we're having a fistfight!" I told him in his office. "Throw me across the table."

Seth grinned, like old times. "Maybe it'll make Page Six?"

"For sure. We'll choreograph it. I'll hit you three times, and then you hit me one time."

"Why do I only get to hit you once?" Seth asked.

"Because you're stronger than me—and I'm prettier."

Jokes aside, things would only get nastier. It boiled over in a marketing meeting for a mobile app product I had envisioned, called Eckō Heads. Seth called a meeting of ten people—I have no idea why it needed to be ten people; three would have sufficed—and he seemed all too eager to shit all over my idea.

"This won't work," Seth said, ending the discussion without offering anything constructive.

I couldn't hold back any longer and vented my anger. "You're saying no to fucking everything!" I felt my blood rushing to my head. "What are you prescribing? What will it take to get a yes?"

"I don't fucking know!" Seth snapped. "But when it's a yes, I'll tell you at that time."

"What's your problem?"

"You're not an expert in this industry," Seth said. "You can't make an accurate prediction. Show me the *data* that this will work." My partner had become so traumatized by the bank interactions that he'd become some sort of weird "born-again" superaccountant, like Alwyn Ernst of Ernst & Young.

Not an expert?! Data!? Who drew the Venn diagram of *Complex* network? Who named this company? Swept up in the fury of emotion, I focused my anger on an innocent bystander, one of the many fleeting boy wonder marketing employees Seth had brought in to save the day. Let's call him Chucky.

"Well, here's a fucking prediction. You see this guy you hired here?" I unconciously glared at poor Chucky, sitting between Seth and me. "I predict he won't even be here in three months. That's what you do: hire and fire, hire and fire."

I'm not proud of that meeting. (I doubt Seth is either.) I know I acted like a prick, but if I'm writing a book about authenticity, I have to own up to sometimes acting like a prick. That meeting was a turning point. Employees quit within the next couple of weeks, and I started to sense that somehow, someway, we would need a new vision for the way everything was structured. We needed surgery. Even if that surgery was painful, and even if we didn't have any anesthesia.

IV. GENERATIONAL DEBT (HUMILITY)

$$\int_0^{100} f(HUMILITY)dx$$

"**B**ANKRUPTCY!" CRIED THE bank.
"Bankruptcy," insisted our advisor.

"Bankruptcy," whispered the Devil, tempting me to just end it, just kill it, just stop the pain.

Not without a fight. One of the many steps we were advised to do was to consult with an expert. So we were fortunate enough to cross paths with a "turnaround guy," Hank Reeves, a former GE'er who's like yet another Winston Wolfe from *Pulp Fiction*: the experienced gray-hair who can be the voice of reason (and dispose of the bodies).

Governance. He helped us untangle the corporate mess, leases, and all the immediate firefights. (These mechanical details are great fodder for some *Harvard Business Review* case study, but they're immaterial to the formula. If you're an accountant seeking the optimal configuration for inventory class 3407B, I suggest a different book. And a stiff drink.)

Seth and I still had another play before we would submit: a potential lifeline from our associates at Li & Fung. During the years prior to the fiasco, they had been very generous partners and had also granted us a significant line of credit. Maybe we could convert that debt into equity in our company? Maybe they'd take on the dysfunctional child and help us operate our way out of the mess. Would they work with us not to sink the ship, despite the cries from the bank syndicate urging us to do just that?

Since 2006, Li & Fung had been both a manufacturing partner and creditor, which is not an uncommon relationship. It did this for many brands; after all, the company is one of the largest exporters in the world. Seth and I traveled back to Hong Kong to meet with them, hats in hand, even staying at the same glitzy hotel where once, only a few years prior, we had clinked our champagne flutes and toasted "to generational wealth!" Now we could sit in that same piano bar and drink away the anxiety of "generational debt."

Once again we met with Victor and his brother William Fung. But this time the conversation wasn't so pleasant. This time Victor didn't ask about Lakewood or how we would "mainstream ourselves." This time he pressed us—understandably—on how, if they gave us more time, we could make good on the debt. You can't blame them. Li & Fung had always been a good business partner and had always given us the benefit of the doubt, but now the Fungs had good reason to doubt.

Seth wasn't on his A game that meeting, and I was probably a D–, or maybe even an F+. "Why would we give you a new line of credit?" Victor asked as I stared at his $10 watch.

YOU MIGHT BE A NEPOTIST IF...

Marci, Seth, and I took care of our family members. (And sometimes family can be your best partner, like Marci, or employees.) In the boom years, we employed our sister-in-laws, our father-in-laws, my brother-in-law, and my God-knows-what-in-laws, happy to help our extended network of family and friends. This always seemed like the right thing to do and I don't regret lending a hand.

Our financial bind forced us to either fire them or ask them to take less. It was awful. If you're a young entrepreneur with money to burn (or you imagine yourself as such), I'm not advising you to be stingy, but the trick is to *be generous in a way that doesn't handcuff you (or them)*.

Here's the deal: Write them a check. Give them a gift. Yes, giving them a job for their birthday is well intentioned, but the road to hell is paved with good intentions.

You might be a nepotist

- *if* your employee's "job interview" involved tequila

- *if* you have staff meetings during Thanksgiving dinner
- *if* you host weddings at a company sales summit
- *if* you share a last name with 10 percent of your company
- *if* you once gave wedgies to your head of marketing.

And, more seriously:

- *if* you can't fire them without being disowned—literally or figuratively.

So don't be a nepotist.

They had no interest in taking on the dysfunctional kid, and why should they? That wasn't their business. But as a testament to their good faith and our years of partnership, they kindly restructured our debt *just enough* to keep a fluttering pulse. *No* on debt-for-equity. *Yes* on time.

After the Li & Fung meetings, around midnight, we still had to do a conference call with the US banks. (Every day, it seemed, we had a conference call with the bank.) I looked around for Seth, as we were supposed to call in together, and couldn't find him. I checked the piano bar where the cheesy Celine Dion singer used to croon, I checked the lobby, I checked the front desk—nowhere. Seconds before the call, I found . . . Seth's *bag*, which he had tossed on the ground and left for me to pick up. The bag was from Hugo Boss and the Boss label stared at me, taunting me.

This was so fitting: Seth had literally left me holding the bag. The "boss." I took the call in the hotel lobby, fuming. Afterward I bunkered myself in the hotel room and wrote in my diary, livid, vomiting out my crazy, ballistic feelings about Seth and the state of our business. I barfed all of this nastiness into my Moleskine notebook, like a teenager, pissed and righteous. It was cathartic. I took a blowtorch to all those

C . H . I . L . L .   G

Old dirty bastard says,
"C.H.I.L.L.- G!"

Business trauma can make you panic. You feel like you're lost in the woods, hungry, alone, and your iPhone doesn't have any service. So how do you get out of the woods? I'm no Smokey the Bear, but I follow the principles of smoked-out Wu-Tang rapper Russell Tyrone Jones aka Ol' Dirty Bastard (RIP), who proclaims C.H.I.L.L. G—a survival guide for both outdoor and corporate meltdowns.

CALM THE FUCK DOWN

Don't panic. Breathe. Separate what you *need* to have versus what you *want* to have. If your hand is pinned beneath a rock and you're delirious, maybe you *want* to have a cream puff, but what you need is a cup of water. (And a knife.)

HEED THE SUN

Find a twig. Plant that twig in the dirt, straight up, and observe the sun's shadow. You just created a sundial. The sun is the one source of energy that will always be there.

The sun is never more important than when you are lost. Dig deep and think about your sun. Is it your creativity? Your spouse and kids? Your faith? Whatever it is, find it, embrace it, don't lose sight of it. Find your sun. With the sun behind you, informing your direction, there can be *no* wrong path.

INSPECT WHAT'S AROUND YOU

Do some recon. Are there signs of any roads? Does the ground have a slope? That slope is important—find the high ground. The high ground will give you a better vantage point, and every farmer knows that shit rolls downhill. In business, you need to take that high ground, even if you're tired, even if it's steep, even if your feet slip in the mud and you bloody your nose.

LISTEN

Cup your ear to the ground. Any signs of running water, a road, a train track? Don't just listen once and

give up—move around, listen more, and then move and listen more. The process is iterative. When you panic in business, it's easy to listen only to the ramblings in your head. Seek other input. Even listen to the critical feedback that's hard to hear. Can you decipher what you need to hear versus what you want to hear?

LAY OUT A PLAN

Are you going to go to the source of the water, head to the road, look for the high ground? Don't try to do everything at once. Create your plan in discrete blocks of time. *Tonight I will build a fire. This will keep me warm. Tomorrow I will search for the road.* With your company, don't play for Year Ten when you might go bankrupt tomorrow. Find the wood for your fire.

GO

Take your action. Don't begrudge it. Don't second-guess it. Don't think about how painful it will be. Just go.

institutions that I had been clinging to (even the ones in my head or the ones I made), and it felt good. It sounds corny. Juvenile, even. Especially by the standards of being a badasss "entrepreneur"—but it worked. Suddenly I was in a conscious state of *now*.

The next morning, I felt a new sense of calm. I knew what I had to do. Maybe it was the symmetry of toasting generational debt in the same Hong Kong hotel where we had shouted "generational wealth!" Maybe it was the vomiting session in my notebook, which exhausted my emotions and let me see more clearly.

You know the real-life character that James Franco played in the movie *127 Hours*? Aron Ralston, a canyoneer, was pinned under a rock, dying of dehydration. This is how I FELT. Alive but losing oxygen, delirious, and unable to focus on the *now*. Trapped under one of the fallen rocks from my ivory tower of debt, my desperate mind had been able only to fathom the past, suffocated by a LOYALTY TO NOSTALGIA.

I now knew that if we wanted to see the future, the only option was to do something drastic. This would be hard. This would be bloody. This would *sacrifice a part of me*. But I had to do it. You have to. Even if you have to lose a finger, a hand, an entire leg, the idea of not breathing and giving up is not an option.

So you do it. You don't wait for the doctor. You don't wait for the sterile environment. You take the dull blade, you put the towel in your mouth, and you bite down and cut off the bitch. You don't begrudge it.

On the cab ride back to the Hong Kong airport, as Seth and I stared out the windows, I mentally took out the dull blade and held it to my wrist.

"Let's just fix this," I said.

"Meaning?"

"We can't 'own it' all anymore."

"We can talk back in Jersey," Seth said.

It was time to cut off my hand. And I had made peace with that.

V. CUT OFF THE HAND. SAVE THE HEAD.

ALMOST TWENTY YEARS ago, Seth and I discussed our VISION FOR THE FUTURE. We were barely old enough to buy beer, and Seth was still wearing the nut-hugging jeans shorts. The day we discussed becoming partners, Seth asked me, "Where do you envision yourself when you're forty?"

"Forty?" I laughed. "I'm barely thinking about this afternoon."

"I'm serious."

"Okay . . ." I said modestly. "*Chillin'*?"

Seth found this hilarious. "At forty, that's the point in your life when you'll be working your hardest. We'll be so big, we'll be so entrenched, we'll be working our asses off. Chilling??"

I thought about that conversation as I pulled my car into Seth's driveway in Highland Park, New Jersey. This was the night: the end of one era, the beginning of another. Tonight was our face-to-face, a meeting that would resolve the future of Eckō. No lawyers, no lieutenants, no consiglieres. Just the two of us, just like how it began.

"Hmm. Chillin'?"

As I parked the car, it felt like a mirror image of our first meeting all those years ago. Back then, as I was painting, Seth had roared up to my garage in his Mustang, hopped out the window like some action movie star, and shook my hand. Now our roles were reversed: I drove up to his home, and *he* was the one running the operations machine of Eckō Unltd.

That night we hatched a plan to:

1. Avoid bankruptcy.
2. Protect the brand.
3. Reconfigure the ownership.
4. Shed our LOYALTY TO NOSTALGIA by bleeding out parts of the overly engorged jack-o'-lantern that was our company.
5. Let each of us pursue his own VISION FOR THE FUTURE.

The goal was to *reconfigure* it without *disfiguring* it.

I knocked on the door, and Seth greeted me with a bro-hug, no trace of acrimony in his voice.

"Hey."

"Hey."

He escorted me to the basement, and then we proceeded to have a mostly unemotional, uneventful negotiation that did the right thing for Eckō the company and Eckō the man (and Seth). There were no fireworks.

We needed to unwind this mammoth machine. We had so many brands and subbrands and layers of complications. It's like a forest, and sometimes that forest needs a controlled burn. You might have plenty of strong, healthy trees in that forest, but they're choked by the deadwood. We needed to preserve the core creative machine that drove product development, retail, and marketing. Everything else was up for discussion. Molt what's wasteful. Preserve the core. Shed your skin.

EQUITY HOARDING

We were equity hoarders. Except for the period of time with the Austrians, who were only silent partners, Seth, Marci, and I wanted no part in diluting our ownership, finding new investors, or exploring other means of financing. We thought that wasn't "keeping it real." This was naive. You don't have to literally *own* every percent of your stock to truly own your brand. (Do you think Phil Knight, the guy who cofounded Nike, still owns the company? He doesn't. (There are 0 individual people who own more than 5% of Nike. Zero.) Does that make him, or Nike, any less authentic? Does that make him a sellout?) This is a lesson it would take us a while to learn. Distribute your interests. Distribute your risks. Don't hoard.

Some of this we cracked in Seth's basement, and some of it we worked out with our lawyers and turnaround guys. Leveraging a play that Seth had been developing for months, we could find a new partner in Iconix, the fashion brand conglomerate. Neil Cole, its CEO, had the vision to see our potential. He was a welcome voice of reason, and he saw the opportunity and gave us a landing. A new configuration. We could get an immediate injection of cash (alleviating the CIT burden) in exchange for shedding 51 percent of our equity in our trademarks (I.P.). Yes, this meant that we wouldn't *own* it all, but you know what? Did we really ever own it all? That's what happens when you hit a certain scale, age, or sense of awareness. You appreciate that despite "the Numbers," you didn't build it by yourself. You always worked for someone. The bank. Your kids. Your community. (And that's how it should be.) Finally, I came to terms with this.

Seventeen years after starting the company, Seth and I still had 100 percent equity and complete control. Can you say that about Calvin or Ralph? Seventeen years after starting Calvin Klein, he didn't have complete control. Who ever really has complete control? And holding it too tightly can be perilous . . . and lonely. Or look at Nike: seventeen years after launching, it was a publicly held company; Phil Knight didn't own it all. This is what grown-ups do.

You

100%

YOUR BRAND

— *vs.* —

NIKE

No single individual owns 5% or more of Nike.

Held by insitutions and mutual funds.

82%

18%

Phil Knight
(Nike cofounder and chairman)

The deal with Iconix would save the company in a brutal market. And then, within the remaining 49 percent of the pie, Seth and I hammered out a deal where I could step away from the day-to-day operations but still be incentivized to be a part of the family and the brand's identity.

The new arrangement saved our brand, saved our ecosystem, ensured a path with less resistance, and freed me up to focus on my intellectual curiosities and passions.

The company—though changed—was saved. In the most savage credit market since the Great Depression, Seth and I had not only averted the disaster but also tacked down a foundation that allowed for future growth. I spun *Complex* off as its own entity (funded by venture capital, which probably should have been the case all along), and under the leadership of Rich Antoniello, my partner and CEO, it has evolved into a media juggernaut. Our Eckō retail stores—which once threatened to cripple us—sustained us as the economy continued to shrink.

We cheated death. Looking back on my career, this deal was my most unlikely, most surprising, most *successful* entrepreneurial coup. I sawed off my hand, but I saved my body. It's painful and it's bloody, but this is what you do. I was proud of it then, and I'm proud of it now.

So, back to our friends at Ernst & Young.

When they called me a *failed entrepreneur*, I gave them a lame, defensive answer, trying to use the vanity of my *stuff*, my *home*, *my fortunes*, as some proof of my success as an entrepreneur. Weak.

Those are external standards. Those are the rules of *their* game. That's the language of the gatekeepers, and it's not authentic to me.

Here's the better answer:

By clearing away that brush—the debt, the old configuration, the misguided "Marc Eckō in 2010"—I had allowed myself to finally see clearly. I had shed my LOYALTY TO NOSTALGIA, and that allowed me to focus on the NOW. This allowed a new VISION FOR THE FUTURE, a future that held a more authentic self. And now I can share that story, and my prescription with others.

Today I'm less involved in the day-to-day operations of Ecko Unltd., but I will be forever attached to the platform—it's been so good to me. Once a Yankee, always a Yankee. I want to see her built to last, and I'll continue to lend her my insights and creative chairmanship. Good, bad, or indifferent, she will always be my baby.

That guy from Ernst & Young who reached out initially eventually called me up to apologize, saying, "Next year, we'll put you up for consideration for an honorary lifetime-achievement award."

No thanks. I finally realized that *who I am* and *what I do* is more important than its institutional measures of success. And as it turned out, I learned a little more about this institution, which, as the ultimate gatekeeper—the final Big Boss—is trusted with the scorekeeping of corporate America.* Ya know what they say about casting stones and glass houses, right?

Ernst & Young* is an accounting firm. But think about that word. What does it mean to be *accountable*? What does it mean to "comply with standards of excellence?" Whose definition of *excellence*?

It's important for you—for all of us—to be accountable to our own measures for success, not just the arbitrary rubrics of others. We live in a world that measures wealth by numbers, and schools that measure learning by standardized test scores. Who's testing the testers? Who's measuring the measurers?

Of course, there's no getting around the need for some basic external standards—I'm not endorsing anarchy—but at the end of the day, the criteria for accountability should ultimately be based on your GUTS-TO-SKIN brand. Refuse to be packaged in what "they" see and say. Push yourself hard. Set your bar high. And focus on jumping *your* bar, not theirs.

I've learned to set my own bar. And instead of relying on the gatekeepers' formula for success in building authentic brands, I decided to create my own.

*Accountability: Look, I've had the media say unsavory bits about me. They've speculated on my company, and often they've been wrong. So I won't try to be the "Where there's smoke there's fire" guy, because sometimes there's not. But I do have to imagine that an institution that claims to be the purveyor of accountability and entrepreneurship may want to do some self-accounting of its own. Some of the headlines make you wonder, jus' sayin':

"Ernst & Young Accused of Hiding Lehman Troubles . . . Accounting Firm Ernst & Young was sued by New York prosecutors over allegations it helped to hide Lehman Brothers' financial problems, in the first major government legal action stemming from the Wall Street company's 2008 downfall. The civil fraud case contends that Ernst & Young stood by while Lehman used accounting gimmickry to mask its shaky finances." —Reuters, December 21, 2010

"Ernst & Young Sued for $900 Million by Liquidators of Madoff Feeder Fund . . . Ernst & Young LLP was accused of negligence, malpractice and breach of contract in a lawsuit filed by the liquidators of M-Invest Ltd., a so-called feeder fund for Bernard Madoff's bankrupt investment firm."—Bloomberg, December 5, 2011

"Ernst & Young Accused of Covering Up Bribery . . . Ernst & Young has been accused of covering up a case in which a Russian judge was set to rule on a tax case worth several million dollars. The allegation comes from former Ernst & Young partner Cathal Lyons, who blew the whistle on the case after Herve Labaude, a senior partner for the firm, closed an investigation into the case. Lyons is also suing the firm for breach of contract for $6 million."—Big4.com, July 7, 2012

$=$ *delta of*

IMAGINE FACTOR

"T.B.D."

—YOU

"Jane! Stop this
crazy thing!"

—GEORGE JETSON,
The Jetsons

CHAPTER 10

VISION FOR THE
FUTURE

VISION FOR THE FUTURE. This is the final piece of the jigsaw puzzle. To understand it, to "see it"—requires a full, complete understanding of the rest of the AUTHENTICITY FORMULA ($\Delta W\exists!$). By now you know that a UNIQUE VOICE ($\sqrt[Unj]{}$) is established only once your ACTION overcomes your FEAR, and once you have a sufficient sense of SELF. This UNIQUE VOICE ($\sqrt[Unj]{}$) is truthful, because WHAT YOU DO is greater than WHAT YOU SAY. Your CAPACITY FOR CHANGE ($\subseteq$) will be the multiple of your humanity and your know-how, which will help you adapt to life's rocky waters. Because your personal brand will be defined by more than WHAT YOU MAKE, your pursuit of a maximized EMOTIONAL IMPACT ($\exists!$) will remind you to never underestimate how YOU MAKE PEOPLE FEEL. This is then raised and amplified by the power of your IMAGINATION (Ω). Once you sever your LOYALTY TO NOSTALGIA, once you inhabit the NOW ($\overline{N\vee W}$), finally, you can visualize a future that delivers the promise of your brand.

Not a vision that's full of fairy tales and unicorns. A vision of the future that has been earned, fought for, and worthy of your creations. A future that's authentic. Not some faraway George Jetson on-a-spaceship future but a future of what will and can be. Not just a future of twenty years from now but a future of twenty minutes from now. A future where you're comfortable in your own skin. A future where you can unconditionally shed your skin. A future that's UN-Labeled.

THE GUTS OF Marc Eckō Enterprises moved from the Twenty-third Street office to other locations, leaving only *Complex*, my assistant Katie, and my own personal executive office. It still had the indoor basketball court, but I no longer played the part of Andy Warhol, and the rabbit hole had long since been filled in.

I was sitting alone in my office, staring at the empty basketball court, feeling hung over. It wasn't a hangover from binging but from the ride itself. I was exhausted from my lap dance with the Devil, and I just wanted to put my head on the pillow and take a five-year nap.

A knock on the door. It's Katie, the same assistant who had once driven me to Beth Israel Medical Center during my panic attack phase.

"Marc." She knocked again, opened the door. "There's this company on the phone, they want you to give a speech."

"I'm busy that day," I told her.

"It's in Singapore," she said.

"When?"

"February." She tossed me a bottle of Advil.

"Oh God. It's the rainy season. No way." I had sudden flashbacks of traveling to Asia to meet with Wu, to meet with Li and Fung. *Enough.* Just let me sleep.

"They'll pay you. They'll fly you out," she said.

"Tell them I need a first-class ticket."

She came back a few minutes later. "No problem."

"*Two* first-class tickets?" One for me, one for wifey.

A few minutes later. "No problem."

I thought about it some more and asked her, "Who else is going to be speaking at this fucking thing?"

"A guy named Malcolm Gladwell." She checked her notes. "He wrote a book called *The Tip—*"

"*The Tipping Point!*" I interrupted. "Malcolm Gladwell?"

"That's it. It's a conference about entrepreneurship. It's in four months."

I was too tired to think of any more BS excuses, so I agreed to go and give a speech on entrepreneurship. *Entrepreneurship.* Fuck. I hate that word. And not just for the fact that it's a French word (kidding . . .) but because it's obtuse, it's passive, and it doesn't express the spirit of artists and creators. So a week passed. A month passed. Then it occurred to me that I actually had to *write* something. And with Gladwell holding court, I had better not come off Junior Varsity.

As the weeks ticked by, I thought more about my life, my brand, and my herky-jerky ride that you've just read about. I went deep into my black book. I drew, I scribbled, I diagrammed. I thought about the forces in life that made me successful, and I thought about the times when I screwed up. I thought about the many brands I had created. I thought about all of those *Alice* paintings, the jack-o'-lanterns, and my journey down the rabbit hole. What compelled me down that rabbit hole? I learned that when Charles Dodgson (aka Lewis Carroll) wrote *Alice's Adventures in Wonderland* and *Through the Looking Glass*, he laced them with a hidden mathematical undercurrent. Supposedly the text has algebraic riddles, high-concept metaphors, and sly critiques of other branches of mathematics. *Interesting.* This got me thinking. The deeper intent (consciously or subconsciously) of my paintings began to snap into focus. Suddenly all of this began making sense. In a way, those paintings *became* the formula.

And the more I thought about *entrepreneurship*, the more I realized that the key to my success—and my peers' success, the success of folks I've looked up to—has nothing to do with the buzzwords you read in the usual business-speak books. ("Paradigm shifts!" "Synergy!" "Create Your Own Vision!") It's much simpler than that. The success or failures in my story, my company's story, and *all of our stories* boil down to AUTHENTICITY (AWƎi).

So I flew to Singapore and I didn't give some puffed-up, alpha-male, chest-beating speech about business. It occurred to me that words alone don't suffice in explaining the concept of authenticity. Instead, I presented the authenticity formula, fleshing out each variable not with words or even just numbers but with visuals, including my paintings. The crowd seemed to like the speech, and Gladwell himself stuck around to watch and later acknowledged that tackling the definition of authenticity is "ambitious and really, really hard to do." He seemed to respect the effort. "What you're doing with this formula thing—what you're trying to express is really, really hard. I respect that."

Hmmm. Cool.

That brings us full circle to what brought me the formula and allows me to bring this book to you. VISION FOR THE FUTURE is about having the courage to dream big, but it's also about having the discipline and the focus to look at what's in front of your face. And, hey, I'm a realist, and part of me can visualize a future where your eyes may have glazed over from a bunch of mathematical expressions. So just in case you missed it, before I drop the mic, I'll leave you with these five final prescriptions:

℞   Prescription 1: BE A CREATOR

RAISE YOUR HAND if you're an artist.

Try saying that to a room full of kindergarten kids. Nearly every kid raises their hand. Then say it to grown-ups at a business conference or in an executive meeting: almost no one.

Shame on you. Shame on me. Shame on all of us.

What happens to us when we get older? Why did we let them beat the creative spirit out of us? When we were children, we all played with crayons and Legos and finger paint. What happens in adulthood that leeches our desire to create, to build, to get messy and explore? Or at least *try*?

When I was eighteen, I had such big aspirations for my brand. *I want to see my name on clothing across the planet. I want the world to wear my shit. I want to be rich and famous.* And, yeah, I'm not gonna pretend that none of that matters, but at the end of the day, that's just the tactical *X*s and *O*s of *building* the company's brand. None of that has anything to do with *creating* the brand that's *inside*.

Just because you are checking boxes or executing a punch list does not mean you are creating. I've checked off enough boxes for three lifetimes, and none of those boxes provided lasting nourishment.

Sometimes I am doubtful and question myself as an *artist,* and say, *"At least I am an entrepreneur!"*

Pssstt. "Entrepreneur"? Being an entrepreneur alone will not satisfy this mandate to create. The word sucks, like I joked earlier. I do really disdain the word. It has a passive, checking-of-the-boxes connotation, and it comes from the French word *"entreprendre,"* which means "to undertake."

I don't undertake. I *CREATE*.

If you can reconnect with the creator inside you—the creator who's always been there, buried deep under the skin of labels—then you will see that the external forces don't really matter. The gatekeepers don't matter. The haters don't matter. So instead of getting hung up on the fear of *"what"* you create on the canvas, just jump into the simple act of doing it. Art is not what you do with paint on a canvas. It's not about any medium. Art is what you do with the oxygen you breathe and the experiences you create.

Whether you're an artist, doctor, inventor, musician, skater, athlete, or engineer—the *act* of creation is what counts. And just because you can't draw, paint, or sing doesn't mean that you can't create like an artist. (And I don't mean simply dressing up and putting flourishes on the outside of the stuff you make.)

As a teenager, I used to paint in my parents' garage. And now, even after so much has changed, I still follow that ancient ritual of retreating to my office or studio, blocking out the noise, and unrolling my canvas bag of markers and color pencils and bristle paper. *Creating.* It is in that quiet where I harvest and mine inspiration. It is entirely a self-directed pursuit. I gather data with my eyes and senses in the world, but I *mine* the *inspiration* by creating it from the inside out. It's those quiet, often mundane moments in batting practice—swing and miss, swing and miss, rinse and repeat—that are the moments when you will create your personal brand. Don't expect fanfare or flashing lights at those moments of eureka.

This is what I thirst for. This defines my purpose. I was an artist when I traced *Spider-Man* comics. I was an artist when I first dabbled in graffiti. I was an artist when I sketched the rhino logo, and I was an artist when I painted *Alice* and *Jack of the Lantern*. These are the quiet moments when I create and work on the brand of me. What are your moments?

| Rx | Prescription 2: SELL WITHOUT SELLING OUT |

SELLOUT. **THEY SAID** it behind my back, they said it to my face. I've had an army of naysayers: the high school haters; the cynics at Rutgers who snickered at me selling T-shirts at the Lyricist Lounge; the "other Echo" graf artist who claimed he was "realer"; the critics who said I was too white for black kids, too black for white kids; "the institutions" (fashion, financial, and everything in between), and the endless parade of gatekeepers.

We like to imagine that there's a holy war between art and commerce. "One is creative and pure, the other is crass and dirty." But the two aren't mutually exclusive. I've learned how to be a starving artist without literally having to starve. Starve for the *right* things. Starve to create something new. But never starve your brand.

This reminds me of the old "No logo" meme. The 1999 book, and the overall movement, took a strong antibrand stance and said, basically, that artists need to suffer for their work. That starving makes you somehow more divine. That the mere association with a brand or a dollar sign strips you of credibility. That branding ultimately sucks the life out of culture.

I call bullshit.

Creation need not only be the work of the divine. And branding need not only be the dirty work of the ad man on Madison Avenue. In this fragmented media culture hyperenabled by efficiencies of social media and self-publishing, YOU ARE A BRAND. Deal with it. You must strive to be both commercially responsible in your business and creatively fulfilled by the exhibition of your ideas. If you find that balance (which, in itself, will be more of an art than science), you will see *that what makes you a good artist is what will make you a good entrepreneur.* If you're authentic in the one, you'll be authentic in the other. The labels "they" will project on you *will not* matter. And if you're willing but *unable* to commercialize your art? That's okay, too. You're still an artist.

Every artist should live by these words:

Never feel bad about successfully selling your creations.

Never feel bad about creating art you can't sell.

Just create.

THIS BOOK IS about understanding the anatomy of a personal brand and then, in turn, the brand's spine of authenticity. So in the spirit of being authentic, I do need to share one more thing. (Brace yourself for a #HUMBLEBRAG. . .) I've never been more financially stable or "worth more" than I am now. Okay, I said it. Why? You know when you go to the gym, you don't want a personal trainer who's fat, right? I say this because culturally, you, the reader will only believe my advice if somehow what's in my bank correlates with smarts. Fame=success. Right? Wrong.

Even though we went through the shit-storm of 2008, I came out more emotionally authentic and more *financially* authentic, no longer weighed down by the yoke of unrelenting debts.

Since 2008, a funny thing happened. I didn't check all the boxes on "Marc Eckō 2010," but I did okay in the end and I successfully landed the plane. I stopped making appearances on the *Today* show, but I started making investments in companies and quietly launched my latest platform, Artists & Instigators. We put the brakes on retail expansion, but I put the pedal to the metal on *Complex*, and it repaid us with tremendous growth. I've focused on execution verus "splashing." I stay in the pool. Dig?

Am I "wealthy"? All I care about now is being wealthy in the currency that matters most. Wealthy with an authentic, actualized awareness of my personal brand and how it fits into the world. Wealthy with creation. That's what makes me most rich. With respect to Wu-Tang, I'm still living 'bout that CREAM, but now *Creation* rules everything around me.

I've gotten so much value in life from Eckō Unltd. and the rhino brand. And I continue to do so. It has been a platform that has granted not just material wealth but also an education that could not have been granted in any other way than having lived it. The platform, the amazing people, the sights, the sounds, the world(s) I've traveled—all from a tiny garage in Lakewood, New Jersey. That's something special. I wouldn't change a thing about it.

FAME $\neq$ $UCCESS

I don't begrudge any of my dustups. I wear my scars with pride. Even the ones you can't see.

So you're more financially stable today, but you got less heat, right? Where's the spotlight?

The "spotlight" is not a factor that goes into authenticity.

Does this mean that the "spotlight" isn't "authentic"? Are the two mutually exclusive? No. You can do both. But be careful of equating fame with success. The authenticity formula isn't about *W*s and *L*s, successes and failures. And I hate talking about what's in my bank account as some measure of compliance to success. The reason I am most wealthy today is because I'm free to better serve the Eckō beast, to steward and support new start-ups, to grow Complex Media, and actually wax philosophical about life here with you. And I count my blessings for that and the value of that currency that has made me wealthy in ways far beyond the value of just a dollar.

Rx Prescription 4: BE AN UN-LABEL

WE, AS A society, put things in a certain taxonomy and groupings, just like we do when shopping in the grocery store. We buy our dairy in the same place, the baked goods in the same place, the toilet paper in the same place. These labeling frameworks help us, as consumers, navigate the world. Ideas, places, and things are labeled so we can make sense of them. Without labels, we'd be unable to tell a can of peaches from a can of beans.

But this has unintended consequences. If we're not careful we find ourselves acting out the label that society has slapped on our tin can, wearing pleated khakis, making our résumé look just like everyone else's, and joining the herd of sheep. Human beings are programmed to pattern match. Even when we try to avoid pattern matching and shake free of the herd, sometimes we just end up as a black sheep in an identical herd of black sheep. (Exhibit A: The "rebellious" goth high school kids who all wear the same eyeliner.)

Fight this label.

Peel off this label.

UN-Label.

And like I said way back at the beginning, I don't mean "un" in the nihilistic or negative sense but in a defiant sense of the word. *Refuse* to be labeled by the gatekeepers. Or if you're going to be a label, be an UN-Label.

This takes work. In the same way that you exercise your body, you need to challenge yourself to shake free of the herd, find your own UNIQUE VOICE ($\frac{Uv}{V}$), and create your personal authentic brand. Make it hard for them to classify you. Make it hard for them to label you.

Don't let yourself be labeled as black or white or Jewish or a pharmacy student or a graf artist or a fashion designer or a CEO. Don't let yourself be placed in a silo. It's okay if the grocery store doesn't know whether to fit you in aisle 3 or aisle 7.

When you refuse to be labeled, suddenly you play by your own rules, not theirs. You measure yourself by your own standards, not the gatekeepers' standards. You define the test, the rubric of compliance for your brand, your creations, and your success.

R_x Prescription 5: AUTHENTICITY IS A PURSUIT. NOT A DESTINATION.

WE WANT TO organize our life in rational, logical, quantitative ways. How much you have versus them. Him versus her. But humans are not rational. We are emotional creatures. And just like there is no straight line in nature—or in your body—it's impossible to imagine your life in such an organized fashion. We are, after all, just one big work in progress.

The formula is designed with the understanding that *AUTHENTICITY* is a work in progress. While the basic concepts of this formula are rooted (mostly) in reality and philosophy, I suppose any second-rate mathematician can punch holes in it. But that's missing the point. The formula is useful for organizing the values that matter, but there will never be a quantified finite output.

Hate to break it to you, but the formula is intentionally overly complex as a bit of satire. It's not an accident that I included all these opaque mathematical symbols, weird variables, and math gobbledygook. Too many business and self-help books give tidy little formulas and Venn diagrams for success like $A + B = C$. Shit's not that simple. There's no easy formula.

Even if some Doogie Howser–type brainiac could actually crunch the numbers and compute a number—authenticity score of 72.0829, say—that score of "72.0829" is constantly changing.

The answer, like the formula itself, is a constantly iterative thing. Brands are not built upon finite numbers, but rather a curve composed of points along the axis of time and actions. The forces of life are always changing. But somehow we seek the validation that can only be found quantitatively in absolute numbers.

And the forces of life can hurt like hell; they're designed to. It's supposed to hurt. You thought it would be easy? They can make progress look like failure. Imagine that you're a sculptor and you have a piece of clay. You strike that clay, at first with blunt, powerful strokes. You strike again, now creating a huge recess in the clay, and just when you think you've created an eyeball, you accidentally strike too far to the left. You think it's a step back. But then maybe you take your thumb and you press it down with your nail, you undulate it, and suddenly what looked like a mistake is now the top of an eyelid, giving your sculpture more clarity. You are establishing the data points that shape the curve along the axis of creation. A work in progress. These forces can at times seem subtractive—maybe they smack your ego, maybe they look sloppy—that's okay. That's part of the ride of creating that will eventually reveal itself with the texture, the essence, the very *definition* of what it is you seek to create.

For me, the formula has clarified these forces in life. But this dogma isn't something you can just slavishly follow and this equation can (and should) be different for everyone. It's not important that you use *my* formula to build an authentic brand, but it's critical that you develop your own.

It's critical that you dig deep down, from the inside out, and look outward and upward for your VISION OF THE FUTURE. Not a vision of *their* future. Not a vision of the gatekeepers' future. And not a vision of the future that's so far away that it's only achieved once cars are flying through space. But a future that's *AWETHENTIC*.

I am a brand.

I've shown you my brand. I've peeled back the label and showed you its guts.

You are a brand.

And your brand is . . . ?

MANIFESTO

I, _____ , on this Day ____ ____ ____ declare that

I am not a Label. I am not a resume. I am more than just a consumer. I am a creator. I am not fearless. But I will overcome my fear with action. I have a unique voice. This voice is true. I will focus on the goalkeepers, not the gatekeepers. I have a healthy contempt for the status quo. No institution is sacred. I will create wealth that matters. I refuse to be defined by the skin in which I am packaged. I will focus not just on what I make, but also how I make people feel. I know that perception is NOT reality. Reality is reality. I learn by doing. I don't just go to school; school comes to me. For the rest of my life.

I, _____ , am a brand.

I own it.

From the guts to the skin. From the skin to the world.

Signed,

_____   _____
Name   Date

SEND TO:

Unlabel by Marc Eckō
c/o Complex Media
1271 Avenue of the Americas
35th floor
NY, NY 10020

Attach your formula on back

ATTACH YOUR FORMULA HERE

ACKNOWLEDGMENTS

THIS BOOK WOULD not have been possible without the partnership of Marci Tapper and Seth Gerszberg. Thanks for all the great memories in partnering to build the Eckō brands, and in the end helping me to develop my own personal one. Guts to skin. Skin to world.

Most important, a special shout-out and a bow of humility to each and every former, present, and future co-worker. Thank you for being a part of the journey and granting me such a valuable education. I'm only as tall as the shoulders that I have been lifted upon.

Big up to my collaborator on this book, the one and only Jeff Wilser! Not only have you become a great friend but you helped me so much more than the obvious—in channeling the words onto the page. You made this entire process fun and deeply meaningful on a personal and professional level. Thanks for making me seem smarter than I really am.

A special shout-out to Matthew Benjamin and Touchstone, and to Matthew Carnicelli, Paul Kepple, and Katie Hill.

ILLUSTRATION CREDITS